T0319332

Fundamental Analysis and Position Trading

Founded in 1807, John Wiley & Sons is the oldest independent publishing company in the United States. With offices in North America, Europe, Australia and Asia, Wiley is globally committed to developing and marketing print and electronic products and services for our customers' professional and personal knowledge and understanding.

The Wiley Trading series features books by traders who have survived the market's ever changing temperament and have prospered—some by reinventing systems, others by getting back to basics. Whether a novice trader, professional or somewhere in-between, these books will provide the advice and strategies needed to prosper today and well into the future.

For a list of available titles, visit our Web site at www.WileyFinance.com.

Fundamental Analysis and Position Trading

Evolution of a Trader

THOMAS N. BULKOWSKI

WILEY

John Wiley & Sons, Inc.

Published by John Wiley & Sons, Inc., Hoboken, New Jersey.
Published simultaneously in Canada.

For general information on our other products and services or for technical support, please contact our Customer Care Department within the United States at (800) 762-2974, outside the United States at (317) 572-3993 or fax (317) 572-4002.

Wiley publishes in a variety of print and electronic formats and by print-on-demand. Some material included with standard print versions of this book may not be included in e-books or in print-on-demand. If this book refers to media such as a CD or DVD that is not included in the version you purchased, you may download this material at http://booksupport.wiley.com. For more information about Wiley products, visit www.wiley.com.

Library of Congress Cataloging-in-Publication Data:
Bulkowski, Thomas N.,
  Fundamental analysis and position trading : evolution of a trader / Thomas N. Bulkowski.
      pages cm. — (Wiley trading series)
  Includes bibliographical references and index.
  ISBN 978-1-118-46420-5 (cloth); ISBN 978-1-118-50874-9 (ebk);
  ISBN 978-1-118-50875-6 (ebk); ISBN 978-1-118-51695-9 (ebk)
  1. Stocks—Prices. 2. Price-earnings ratio. 3. Dividends. I. Title.
  HG4636.B85 2012
  332.63'2042—dc23

                                                              2012032676

Printed in the United States of America

10 9 8 7 6 5 4 3 2 1

Contents

Preface

A re you like John?

He learned early in life to save his money for a rainy day. Instead of putting it into the bank, he put it into the stock market. He bought Cisco Systems in mid-1999 at 35 and watched the stock soar to 82 in less than a year.

"I'm looking for my first 10-bagger," he said, and held onto the stock.

In 2001, when the tech bubble burst, the Cisco balloon popped, too, and it plunged back to 35. He was at breakeven after seeing the stock more than double.

"It'll recover," he said. "It's a $200 stock. You'll see."

The stock tunneled through 35 then 30, then 20, and bottomed at 15, all in *one* month. When it hit 10, he sold it for a 70 percent loss.

"I should have sold at the top. Buy-and-hold doesn't work." But it did work. Cisco more than doubled, but he held too long.

Next, he tried position trading to better time the exit and chose Eastman Chemical. He bought it in 2003 at 14, just pennies from the bear market bottom, and rode it up to 21 before selling. He made 50 percent in a year. Was he happy?

"I sold too soon." The stock continued rising, hitting 30 in 2005. He disliked seeing profits mount after he sold, and wanted to profit from swings in both directions.

He switched to swing trading in 2005 and tried his old favorite: Cisco. The stock bounced from 17 to 20 to 17 to 22 over the next year, but he always bought too late and exited too early. He made money, but not enough.

He took a vacation from his day job and watched Applied Materials wave to him on the computer screen, inviting him to come day trade it. So he did. He made $400 in just 15 minutes. "If I can make $400 a day for a year, I'll make"—he grabbed his calculator and punched buttons—"$146,000! No, that's not right. How many trading days are there in a year?"

He redid the math and discovered that he could make $100,000 a year by nibbling off just 40 cents a share on 1,000 shares every trading day. "Wow. Count me in."

After paying $5,000 for a trading course and more for hardware, software, and data feeds, he took the plunge and started day trading full time.

It took a year to blow through his savings. Another three months took out his emergency fund. He moved back in with his parents while he looked for a real job.

Now, he is saving again and putting it to work in the market. "After reading the manuscript for this book," he said, "I found a trading style that works for me. I'm a swinger—a swing trader. And I'm making money, too." He handles not only his own money but his parents and siblings as well, providing them with extra income and building a nest egg for their retirement.

EVOLUTION OF A TRADER

John represents an amalgam of traders, a composite of those searching for a trading style that they can call their own. He suffered through many failed trades before finding a trading style that worked for him. I wrote the Evolution of a Trader series to help people like John.

Evolution of a Trader traces my journey from a buy-and-hold investor to position trader to swing trader to day trader as I searched for styles that worked best when markets evolved. However, these are not autobiographical. Rather, it is an exploration of what has worked, what is supposed to work but does not, and what may work in the future.

This series dissects the four trading styles and provides discoveries, trading tips, setups, and tactics to make each style a profitable endeavor. I have done the research so you do not have to. I show what is needed to make each style work.

CONTENT OVERVIEW

The three books in the Evolution of a Trader series provide numerous tips, trading ideas, and setups based on personal experience and that of others.

Easy to understand tests are used to confirm trading folklore and to illustrate ideas and setups, and yet the books are an entertaining read with an engaging style that appeals to the novice.

Each section has bullet items summarizing the importance of the findings. A checklist at chapter's end provides an easy-to-use summary of the contents and reference of where to find more information.

At the end of each book is a topic checklist and reference.

Trading Basics

The first book in the series begins with the basics, creating a solid foundation of terms and techniques. Although you may understand market basics, you will learn from this book.

How do I know? Take this quiz. If you have to guess at the answers, then you need to buy this book. If you get some of them wrong, then imagine what you are missing. Answers are at the end of the quiz.

From Chapter 2: Money Management

1. True or false: Trading a constant position size can have disastrous results.

2. True or false: A market order to cancel a buy can be denied if it is within two minutes of the Nasdaq's open.

3. True or false: Dollar cost averaging underperforms.

From Chapter 3: Do Stops Work?

1. True or false: Fibonacci retracements offer no advantage over any other number as a turning point.

2. True or false: A chandelier stop hangs off the high price.

3. True or false: Stops cut profit more than they limit risk.

From Chapter 4: Support and Resistance

1. True or false: Peaks with below average volume show more resistance.

2. True or false: Support gets stronger over time.

3. True or false: The middle of a tall candle is no more likely to show support or resistance than any other part.

From Chapter 5: 45 Tips Every Trader Should Know

1. True or false: Fibonacci extensions are no more accurate than any other tool for determining where price might reverse.

2a. True or false: Only bullish divergence (in the RSI indicator) works and only in a bull market.

2b. True or false: Bullish divergence (in the RSI indicator) fails to beat the market more often than it works.

3. True or false: Price drops faster than it rises.

From Chapter 6: Finding and Fixing What Is Wrong

1. True or false: The industry trend is more important than the market trend.

2. True or false: Holding a trade too long is worse than selling too early.

3. True or false: Sell in May and go away.

The answer to every statement is true.

Fundamental Analysis and Position Trading

This book explains and describes the test results of various fundamental factors such as book value, price-to-earnings ratio, and so on, to see how important they are to stock selection and performance.

The Fundamental Analysis Summary chapter provides tables of fundamental factors based on hold times of one, three, and five years that shows which factor is most important to use for those anticipated hold times. The tables provide a handy reference for buy-and-hold investors or for other trading styles that wish to own a core portfolio of stocks based on fundamental analysis.

Chapters such as "How to Double Your Money," "Finding 10-Baggers," and "Trading 10-Baggers" put the fundamentals to work. The chapter titled "Selling Buy-and-Hold" helps solve the problem of when to sell long-term holdings.

Position Trading   The second part explores position trading. It introduces market timing to help remove the risk of buying and holding a stock for years.

Have you heard the phrase, *Trade with the trend*? How often does a stock follow the market higher or lower? The section in Chapter 19 titled, "What Is Market Influence on Stocks?" provides the answer.

This part of the book looks at how chart patterns can help with position trading. It discloses the 10 most important factors that make chart patterns work and then blends them into a scoring system. That system can help you become a more profitable position trader when using chart patterns.

Six actual trades are discussed to show how position trading works and when it does not. Consider them as roadmaps that warn when the road is bumpy and when the market police are patrolling.

Swing and Day Trading

The last book of the series covers swing and day trading. The first portion of the book highlights swing trading techniques, explains how to use chart patterns to swing trade, swing selling, event patterns (common stock offerings, trading Dutch auction tender offers, earnings releases, rating changes, and so on), and other trading setups.

It tears apart a new tool called the chart pattern indicator. The indicator is not a timing tool, but a sentiment indicator that is great at calling major market turns.

Day Trading   Day trading reviews the basics including home office set-up, cost of day trading, day trading chart patterns, and the opening range breakout. It discusses research into the major reversal times each day and what time of the day is most likely to set the day's high and low—valuable information to a day trader.

An entire chapter discusses the opening gap setup and why fading the gap is the best way to trade it. Another chapter discusses the opening range breakout setup and questions whether it works.

Ten horror stories from actual traders complete the series. They have been included to give you lasting nightmares.

INTENDED AUDIENCE

The three books in this series were written for people unfamiliar with the inner workings of the stock market, but will curl the toes of professionals, too.

Research is used to prove the ideas discussed, but is presented in an easy to understand and light-hearted manner. You will find the books to be as entertaining as they are informative and packed with moneymaking tips and ideas. Use the ideas presented here to hone your trading style and improve your success.

Whether you are a novice who has never purchased a stock but wants to, or a professional money manager who trades daily, these books are a necessary addition to any market enthusiast's bookshelf.

Acknowledgments

S many people are involved in bringing a manuscript to life, and I play a small role. To all of those workers at John Wiley & Sons, I say thanks for the help, especially to Evan Burton and Meg Freeborn. They ironed the wrinkles and made the trilogy presentable, even fashionable

CHAPTER 1

Introduction to Buy-and-Hold

I started dabbling in the markets by researching companies using their annual reports. I pored over the numbers and checked the ratios to make sure the company would not fold anytime soon.

In those days, I learned to love cash dividends and stock dividends as well. They added to the bulge in my wallet and slowly increased my net worth one share at a time. During the bull market of the 1980s, I had a win/loss ratio of 63 percent and made an average of 39 percent per trade. I achieved that without knowing what I was doing.

For example, I bought a stock called Sparton Corp. This was a wonderful stock that never heard of going up while I owned it, but it paid a huge dividend. That is, until they stopped paying it! I bought it three times and lost 23 percent, 39 percent, and 53 percent of my money.

I grew to mistrust the method of holding a stock forever (well, 3.6 years was my average hold time for stocks bought in the 1980s). I was tired of seeing a stock like ASA Holdings (acquired by Delta), which I bought four times in the late 1990s at an average price of 23.36, more than double to 51 and then drop to 34 before I sold it.

Nevertheless, I still like investing, which is a synonym for buy-and-hold. You can make a lot of money with little work. The hardest part is ignoring the daily rollercoaster movements of the market.

As I mentioned in *Trading Basics*, Chapter 2, under "Hold Time: My Trades," my best hold time is between three and four years. Research a company, buy the stock, and then hold it until it realizes its full potential. Then sell it.

WHAT IS BUY-AND-HOLD?

You probably know what buy-and-hold means, but let me tell you how I define it. If I buy a stock with the intention of holding it for years, then that is a buy-and-hold position. I expect bumps along the way, such as a quarter or two of weak earnings, but I am focusing on their long-term potential for growth.

Despite the name, I do not interpret it as buy-and-hold *forever*. Buy-and-wait is a better description. My guess is that I will never hold a stock as long as I did Michaels Stores. Some of those shares I bought in 1990 and sold in 2006 when the company went private. Now, my inner voice—call it the voice of experience—sees that I have doubled my money and will want to capture profits before a dead-cat bounce pattern takes away 70 percent of it in one session.

Often that voice speaks only after the stock has given back too much from a peak, such as in the case of Interface (IFSIA), where I sold 25 percent below the high, or Steelcase, down 26 percent. In fact, I thought we were sliding into a bear market in July 2010 and sold over half of my portfolio in a flight to cash.

I was wrong.

The market bottomed and then went on to new highs. I am more sensitive to price fluctuations because of the recent 2007 to 2009 bear market, especially when I have good gains.

I began concentrating on buy-and-hold positions because I found it more difficult to make money by short-term trading. That was in 2007, just months before the bear market started. Big mistake. Fortunately, it took only nine months after the bear market ended to recover my losses.

That brings up an important question: Who should buy and hold?

WHO SHOULD BUY AND HOLD?

Trading Basics, Chapter 2, "A Better Way? Portfolio Composition," discusses my thinking about diversification. Build a core portfolio of stocks from the buy-and-hold category and pepper it with other trading styles that fit your needs, such as swing trades or position trades. Diversify your holdings not only by industry, but trading style as well. That way, when the market favors swing trading over other styles, you will have positions ready to take the lead to greater wealth.

This guidance applies to day traders, too. I have heard that day traders tend to burn out after several years of trading (four years comes to mind, but I do not know if that is true). The constant pressure to perform each day coupled with lack of exercise and inability to relieve stress tends to fry the adrenal system. Having buy-and-hold positions available in which to place excess cash will create a cushion if the pressures of day trading become too much to bear. Swing and position trading can give the day trader a more relaxed ride in which to recover while still having the emotional feel of being in the game.

Regardless of your trading style, consider adding to your portfolio positions held for the long term. These are not buy-and-forget positions, but they need not require constant attention, either. Think long-term growth.

MY NUMBERS: BACKGROUND AND TERMS

In the pages that follow, I use almost a thousand stocks covering the period from 1992 to 2007. Not all stocks covered the entire period and dividends were not included unless noted otherwise. The test period includes the 2000 to 2002 bear market.

I refer to year 0 through year 5. Year 0 refers to the first year in which fundamental data and prices for a particular stock were available. It serves as the base year in which other years are compared. Year 5 is the last year. Year 0 through year 5 use the closing price at year's end.

Since I use 16 years worth of data but present only a five-year-wide window, the analysis uses data like a moving average. I use the fundamental number from the new year and drop off the old year. Year 1 becomes year 0, year 2 becomes year 1, and so on in a series of overlapping years as the five-year window slides from 1992 to 2007.

In this manner, each year 0 has the opportunity to see how price behaves during the next five years.

I am sure that none of this makes much sense and you may be asking, "Who cares?" but that is fine. When I start discussing tests, it will become clear and you will understand my thinking.

NOW WHAT?

If technical analysis tells you what will happen in the short term, fundamental analysis tells you what to expect in the long term. Both are useful tools for making money, but a brief review of important fundamentals will help when selecting companies to buy and hold. Those chapters follow.

Even if you are a day trader, some of the discoveries discussed in the coming chapters are worth learning. They may help you select stocks to trade. They may spark a new avenue of investigation that may well send you on a path to greater riches.

CHAPTER 2

Stock
Selection

This chapter is about selecting stocks for investors using methods that have proved helpful. Other tips follow in the coming chapters, so you can create selections that are ideal for your situation.

When I created my website (http://thepatternsite.com) in late 2006, I started receiving emails from people asking how I selected stocks in which to trade or invest. I thought back to the 1980s in the public library when I hunted for stocks in Value Line to populate my watch list. I took my picks home and then typed the quote information into my computer each day from the *Wall Street Journal*. That was easy enough to do until the list grew to 500 stocks, but it usually took less than an hour to update my database manually.

Some old timers will claim that you get a better feel for the stock if you manually type in the quote information. My reply to that is hogwash. With 500 stocks, there is no way I can keep them separate in my mind. I am not that smart.

Anyway, here are the Value Line criteria I used, and they still apply today.

- The stock needs a heartbeat. That means in two of the past five years, the yearly high must be at least twice the yearly low.
- If the stock was too expensive, I threw it out. The preferred price range is $10 to $20. In fact, a study I conducted (see http://thepatternsite.com/prices.html) shows that chart patterns in stocks priced from $0 to $10 outperformed the other ranges, but I did not know it back then.
- The stock must have a price-to-earnings ratio, meaning I tossed any stock with NMF (not meaningful) showing in the P/E box.

- I selected stocks with high three- to five-year price appreciation potential. Triple-digit percentages are tasty, but unrealistic. I relied on it anyway.
- I selected at least five stocks per industry, so I had to relax my requirements to admit some of them. Having many stocks from one industry gives me a better feel for how they are doing as a group.
- I checked the list of insider buying and selling. I wanted to see many insiders buying and few selling. I will discuss this later in the chapter.
- Fundamental factors included a low P/E ratio, climbing sales, positive earnings for the past several years, low debt, and so on. The chapters in this volume will tell you what works best.

WHAT COMES AFTER LARGE PRICE MOVES?

In the first bullet item in the list—the yearly high price must be twice the year low—I interpreted that as price doubling, but it could have been cut in half, too.

I decided to do some research to see if price doubling or cut in half led to better performance the following year. I used 567 stocks from 1990 to 2008 in the test. Not all stocks covered the entire range. For each stock and each year during the test period, I found the yearly low, the yearly high, and the close-to-close move the following year. I sorted the results into two buckets (stocks more than doubling versus not doubling) by years, giving 19 annual performance contests.

The median rise a year *after* a stock doubled beat the median rise of those not doubling 53 percent of the time. Yawn. Summing the median gains or losses of those 19 contests gives gains of 385 percent versus 165 percent for year-ahead performance of stocks doubling (or better) versus not doubling, respectively. Substituting the *average* gain instead of the *median* gives 916 percent versus 273 percent, respectively. In other words, stocks that do well continue doing well.

- Stocks that double substantially outperform the following year 53 percent of the time.

Here is the exciting news. Stocks that drop by 50 percent or more tend to zip higher the following year. They win 13 of 19 performance contests, or 68 percent of the time. The cumulative median rise of those 19 annual contests is 253 percent for those stocks dropping in half (or more) compared to next year gains of 152 percent for those not dropping by at least 50 percent.

Substituting averages for medians gives cumulative gains of 588 percent versus 293 percent, respectively. In other words, stocks that drop in half tend to not only bounce back the following year, but also do so with gusto.

- Stocks that drop 50 percent or more outperform the following year 68 percent of the time.

Let me issue this caution about my studies. They are not academic quality, meaning I did not include stocks that went bankrupt or merged out of existence. However, it has been my experience that the conclusions of the studies will match those from the academic world. We will see that later in this volume.

When selecting stocks for a watch list, pick those that have made large moves in the past, either up or down. Compare the yearly low to the yearly high and look for a ratio of at least 2 to 1.

If stocks are coming out of a bear market, buy stocks that have declined the most. They tend to recover further.

MYTH: STOCKS THAT DROP LEAST IN A BEAR MARKET THEN SOAR

One of the things I take pride in is that I prove what I say. How many times have you heard that stocks that drop least in a bear market tend to soar most after the bear market ends? A financial consultant said that to me just two weeks ago. That belief is wrong. Here is the proof.

I used 472 stocks from my database that stretched back as far as the 2000 bear market and followed them through the 2007 bear market plus a year later, tracking their performance into 2010. I found that stocks that declined most bounced highest. Stocks that declined least bounced, but not nearly as high. **Table 2.1** shows the results.

TABLE 2.1 Price Recovery After a Bear Market

Market	Median Bounce 1 Year Later	Average Bounce 1 Year Later
Bear market 3/24/2000 to 10/10/2002		
Above median 49% decline	107%	158%
Below median	29%	45%
Bear market 10/11/2007 to 3/6/2009		
Above median 57% decline	145%	223%
Below median	61%	69%

For example, in the 2000 to 2002 bear market, the median decline of all 472 stocks in the test was 49 percent. Those stocks that dropped more than 49 percent bounced a median 107 percent a year later (or an average of 158 percent, if you prefer). Those that dropped less than 49 percent during the bear market bounced only 29 percent (median) and 45 percent (average) a year after the bear market ended.

The 2007 to 2009 bear market follows the same trend with stocks that dropped more than the median 57 percent bounced higher than did those with shallower drops during the bear market.

This agrees with a finding mentioned in Fosback's book (The Institute for Econometric Research, 1976). He writes, "At major bear market troughs, for example, relatively weak stocks tend to bounce up faster, while stocks which have failed to decline much in the preceding bear market are often stodgy issues which rarely provide outstanding profits in any kind of market."

- Stocks that drop most in a bear market bounce higher one year after the bear market ends. Stocks that drop least perform worse.

STOCK SELECTION THE EASY WAY

One financial adviser I know watches television for her stock leads. When the news reports on an exciting drug breakthrough, she is at her computer, researching the company for a possible investment. When BP had a rig explosion in 2010 that blasted oil into the Gulf of Mexico, she bought the stock near the bottom, hoping for a recovery.

Some of these stock picks are gold and some are pyrite. Overall, though, she does well. One of her favorite techniques is to monitor Yahoo! Finance to see what stocks are making big moves. If they are bio-tech companies, she researches them and waits for them to come back to earth. Then she pounces. That is where she gets her most promising leads.

For more mundane stocks, she pounds the pavement looking for goods or services she likes, and visits stores with crowded parking lots.

Let me give you a personal example. Near the end of the 2007 to 2009 bear market, I kept reading in the letters to the editor section of the local newspaper how customers loved Steinmart. The people in town wanted more stores just like that one. In late March 2009, I started my research on the stock for a possible investment. They announced earnings on the 19th and the stock shot up and then moved sideways in an event pattern I call an earnings flag. My trading notebook says that I wanted to buy on

March 31, which would have filled near 2.82, the opening price the next day.

Just over five months later, the stock peaked at 13.75. Unfortunately, I watched it all from the sidelines, because I never bought the stock.

The moral of this anecdote is to buy stocks you know and like. Finding retailers is easy since they are where you shop. You can check how full the parking lot is and how full the shopping carts are. Visit a few outlets. Are the stores clean? Do the shoppers look happy?

This method was how I found Michaels Stores, the best-performing stock I have ever owned. I had just bought my house and had bare plant ledges. I stopped in at Michaels MJ Designs and bought several baskets of silk plants. I visited the store often for more decorations.

When I researched the company, I discovered that Michaels and Michaels MJ Designs were different companies. They used to be part of the same company but split up and divided the world between them. The first chapter in *Trading Basics*, describes what happened to my investment.

If you like a company, why not buy a piece of it? That is what happens when you become a shareholder.

- Pick stocks of companies that you know and like. Popular retailers are easy to spot. They have full parking lots with shoppers carrying cartloads of merchandise to their cars.

TWO TIPS FOR STOCK SELECTION

You may find the following tips useful when looking for stocks to buy.

1. Check for poor earnings or earnings warnings in other stocks in the same industry. For example, if Lowes Companies reports poor earnings before Home Depot, then there is a good chance that Home Depot is suffering, too, and the stock will take a bullet.

2. Check for rating upgrades or downgrades of other stocks in the industry. If many companies in the same industry are suffering, then now is probably not the time to buy unless your crystal ball sees improvement coming. Play it safe and wait until the stocks show signs of responding to good news and downplaying bad news.

Both of these items will tell if the whirlpool swirling around your stock will suck it lower. Even though your stock may have announced better than expected earnings, it will likely suffer as those around it sink.

BUY FALLEN ANGELS

Another easy way to select stocks is to consider *fallen angels*. Gabriel Wisdom (*Wisdom on Value Investing*, John Wiley & Sons, 2009) uses a fundamental philosophy to select beaten down stocks called fallen angels. "The term originated on Wall Street many years ago," he writes, "and it describes a stock or bond that has fallen but should rise again."

The book is packed with tips on stock market investing. He splits the buying decision into two screens: Business Quality and Paying the Right Price. The quality screen focuses on common metrics for companies such as sales and earnings growth rates of at least 10 percent with low debt. Paying the right price means studying ratios, such as earnings yield and price to sales, to help value a company.

He also likes companies spun off from a parent as an investment opportunity. In my experience, I have found them to be valuable investments as well. Imagine that you are a vice president in a company and they decide to spin off their manufacturing operations with you in charge. This is your chance to prove you know what it takes to build a company into a powerhouse.

The company spinning off the operations will want the newborn to prosper, so they will stuff it with solid financials, a healthy business plan, and strong leadership.

- Select quality stocks beaten down in price but with solid prospects.
- Spin-offs can represent a good opportunity to buy an established company with management motivated to succeed.

WHAT CHART PATTERNS APPEAR BEFORE MERGERS AND BUYOUTS?

In searching for stocks to buy, I wondered if there were any chart patterns common to stocks that receive buyout offers. Clearly, insiders know about impending buyouts or mergers and perhaps some of them trade on that information (even if it is illegal, it may happen anyway). Maybe they tell a friend who trades on the information or perhaps an analyst guesses correctly that a company is undervalued and ripe for purchase. Whatever the cause, perhaps the footprints left by the smart money appear on the stock charts as recognizable patterns. It is an interesting thought worth exploring.

I have an archive folder on my computer that holds securities that I no longer follow. When a buyout or merger occurs, I move the data into that folder. That is where I went to search for chart patterns in mergers and buyouts. I found 111 of them.

FIGURE 2.1 Building Materials Corporation of America buys ElkCorp

What did I discover? I found patterns that occur surrounding the merger/buyout offer (I will just call it a merger from here on). **Figure 2.1** shows an example on the weekly chart. On November 6, 2006, the company announced that they were seeking strategic alternatives—often code words for seeking a merger partner. The stock gapped higher on the news (point A). On December 18, the company announced that an affiliate of The Carlyle Group would eat the company. The stock again gapped up again (B).

Instead of merging with Carlyle, the company first rejected a $40 bid from Building Materials Corporation of America, but then accepted a higher offer of $43.50.

I receive an email from a person who wrote, "I found a new chart pattern!" His enthusiasm reminded me of an oil driller changing the drain pan on his car yelling, "I struck oil!"

The email was referring to price action similar to that near C. While waiting for a merger to complete, a stock tends to move horizontally. I checked the news, and sure enough, the company had announced a merger. The quick rise followed by a horizontal movement was not a new pattern, but a typical reaction to merger news.

Overpaying?

If the company is willing to sell itself for $43.50, why would anyone pay more for the stock? Sometimes a stock will rise above the merger price if shareholders think the offer will be raised or feel as if the offer does not represent fair value. I usually take the money and dump the turkey after the merger announcement. The merger sometimes falls apart and the stock will drop back to where it traded before the merger announcement, so keep that in mind.

Returning to Figure 2.1, one of the chart patterns that popped up repeatedly was a double bottom. The one I highlighted on the chart is an Adam & Adam double bottom, so called because of the shape of each bottom. Adam has a long and narrow configuration, often a day or two wide. That contrasts to an Eve bottom, which is wider and appears more rounded. If Eve has price spikes, they are more numerous than the one or two that Adam has. Performance is slightly different between the various combinations of Adam and Eve bottoms.

Table 2.2 shows the names of chart patterns and how often they appear before the merger announcement. The most frequent pattern is none at all mixed with patterns that occur so infrequently that I lumped them into the "none" category.

In second place is a double bottom, which I have discussed. Following that is an ugly double bottom. That is a double bottom in which the second bottom is priced more than 5 percent higher than the first, making it look ugly.

Do not expect stocks showing double bottoms to lead to merger announcements 31 percent of the time. The table does not work like that.

Just before a merger announcement, price is usually trending higher. In fact, it does so 63 percent of the time. I used a 50-day simple moving average to gauge the trend.

Figure 2.1 shows an exception when the stock dips to form the double bottom. After the announcement becomes public, price often gaps up, but usually remains slightly below the merger price. After that, the stock stays in a horizontal trading range unless news events power the stock in one direction or the other.

TABLE 2.2 Chart Patterns That Appear Before Mergers

Chart Pattern	Pre-Merger Frequency
None (other)	50%
Double bottom	31%
Ugly double bottom	14%
Head-and-shoulders bottom	5%

- The chart pattern found most often before a merger announcement is a double bottom.
- Stocks trend higher 63 percent of the time before a merger or buyout announcement.

WHAT ARE INSIDERS DOING?

Who better to know how a business is doing than the people running it? Those people are called insiders. Although insiders may know the business, can they translate that knowledge into buying and selling their company's stock in a timely manner? The answer to that question has kept academics battling, but seems to be yes, although skirmishes in the war are ongoing.

A Tweedy, Browne paper (2009) cited five studies that tracked the performance of stocks in which multiple insiders (corporate officers, directors, or large shareholders) bought and few, if any, sold. The annualized returns of those stocks beat the market index by two to four times.

Many cite Donald T. Rogoff's dissertation (Michigan State University, 1964) when researching insider transactions. He examined insider transactions of 45 companies in which three or more insiders bought stock and none sold during one month. The gains in the stocks during the following six months exceeded the market's gain by 9.5 percent.

Gary S. Glass (Ohio State University, 1966) used eight securities that had the most insider buying over selling during one month in 14 monthly contests and found that the performance of those stocks seven months later beat the market by an average of 10 percent.

Let us take an example of how I use insider buying to determine whether to invest in a stock.

Figure 2.2 shows the stock of Caché Inc. (CACH). In early January 2010, four insiders were awarded 5,000 shares of stock. A few days later, director Andrew Saul bought almost 21,000 shares. In mid-March, he bought 35,000 shares and did so again in a series of transactions amounting to about another 35,000 shares.

At first, I thought that he was buying because of perceived value, but it bothered me that no other insiders were buying too. Then I thought that he was averaging down his buy price, but further checking showed that he was averaging up. He bought over a million shares (most of his position) near $2 a share in January 2009. It also bothered me that his buying seemed to be on a timetable of every two months: January, March, May. Finally, he is not exactly buying when the stock is cheap.

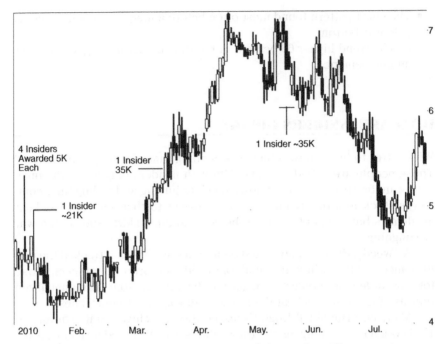

FIGURE 2.2   Insider buying suggests accumulation or does it?

Although the stock was trading near the bottom (support) of an up-sloping channel (not shown in the figure, but you can see it best on the weekly scale, starting with the peak in May 2009 and the valley in July 2009), I expected the general market to be weak. That weakness would likely force the stock below the bottom channel line, so I elected to wait and see.

When using insider transactions, I like to see many different insiders buying with little or no selling. I am not talking about 10 directors buying 300 shares each. I am talking about them backing up an 18-wheeler and filling it with stock. I want them to own a significant amount, too. If the stock declines, I want their wallets or pocketbooks to bleed just as mine will.

- Look for many different insiders buying a ton of stock when price is low, with few selling—but selling small amounts is fine. Does the buying appear regularly, as if on a schedule? If so, that is not as good as insiders buying value at a low price.

CHAPTER CHECKLIST

Based on findings in this chapter, here are some tips to consider when shopping for stocks.

☐ See this chapter's introduction for criteria I use to select stocks.

☐ Stocks that double substantially outperform the following year 53 percent of the time. See the section "What Comes After Large Price Moves?"

☐ Stocks that drop 50 percent or more outperform the following year 68 percent of the time. See the section "What Comes After Large Price Moves?"

☐ Stocks that drop most in a bear market bounce higher one year after the bear market ends. Stocks that drop least perform worse. See Table 2.1.

☐ Pick stocks of companies that you know and like. See the section "Stock Selection the Easy Way."

☐ Check for poor earnings or earnings warnings in other stocks in the same industry. See the section "Two Tips for Stock Selection."

☐ Check for rating upgrades or downgrades of other stocks in the industry. See the section "Two Tips for Stock Selection."

☐ Select quality stocks beaten down in price but with solid prospects. See the section "Buy Fallen Angels."

☐ Spin-offs can represent a good opportunity to buy an established company with management motivated to succeed. See the section "Buy Fallen Angels."

☐ The chart pattern found most often before a merger announcement is a double bottom. See Table 2.2.

☐ Stocks trend higher 63 percent of the time before a merger or buyout announcement. See the section "Overpaying?"

☐ Look for many different insiders buying a ton of stock when price is low, with few selling—but selling small amounts is fine. Does the buying appear regularly, as if on a schedule? If so, that is not as good as insiders buying value at a low price. See the section "What Are Insiders Doing?"

CHAPTER 3

Book Value

The way to a small fortune in the stock market is to start with a large one! That is a joke, of course, but I think that the way to make a million dollars in the market comes one dollar at a time, beginning with selecting the right stocks. The fundamental factors that I discuss in the following chapters will serve as a strong foundation for your stock-picking endeavors. Select stocks for value, and then I will show you how to time your entry and exit using technical analysis.

There will be some pain involved. I will throw at you a few terms that make it sound like learning a new language. Push past your fear and discover that the pain will be brief, like ripping off a bandage. One of those moments is coming in just a few paragraphs.

According to the statistics summary in Chapter 12, book value is one of the key ingredients of stocks that increase in value. It takes three of the top five slots for performance over one and three years, and two of five slots for a hold time of five years. If you want to make money in the stock market, basing your stock picks on book value is a good choice.

When I started investing over 30 years ago, one of the fundamentals I looked at was book value. I figured that if the company was trading below book value, then even if they went bankrupt, I could still get some of my money back. That is not always true because book value and market value are different. I will explain that later.

BOOK VALUE DEFINED

How do you define book value? Unfortunately, the answer depends on whom you ask. I checked three sources and all three have different definitions. Since I am using Value Line data, let us use their definition (Value Line Publishing, 2007). Book value is "net worth (including intangible assets), less preferred stock at liquidating or redemption value, divided by common shares outstanding."

Intangibles include goodwill (how much a company overpaid for assets), patents, trademarks, unamortized debt discounts, and deferred charges. Of the sources I checked, Value Line is the only one to include intangibles in book value.

If book value is the worth of a company after it liquidates and all debts are repaid, then I have to believe that any patents and trademarks the company owns might be worth something. Therefore, I like Value Line's definition. However, including intangibles does create a problem—valuing them.

- Book value is net worth minus preferred stock divided by common shares outstanding.

VALUE ASSETS PROPERLY

How much is a patent worth? What is the value of a trademark? Book value can be almost anything an accountant wants it to be, which is why some (but perhaps only a few because book value is popular) deemphasize the method in value investing. Historically, though, book value had prominence when asset valuation determined market value and unscrupulous operators sold watered stock to the public.

Watered stock refers to issuing stock valued considerably more than the assets it represents. The term is said to come from the practice of feeding cattle huge amounts of salt and then letting them guzzle water. The water makes them weigh more and that boosts their value when they touch the scales.

- Book value can be unreliable when the value of intangible assets is inflated.

Try this experiment. Weigh yourself just before going to bed and again in the morning. Chances are that you will weigh less in the morning. What are you doing at night besides sleeping?

INVESTING USING BOOK VALUE

Investing using book value is a lot like buying a used car. Imagine visiting a car lot and seeing a sports car that catches your attention. The writing on the windshield says, "Buy me," and it calls to you with windswept lines, tight curves, and racing stripes. You probably kick the tires just for fun, because you have heard that is what people do.

The salesperson pops the hood and you lean closer to look at things you do not have a clue as to how they work. You grunt, point, and ask questions about changing the oil, gas mileage, and its top speed before the rubber separates from the rims. Of course you take it for a test drive, check the gauges and everything else you can think of. Back at the lot, you ask that important question: "How much does it cost?"

"Since we depreciated it like crazy, we can let you have it for just $5,000. Bluebook is ten. Better buy it now before someone else does. Thirty people have already looked at it this morning." You glance at your watch and they have been open for only an hour, so you know that is a lie.

At the library, you look up the car's value and discover that the dealer was right. The fair value is $10,000. Why is it selling for half that? Then you recall thousands of cars caught in floods, totaled by their insurance companies, and then resold illegally. This could be one. Or it could have been involved in a dozen accidents. Perhaps the dealer forgot to include something important. "You want an engine, too? That's another five grand!"

In other words, the value of the car is subjective, just like book value. How much is a factory worth that makes buggy whips and microchips? Is a pile of widgets sitting in inventory worth a million dollars or a buck? The answer to both questions is this: It is worth as much as someone is willing to pay.

Book value is often far removed from market value, so do not get the two confused as I did over 30 years ago. The price of property, plant, and equipment is carried on the books starting at its original cost and reduced over the years by depreciation or increased after improvements.

- Book value is not the same as market value.

WHEN IS BOOK VALUE IMPORTANT?

Sometimes the value of assets kept on the books is outdated, and you do not know how much something is really worth until you try selling it. Each potential buyer may value an asset differently. You can test this yourself by hosting a yard sale or visiting an auction. One person might think they found a Picasso and bid highly for it, but you know the truth: You watched Grandma paint it in her garage last spring.

Book value is important under three conditions.

1. You expect the company to go out of business. It gives you an estimate of what the company is worth after all the bills are paid.
2. If the company were to merge with another, book value may be used to price the company.
3. In a tender offer, if others perceive value in hidden assets, they may bid more for the company.

- Book value is important if the company goes out of business, merges with another, or is bought for its hidden assets.

THE VALUE OF HIDDEN ASSETS

Hidden assets are one reason why book value is popular. Natural resource companies (oil, gas, metals, timber, and so on) can be loaded with assets valued at pennies on the dollar. If you can discover these gems, then you can make a bundle providing (yes, there is a catch) others recognize that value, too. If whispers of a possible takeover arise, then the stock could soar. Like Grandma's Picasso, if several bidders want to buy the painting, then the price will climb.

Let us return to our sports car analogy, the hot red number we saw on the dealer's lot. What if the reason for selling the car is because no one is buying, and the dealer is trying to move inventory? He prices the car to sell. Paying five grand for a car worth double that is a bargain. You can sell it to your rich brother-in-law at full price and walk away with a smile on your face and a bulging wallet.

Finding companies selling below book value and investing in them is better than the alternative, but I will prove that with numbers later in this chapter. If all else remains the same, would you be better off buying a company with a low price to book value or a high one?

A high price to book value means paying more than what the company is worth. People do that all the time in momentum trading when they buy high and sell higher. I have made a lot of money doing that.

Another way to look at it is this. A company selling at or above book value has limited upside potential if everything goes right, but a huge downside if things go wrong. A company selling below book value has a huge upside if things begin to turn around. Which is a better setup?

- A company selling above book value has limited upside potential if everything goes right, but a huge downside if things go wrong. A company selling below book value has big potential when things turn around.

LIMITS OF BOOK VALUE

Book value does have its limitations, according to sources I checked. Peter Lynch and John Rothchild (Penguin Books, 1990) write, "Penn Central had a book value of more than $60 a share when it went bankrupt!" Here are a few limitations.

- The price-to-book ratio is wonderful for asset rich or capital-intensive businesses.
- If you ignore intangible assets (goodwill, patents, trademarks, brands, and other intellectual property), then that hurts service-based firms with few tangible assets.
- Firms with lots of debt on the books coupled with overvalued assets or hard to dispose of assets can pose a hazard to your wealth. If those assets are liquidated for pennies on the dollar, then a high book value gets swallowed up by a mountain of debt.
- Companies that have years of losses or one massive loss can have a negative book value. AMR Corporation is an example. Earnings per share went negative starting in 2001 and remained that way until 2006. The people flying the company could not pull up in time and book value joined earnings by going negative in 2004 and staying underground until 2007.
- Share buybacks can decrease book value by reducing capital on the balance sheet. Weight Watchers is an example. The company bought back a substantial amount of shares (19 percent), taking book value in 2006 from –0.70 to –11.67 a year later.
- Companies that play with cash reserves can change book value. For example, book value drops when the company transfers cash from the balance sheet into reserves for funding pension plans.

Does any of this matter? I think it is like making lasagna with cottage cheese instead of ricotta. If you drink enough wine while cooking, it will not matter how the lasagna tastes.

I use the Value Line numbers for book value prudently and do not sweat the details. As we will see, a low book value can produce some tasty results even if you ignore the limitations.

BUYBACKS LOWER BOOK VALUE

In the last section, I mentioned that share buybacks can lower book value. Let us take a closer look at this by citing an example. Say IBM has $500 billion in assets and $250 billion in liabilities. For simplicity, say book value is the difference between the two, or $250 billion (forget intangibles, preferred stock, and anything else) and that they plan to retire the shares (never issue them again). If the company has a billion shares outstanding, then book value per share is $250.

Suppose the stock is trading at $500 and the company buys back 20 percent of shares outstanding, costing $100 billion, which they fund with cash. Assets drop by $100 billion to $400 billion. The new book value would be $400 billion (assets) – $250 billion (liabilities) or $150 billion. The buyback hurt book value.

This is a simplified example because the company can fund the buyback program by issuing debt or holding the shares as treasury stock. Also, if the company were to buy back the shares at below book value, then the book value per share would go up.

- Share buybacks can change book value.

HISTORICAL RESEARCH

Before I get to my statistics, let us review what other researchers have found in several important studies.

De Bondt and Thaler (American Finance Association, 1987), ranked all companies listed on the NYSE and AMEX (except for those in the S&P 40 Financial Index) between 1965 and 1984 according to price (market value) to book value. They split the results into five groups, from lowest average price to book value (.361) to highest (3.417) and found that the cumulative average return in excess of the index four years after forming the portfolio was 40.7 percent for the lowest price to book value securities and –1.3 percent for those with the highest price to book value.

- Greater returns were achieved by companies with low book value.

Lakonishok, Shleifer, and Vishny (American Finance Association, 1994) looked at stocks with data from April 1963 to April 1990. Using a five-year buy-and-hold approach, they showed that the average annual return ranged from 9.3 percent for high price-to-book-value stocks to 19.8 percent for low price-to-book-value stocks.

The authors computed the returns over time, from 1968 to 1989 in a series of annual contests and found that low price-to-book-value stocks outperformed high price-to-book-value stocks in year ahead performance in 16 out of 22 years, or 73 percent of the time. Using a 3-year hold time, low price to book value won 18 out of 20 contests, or 90 percent of the time. A five-year hold time showed low price to book value winning all 18 contests.

- Low price to book value won 73 percent of contests when held for three years and won all contests when held for five years.

Does low price to book value show higher returns during the best and worst periods? The authors tested this using the 25 worst performing months from April 1968 to April 1989 and found that low price to book value beat those stocks with high price-to-book-value ratios. Excluding those 25 months, they conducted another test when the market declined during 88 months and still found that low price-to-book-value stocks had higher returns.

- Stocks with low price to book value outperform in good and bad times.

Two additional tests using the 25 best performing months and 122 months other than the 25 best, found the same result: Stocks with low price to book values outperformed those with higher ratios. The authors concluded that using a low price-to-book-value approach did not lead to greater downside risk.

- Using a low price-to-book-value approach does not lead to greater downside risk.

In 2009, Tweedy, Browne Company LLC revised their booklet and used information on 7,000 public companies, including those bankrupt or merged out of existence, and filtered them by the following criteria:

- $1 million minimum market capitalization;
- Stocks priced no more than 140 percent of book value on each April 30 from 1970 to 1981.

Filtering removed 1,820 stocks from the search. They found that rolling over a million-dollar investment in stocks selling at less than 30 percent of book value each April 30 from 1970 to 1982 would have grown to $23,298,000. A million dollars invested in the S&P 500 over the same period would have grown to just $2,662,000.

Besides giving me a cut, now you know what to do with those millions.

PRICE TO BOOK VALUE: A GOOD MEASURE

Can we confirm some of the research results using a different data source and methods? Yes, and this section looks at the statistics to see how book value and stock price behave.

A book value of $5 is more important when the stock is selling at $1 than when it is selling at $50. To make comparisons fair between companies and stocks, divide the stock's price by book value. A stock trading at $20 with a $5 book value would have a price-to-book-value ratio of 20 ÷ 5 or 4. Most of the discussion in the following sections concerns the ratio of price to book value.

For investors, a low price to book value can mean several things.

1. The assets are overstated. The stock's price may tumble should assets fall back into alignment with their fair value.

2. Poor return on assets. New management could restructure the company or sell off some of those assets, returning to shareholders locked-in value. Improved business conditions could be all it takes for the company to turn around and the stock's price to soar.

3. The company is undervalued. Hidden assets, like real estate on the books at cost even though inflation has multiplied its value significantly, can boost the value of a company, but only if the market discovers those assets. That can take years to happen.

4. Low price. It may be that a bearish stock market devalued nearly *all* companies to the point that low price to book values make them look as exciting as money found lying in the street.

Do stocks with high or low price to book value perform better over time? The answer is low price to book value beats the high flavor. **Table 3.1** shows the results.

TABLE 3.1 Average Price Change over Time, Sorted by Median Price to Book Value

Condition	Year 1	Year 2	Year 3	Year 4	Year 5	$10,000 Invested
Above median P/ BV 2.11	9%	8%	8%	8%	9%	$14,947
Below median	14%	14%	14%	13%	13%	$18,924

Using book value and price of the stock on the last trading day of year 0 gives the ratio of price to book value. The median price to book value during year 0 was 2.11. I evaluated each stock upon whether it was above or below the median price to book value and then gauged how well it performed during the following five years, based on year-end price changes.

For example, the average rise one year after stocks had a price to book value above the median was 9 percent. Those with below-median values showed rises averaging 14 percent. At the right side of the table, as another example, stocks with above-median price to book values showed average gains of 9 percent. That compares to gains of 13 percent for those stocks with price to book values below the median.

In all contests, stocks with price to book values below the median performed better than did those with ratios above the median. Over a five-year hold time, $10,000 invested in stocks with below the median price to book value would have climbed to $18,924.

- Find stocks selling below the 2.11 median price to book value.

SMALL CAPS: BEST CHOICE

There are many ways to slice and dice price to book value and here is another: by market capitalization. If you multiply the price of the stock times the number of shares outstanding, you get the market cap. I define small-cap stocks as those below $1 billion in market capitalization. Large-cap stocks are those above $5 billion, and mid caps are everything between those two.

Do stocks perform differently when sorted by market cap? Yes, and **Table 3.2** shows what I discovered.

The table uses different median values calculated for each market cap. The percentage values are year-to-year changes, but the $10,000 invested column is for a hold time of five years.

Small-cap stocks with price to book values above the median 1.70 showed average price gains of 16 percent a year later. This compares to a 22 percent average rise for those stocks below the median.

Mid-cap stocks gained an average of 9 percent of their value for those above the 2.25 median compared to gains of 11 percent for those below the median.

Fourteen of 15 contests (93 percent) showed higher gains if the stock had below median price to book values (regardless of market cap).

Now look at the table again. Notice anything remarkable? In most cases, small-cap stocks outperformed mid- and large-cap stocks. For example,

TABLE 3.2   Median Price to Book Value by Market Cap

Condition	Year 1	Year 2	Year 3	Year 4	Year 5	$10,000 Invested
Small cap, above median 1.70	16%	13%	11%	9%	13%	$17,955
Below median	22%	18%	16%	15%	13%	$21,856
Mid cap, above median 2.25	9%	9%	8%	9%	9%	$15,134
Below median	11%	11%	11%	11%	13%	$17,049
Large cap, above median 3.21	2%	3%	5%	4%	2%	$11,782
Below median	12%	11%	12%	14%	13%	$18,150

after holding the stock for a year, small caps showed gains averaging at least 16 percent compared to maximum gains of 11 percent for mid caps and 12 percent for large caps. Out of 20 contests, small-cap stocks win 65 percent of the time (that is, comparing the smaller of the two small-cap values per year to each of the four mid- and large-cap values).

A $10,000 investment in small-cap stocks with below-median price to book values grew to $21,856 after five years compared to $17,955 for those small caps with above-median price to book values.

When selecting stocks to buy and hold, pick small-cap stocks, those with market caps below $1 billion. Be careful when relying on services for their view of market cap. Some define small, mid, and large caps at values other than $1 billion and $5 billion.

The finding that small-cap stocks outperform mid- and large-cap ones is not new. A Fama and French (June 1992) article shows a table of book values to market equities (price) sorted by market cap using data from July 1963 to December 1990.

Adjusting the results for price to book value, we find that small-cap stocks with low price to book values have an average monthly return of 1.92 percent or an annual return of 23.0 percent. Large-cap stocks with high price to book values show average monthly returns of 0.70 percent or 8.4 percent annually. The larger the market cap, the worse the results, and the higher the price to book value, the worse the results. The authors split market cap into 10 categories, and, within each category, the best returns came from stocks with the lowest price to book values.

- Small-cap stocks with low price to book values outperform, so consider buying stocks priced below $1 billion in market capitalization.

LOW STOCK PRICE RULES!

Table 3.3 shows the results of stocks sorted by stock price and price to book value. I wanted to know if low-priced stocks performed better than middle- or high-price ones, according to price to book value.

This table uses split, *unadjusted* stock prices to determine the boundary between low, medium, and high prices. Why? Because a high-priced stock today can appear cheap in a few years due to stock splits. For example, a stock priced at $40 (high) would be considered mid range after a two-for-one split ($20) and low priced after another two-for-one split ($10). The stocks used for the years covered did not have any stock splits.

Low-priced stocks were below $15.80, high-priced ones were above $28.20, and mid-priced stocks were everything else. Those boundaries were set by dividing the samples into thirds and using the associated year 0 closing price. The median price to book values used in the analysis also changed since fewer stocks had no splits.

A scan of the table shows that low-priced stocks outperformed all others in nearly all categories. When choosing stocks to hold for the long term, pick low-priced ones below the median price to book value. This becomes

TABLE 3.3 Performance of Stocks Using Price to Book Value Sorted by Price

Condition	Year 1	Year 2	Year 3	Year 4	Year 5	$10,000 Invested
High price (> $28.20), above median 2.75	5%	7%	8%	7%	4%	$13,502
Below median	6%	7%	8%	8%	11%	$14,681
Mid price, above median 1.96	7%	7%	7%	8%	11%	$14,753
Below median	10%	10%	10%	10%	10%	$16,178
Low price (< $15.80), above median 1.40	20%	16%	15%	9%	11%	$19,345
Below median	28%	18%	13%	17%	14%	$22,651

clear when looking at how $10,000 invested for five years in low-priced stocks grew to $22,651 compared to $14,681 for high-priced ones.

What happens to performance when we consider price to book value? Out of 15 contests, 11 were won by those below the median price to book value, two were won by those above the median, and two tied.

Look at the percentage change in Table 3.3. Low-priced stocks performed much better than higher priced ones. For example, low-priced stocks with below median price to book value returned 28 percent in their first year compared to 10 percent for mid-priced stocks and 6 percent for high-priced ones.

How often do low-priced stocks outperform higher priced ones? Answer: 59 percent of the time. I measured this by comparing stock prices in year 0 and finding that the median percentage return a year later was 7.7 percent. Then I looked for low-priced stocks (less than $15.80) that exceeded those gains, and found that happened 59 percent of the time.

Stocks selling at a low price (less than $15.80) with below median price to book values (less than 1.98, which is the median price to book value for all split unadjusted stocks) resulted in better than the median 7.7 percent performance 61 percent of the time.

- Select stocks priced below about $16.00 for the best results.

BOOK VALUE AND RETURN ON EQUITY

Some sources caution that investing by book value alone can be as dangerous as driving at night with the lights off. One note said that overvalued growth stocks commonly show a low return on equity (ROE), and a high price to book value. Both should move up in tandem, it said.

I decided to test this and combined price to book value (rising or falling) with return on equity (rising or falling) and **Table 3.4** shows the results.

TABLE 3.4   Annual Return on Price to Book Value and Return on Equity

Price to Book Value	ROE	Year 1	Year 2	Year 3	Year 4	Year 5	$10,000 Invested
Falling	Falling	6%	8%	10%	15%	11%	$15,982
Falling	Rising	13%	8%	10%	14%	10%	$16,803
Rising	Falling	9%	8%	14%	13%	13%	$17,131
Rising	Rising	10%	10%	10%	14%	10%	$16,715
Falling, small caps	Rising	19%	11%	7%	23%	15%	$20,108
Falling, small caps priced below $15.80	Rising	41%	10%	7%	25%	17%	$24,080

If both price to book value and ROE are declining from one year to the next, then the stock gained an average of 6 percent the following year. This is the worst of the four combinations. Stocks with the best combination, a falling price to book value and a rising return on equity, had gains averaging 13 percent.

The combination of rising price to book value (meaning either the stock's price is climbing or book value is dropping), and falling ROE (a smaller shareholder's return), gives the best investment after holding for five years: $17,131. This is probably the product of a skyrocketing stock price—exactly the combination that the note warned about.

For year ahead performance, I would suggest finding stocks based on the second-place winner (falling price to book value/rising ROE). The first-year gain averages 13 percent.

Avoid stocks with a falling price to book value and declining ROE. That combination resulted in the worst performance after five years: $15,982.

If you refine the search to small-cap stocks with falling price to book value and rising ROE the year 1 gain jumps to 19 percent. After five years, you will more than double your money, to $20,108.

Adding stock price into the mix along with small caps, falling price to book value, and rising ROE, we find that the year 1 gain shoots up to 41 percent and $10,000 invested and held for five years grows to $24,080. Since I am using stock price, I switched to split unadjusted price data using the $15.80 value discussed in Table 3.3. The various combinations cut the search for the perfect investment down to 37 stocks, but this also smacks of curve fitting.

Curve fitting is tuning the results to achieve optimum performance. That is not always a bad thing, but future performance may fall well short of expectations.

- Stocks with a falling price to book value and rising return on share-holders equity (ROE) result in the best performance a year later. Avoid stocks in which price to book value and ROE are both falling.

WHAT IS THE BEST PRICE TO BOOK VALUE?

If you had to pick one price-to-book-value range in which to search for stocks, what would it be? **Table 3.5** shows a range of price to book values (left column), followed by the average percentage gain that stocks within the range had in one year (year 0 end to year 1 end), and the number of samples qualifying.

TABLE 3.5　One-Year Gain Showing the Best Price to Book Value

P/BV Range	Gain	Samples
≤0	16%	127
0–0.5	36%	202
0.5–1.0	20%	1,073
1.0–1.5	14%	1,883
1.5–2.0	13%	1,751
2.0–2.5	10%	1,291
2.5–3.0	12%	970
3.0–3.5	10%	712
3.5–4.0	13%	514
>4.0	6%	2,199

For example, 127 stocks with zero or less-than-zero price to book values scored an average percentage gain of 16 percent. Those with price to book values above zero but less than 0.5 had the highest average percentage gain, 36 percent with 202 samples qualifying.

For the best year-ahead performance, select stocks with price to book values at or below 1.0. Restricting stock selections to companies with price to book values below 1.0 in year 0 gives a year 1 gain of 21 percent. A $10,000 investment grows to $21,661 after five years—more than doubling.

- Stocks with price to book values below 1.0 tend to do well.

COMBINATIONS AND PERFORMANCE

If I take the combination of stocks priced below $15.80, falling price to book value, rising return on equity, and limit price to book value to below 1.0, I find the performance results listed in **Table 3.6**. Only 21 stocks qualified and that means it is a reasonable number to pour through manually, searching for the best stocks to add to your portfolio.

In the bottom row, I added a small-cap requirement. This cuts the number of stocks and hurts performance, which I find puzzling since small caps should outperform.

Let me caution you that the results are from in-sample tests using stocks from 1992 to 2007. That means your results may vary, and additional testing is needed to prove that the combination described works well under other market conditions and with other stocks.

TABLE 3.6 Combinations of Factors and Performance

Combination	Year 1	Year 2	Year 3	Year 4	Year 5	Stocks	$10,000 Invested
Price below $15.80.	50%	24%	11%	30%	35%	21	$36,321
Falling price to book value.							
Rising return on equity.							
Book value below 1.0.							
Same as above but small caps, too.	40%	27%	6%	33%	36%	15	$34,282

The low sample count also means that the numbers are likely to be unreliable. Do not expect that a stock following the criteria outlined in the table will make 40 percent or 50 percent a year after buying it.

TRADING STRATEGY: BEATING THE DOW

Michael O'Higgins and John Downes (HarperCollins, 1992) cowrote a book in which they suggested that buying the 10 Dow stocks with the lowest price-to-book ratios outperformed the complete Dow Jones Industrials. Their table covered the years from 1973 to mid-1991.

I used the Dow stocks as of March 23, 2009, and checked the historical price data on those components. My data for three Dow stocks (Citibank, Kraft, and JPMorgan Chase) did not go back to 1992, and many other components substitutions occurred since 1992, which I ignored.

Table 3.7 shows my results. I ranked the Dow stocks during 1992 and established the 10 lowest and highest according to their price-to-book-value ratios. Then, I measured the price change in each stock and the Dow from the close on the last trading day in 1992 to the last close in 1993. I found that the Dow had climbed by 13.7 percent, without dividends added. Those with the highest price to book values dropped 5.9 percent in 1993 compared to a gain of 14.5 percent for those 10 Dow stocks with the lowest price-to-book ratios.

In the 16 years covered by Table 3.7, the 10 stocks with the lowest price-to-book-value ratios beat the top 10 nine times, or 56 percent of the time. However, the bottom 10 beat the entire Dow average 81 percent of the time.

TABLE 3.7 Top and Bottom Ten Price-to-Book-Value Stocks in the Dow Industrials

Year	Top 10 High P/BV	All Dow Stocks	Bottom 10 Low P/BV
1993	−5.9%	13.7%	14.5%
1994	3.3%	2.1%	8.8%
1995	37.9%	33.5%	43.2%
1996	35.3%	26.0%	34.5%
1997	31.7%	22.6%	30.3%
1998	46.8%	16.1%	17.0%
1999	21.5%	25.2%	27.7%
2000*	−14.9%	−6.2%	2.6%
2001*	0.9%	−7.1%	−1.0%
2002*	−14.9%	−16.8%	−14.1%
2003	13.7%	25.3%	31.0%
2004	1.7%	3.1%	7.9%
2005	−2.7%	−0.6%	−2.8%
2006	13.5%	16.3%	30.2%
2007	9.8%	6.4%	−6.6%
2008*	−31.6%	−33.8%	−41.6%

*Bear market years

Looking closer at the bear market of 2000 to 2002 and 2008, we find that the Dow stocks with the lowest price to book values beat the top 10 half the time and the full Dow complement 75 percent of the time.

A $10,000 portfolio invested equally in the 10 Dow stocks with the lowest price to book values from 1993 to 2008 would amount to $39,718. Another $10,000 invested in the entire Dow stocks covering the same period would amount to $26,586. Dividends, commissions, slippage, and other fees were not included.

- Annually buying the Dow's 10 lowest price-to-book-value stocks remains a winning strategy.

THE EIGHT-STOCK SETUP

Let us say that you do not want to split your money into 10 stocks in the Dow industrials. What would be the optimum number of stocks to hold for maximum gains? Assuming you spent $10,000 evenly spread between Dow stocks with the lowest price-to-book ratios, rebalanced your portfolio yearly, and spent $20 on round-trip commissions ($10 to buy and $10 to sell), **Figure 3.1** shows the result.

For example, if you spent $10,000 on one Dow stock with the lowest price to book value, you would have ended with $1,810 after 16 years, after commissions, and after rotating to the lowest price to book value stock each year. Yuck. Much of that decline was due to General Motors teetering on the brink of bankruptcy in 2008. The results cry out for diversification.

Holding two stocks returns $18,237, which is a vast improvement, but it still pales in comparison to the $46,688 gain by holding 13 stocks. Second best, and my personal choice, is selecting eight stocks with the lowest price to book values each year. That would return $45,737. You get diversification and close to peak performance based on the Dow components in early 2009 while still holding a manageable number of securities. Since the analysis allowed fractional shares and $20 round-trip commissions on the Dow components, you will want to test this yourself.

The eight-stock setup also results in the highest portfolio value over the 16 years, that of $93,406 as of year end 2007, besting the 13-stock portfolio value of $71,436. When the bear market of 2008 began (which really began in late 2007), it was a body blow for all stocks, including those with low price to book values. The eight-stock portfolio dropped by half.

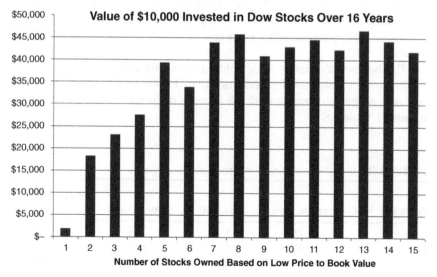

FIGURE 3.1 Investment in Dow stocks with the lowest price to book value versus 16-year average return.

The eight-stock portfolio beats the complete 30 Dow stocks 69 percent of the time (in annual contests) and ends with a balance 72 percent higher, $45,737 versus $26,566.

- To beat the performance of the Dow industrials, buy eight Dow stocks with the lowest price to book value each year.

HOLD TIME FOR BEST RESULTS

Knowing that buying low price-to-book-value stocks results in higher profits over time, how long should you hold a stock?

There are several answers. First, hold the stock until the price to book value rises to the 2.11 median (see Table 3.1), or whatever book value you chose to use.

Second, sell when the stock is valued no differently than (or above) the rest of the industry. This option makes the most sense. Why? Because the industry might have the hot hand in a cold market, and selling at the market median could mean leaving extra chips on the table if the industry has a higher median.

Another answer appears in **Table 3.8**.

I computed the year 0 to year 1 price change for all stocks having a year 0 price to book value below the 2.11 median and found that the average rise was 15.7 percent. The following year, I used the year 1 price to book value and looked at the year 1 to year 2 price change, which turned out to be 16.0 percent. The remainder of the table shows additional results.

The largest gains came after holding stocks for two years.

In another test, I used a frequency distribution to determine when the best and worst performance of the 5 years occurred. Those count totals appear in Table 3.8.

TABLE 3.8   Hold Time for Low Price-to-Book-Value Stocks

Gains Per Year	Average Rise	Best Year	Worst Year	Best/Worst Ratio
1	15.7%	894	788	53.2%
2	16.0%	846	800	51.4%
3	14.1%	804	706	53.2%
4	14.0%	691	700	49.7%
5	13.0%	642	883	42.1%

For example, 894 times the first year's percentage change was the highest of the five years, and 788 times it was the worst performing year. Only stocks with five years of performance were included.

Based on the findings, the best hold time was one to three years because they had the highest best-year percentage to the sum of best and worst years. The worst hold-time ratio was five years because the average rise was 13.0 percent over that period.

This range is slightly shorter than I found for my own trades in *Trading Basics*, Chapter 2 (see the section "Hold Time: My Trades"), which had a range of three to four years where I made 36 percent, but also made 28 percent (which is close) after holding between two and three years.

- Hold low price-to-book-value stocks for one to three years.

CHAPTER CHECKLIST

You may be sick of reading about book value because we tunneled to the earth's core for answers. Book value is one of the cornerstones of value investing, so it was worth the trip.

Historical research says that stocks outperform when they have low price to book value. My tests showed similar results.

Combing the research results, we find the following (from "Combinations and Performance"):
- Select stocks priced below $16.
- Look for price to book value below 1.0.
- Find stocks with price to book value lower this year than last.
- Choose small-cap stocks (optional).
- Return on equity should be rising.

In the next chapter, we look at capital spending and find that when it decreases, stock performance improves. Who knew? Before we get there, here is a list of the important tips to consider when using book value.

- ☐ Book value is net worth minus preferred stock divided by common shares outstanding. See the section "Book Value Defined."
- ☐ Book value can be unreliable when the value of intangible assets is inflated. See the section "Value Assets Properly."
- ☐ Book value is not the same as market value. See the section "Investing Using Book Value."
- ☐ Book value is important if the company goes out of business, merges with another, or is bought for its hidden assets. See the section "When Is Book Value Important?"

☐ A company selling above book value has limited upside potential if eve-rything goes right, but a huge downside if things go wrong. A company selling below book value has big potential when things turn around. See the section "The Value of Hidden Assets."

☐ See the section "Limits of Book Value" for a list of problems associated with relying on book value.

☐ Share buybacks can change book value. See the section "Buybacks Lower Book Value."

☐ Greater returns were achieved by companies with low book value. See the section "Historical Research."

☐ Low price to book value won 73 percent of contests when held for three years and won all contests when held for five years. See the sec-tion "Historical Research."

☐ Stocks with low price to book value outperform in good and bad times. See the section "Historical Research."

☐ Using a low price-to-book-value approach does not lead to greater downside risk. See the section "Historical Research."

☐ Find stocks selling below the 2.11 median price to book value. See Table 3.1.

☐ Small-cap stocks with low price to book values outperform, so con-sider buying stocks priced below $1 billion in market capitalization. See Table 3.2.

☐ Select stocks priced below about $16.00 for the best results. See Table 3.3.

☐ Stocks with a falling price to book value and a rising return on share-holders equity (ROE) result in the best performance the following year. Avoid stocks in which price to book value and ROE are both falling. See Table 3.4.

☐ Stocks with price to book values below 1.0 tend to do well. See Table 3.5.

☐ Table 3.6 lists combinations of fundamentals to limit the number of stocks qualifying and to boost performance.

☐ Annually buying the Dow's ten lowest price-to-book-value stocks remains a winning strategy. See the section "Trading Strategy: Beating the Dow."

☐ To beat the performance of the Dow industrials, buy eight Dow stocks with the lowest price to book value each year. See the section "The Eight-Stock Setup."

☐ Hold your low price-to-book-value stock for one to three years. See Table 3.8.

CHAPTER 4

Capital Spending

C apital spending sounds like something Congress does when they pass one of their pork-laden bills. The full phrase is capital spending per share of stock, and it refers to the amount of money a company spends annually to buy property like tools, equipment, factories, and the real estate on which they stand (usually), divided by the number of shares outstanding.

When management discusses their quarterly results with analysts and shareholders, you will hear the term *capex*. It is short for capital expenditures or capital spending.

When I started researching capital spending, I imagined that a company increasing its capital spending would add value to the enterprise, helping to ensure a rise in future earnings and a higher stock price. What I found during testing surprised me.

- Capital spending is the amount of money a company spends annually to buy property, divided by the number of shares outstanding.

IS DECREASING CAPITAL SPENDING THE HOLY GRAIL?

In the first test, I used 788 stocks from 1992 to 2007 that reported capital spending, but not all stocks covered the entire period. Dividends were not included in the results.

TABLE 4.1   Capital Spending versus Change in Stock Price

Capital Spending	Year 1	Year 2	Year 3	Year 4	Year 5	$10,000 Invested
Increasing	8%	10%	12%	10%	9%	$15,919
Decreasing	16%	12%	9%	13%	12%	$17,916

Table 4.1 shows whether a company increased capital spending in year 0 and the resulting change in stock price over the next one to five years. Each column represents the average change in stock price from one year to the next.

If a company increased capital spending, then the following year its stock price climbed an average of 8 percent. In year 4, after increasing capex, price climbed an average of 10 percent before averaging 9 percent in year 5.

Look at what happens when the company cuts capital spending. In year 1, the stock gains almost twice as much as when a company increased capital spending: 16 percent versus 8 percent. The remainder of the years also show better performance except for year 3. Buying stocks that decreased capital spending at the end of year 0 and holding them for five years grew a $10,000 investment to $17,916.

Have we found a method to pick a better stock? Maybe. Decreasing capital spending resulted in performance better than the average between 49 and 55 percent of the time. I expected it to work more often than that.

- When companies cut capital spending, their stocks tend to outperform the next year, but the improvement only applies to half of the stocks.

CAPITAL SPENDING TRENDS VERSUS PERFORMANCE

I looked at the trend of capital spending from year to year, and **Table 4.2** shows the results. For example, a company that increases capital spending in the first year followed by a decrease the next shows an average stock gain of 14 percent the following year. I show that as the year 1 value.

Flipping the test to a decrease in capital spending the first year followed by an increase the next year showed stocks posting their worst performance of the bunch: an 8 percent increase in price the following year.

The best performance comes if the company cuts capital spending two years in a row. The stocks gained an average of 18 percent the following year. In fact, a $10,000 investment would grow to $18,515 after five years from stocks in which the company cut capital spending two years in a row.

TABLE 4.2 Variations on Capital Spending

Capital spending from year to year	Year 1	Year 2	Year 3	Year 4	Year 5	$10,000 Invested
Increase then decrease	14%	13%	9%	11%	13%	$17,440
Decrease then increase	8%	9%	14%	11%	9%	$16,091
Decrease both years	18%	11%	11%	14%	12%	$18,515
Increase both years	8%	11%	11%	7%	9%	$15,500

Unfortunately, a two-year cut in capital spending resulted in only 58 percent of the stocks showing better-than-average results. That exceeds the 55 percent found in the prior test.

- Companies with capital spending decreases for two consecutive years have the best year-ahead stock performance. This method works 58 percent of the time.

FREQUENCY DISTRIBUTION

Table 4.3 shows a frequency distribution of change in capital spending and the following year's stock price change. For example, companies that increased capital spending at least 10 percent saw their stock prices rise by 8 percent the next year. Those that cut their capital spending at least 10 percent saw their stocks climb by 17 percent, or more than double!

TABLE 4.3 Capital Spending Increases versus Stock Performance

Capital Spending Increase	One-Year Stock Price Change	Capital Spending Decrease	One-Year Stock Price Change
10%	8%	−10%	17%
20%	8%	−20%	17%
30%	7%	−30%	18%
40%	4%	−40%	21%
50%	2%	−50%	24%
60%	1%	−60%	25%
70%	1%	−70%	29%
80%	−1%	−80%	23%
90%	−3%	−90%	26%

If you scan down the columns, you will see that as capital spending increases, stock performance decreases. As capital spending decreases, stock performance mushrooms until reaching –70 percent. After that, the sample counts get too small to be reliable.

The idea you should remember from this chapter is this: Look for stocks in which the company is cutting capital spending, preferably two years in a row, and by a sizable percentage. Stocks that qualify tend to outperform the next year. The performance improvement is often due to a few big winners because just over half of the stocks see improvement using this method.

- As capital spending increases, stock performance suffers. If capital spending decreases, stock performance rises.

PERFORMANCE BY MARKET CAP

Table 4.4 shows the results over time after sorting price-to-capital spending by market capitalization. For example, large-cap stocks in year 1 that were above the median 33.17 price-to-cap spending scored gains averaging just 3 percent. Those with below median spending scored gains of 13 percent.

In all cases except one, performance improved when the price-to-capital-spending ratio was below the median. Small-cap stocks performed better than mid and large caps. Look at the difference between the best and worst performing caps. A $10,000 investment in small-cap stocks with a below the median price-to-capital-spending ratio grew to $20,369 compared to $12,114 for large-cap stocks with above-median ratios.

TABLE 4.4 Median Price-to-Capital Spending by Market Cap

Condition	Year 1	Year 2	Year 3	Year 4	Year 5	$10,000 Invested
Small cap, above median 19.17	18%	14%	12%	12%	13%	$18,933
Below median	18%	17%	14%	13%	14%	$20,369
Mid cap, above median 24.20	9%	8%	9%	9%	8%	$14,891
Below median	12%	14%	11%	12%	14%	$18,234
Large cap, above 33.17 median	3%	1%	5%	6%	5%	$12,114
Below median	13%	15%	15%	12%	11%	$18,530

The results suggest that selecting small-cap stocks with below median price-to-capital-spending ratios can pay handsomely if you plan to hold the stock longer than one year.

- Invest in small-cap stocks because they show the best performance over time, especially if they cut their capital spending.

CHAPTER CHECKLIST

If a company spends big bucks to build a factory, once the factory is running, capital spending can decrease (all else being equal), helping to contribute to profitability. That is the big lesson learned in this chapter.

In the next chapter, we look at cash flow. Analysts love cash flow, but is it as important as they make it out to be?

Here is an itemized checklist of findings for capital spending:

- ☐ Capital spending is the amount of money a company spends annually to buy property, divided by the number of shares outstanding. See this chapter's introduction.
- ☐ When companies cut capital spending, their stocks tend to outperform the next year, but the improvement only applies to half of the stocks. See Table 4.1.
- ☐ Companies with capital spending decreases for two consecutive years have the best year-ahead stock performance. This method works 58 percent of the time. See Table 4.2.
- ☐ As capital spending increases, stock performance suffers. If capital spending decreases, stock performance rises. See Table 4.3.
- ☐ Invest in small-cap stocks because they show the best performance over time, especially if they cut their capital spending. See Table 4.4.

CHAPTER 5

Cash Flow

C ash flow is what keeps a business running. If Joe's Manufacturing runs out of cash, then they cannot pay their employees, and cannot buy materials to make the things they sell. If the shortfall lasts long enough, the operation grinds to a halt like a car running without oil. Another term for that is bankruptcy.

Consider earnings per share. If earnings go negative, what happens? Does the electric utility threaten to turn off the lights? No. The company can exist with negative earnings for years, but if the cash flow dries up, then they are in serious trouble.

Biotechnology companies are a good example. They are often unprofitable for years until their blockbuster drug gets approved and the cash starts tumbling in.

What about the opposite of a cash starved outfit? Let us call it the cash cow. Investors dream of owning cash cows, but what should the company do with all that extra cash?

When a company uses its free cash flow (operating cash flow minus capital spending) wisely, earnings can explode in future years. Dividends can increase, debt can drop, they can buy back shares, or reinvest in the company to continue the trend. Free cash flow is what remains after paying all of the bills.

- Free cash flow is operating cash flow minus capital expenditures.

If we were to look at a cash flow statement, it would appear in three parts:

1. *Operating cash flow* (often called just cash flow) represents the core of cash-generation activities. It is sales less the cost to buy inventory, pay for taxes, pay interest on debt, and other related operating costs. Operating cash flow is the net cash that comes from operating a business.

2. *Cash flow from investing* is just as it sounds. A company might buy and sell investment securities, plus acquire other companies or sell parts of itself.

3. *Cash flow from financing* is the money a company pays or receives from issuing or repaying debt and selling or repurchasing equity (stock), minus the cost of any dividends paid.

HISTORICAL RESEARCH REVIEW

Professors Lakonishok, Shleifer, and Vishny (American Finance Association, 1994) wrote a paper that examined cash flow to price in stocks on the New York and American Stock Exchanges. The analysis covered the period from 1968 to 1989.

They found that the average annual return for glamour stocks (lowest rank based on cash flow to price) over five years was 9 percent compared to a return of 20 percent for Value stocks (highest rank of cash flow to price). To flip the ratios around and put it in our terms, stocks with low price-to-cash-flow ratios dramatically outperformed those with high ratios. My results, discussed below, confirm their findings.

Later in the article they ask, are higher returns from value investing due to increased risk? They answer, "These tests do not provide much support for the view that value strategies are fundamentally riskier."

To test this, they used cash flow to price, among other metrics, and created a portfolio using 1-, 3-, and 5-year holding periods. For the 1-year hold time, value (low price to cash flow) stocks outperformed glamour (high price to cash flow) stocks in 17 of 22 years. Using the 3- and 5-year hold times, value beat glamour in 18 out of 20 and 18 out of 18 contests, respectively. They concluded that "value strategies have consistently outperformed glamour strategies," and "These numbers pose a stiff challenge to any risk-based explanation for the higher returns on value stocks."

Using a second method, they compared the returns of value and glamour portfolios during the best and worst performing months using cash flow to price divided by the 5-year weighted average rank of sales growth. They concluded that "The value portfolio outperformed the glamour portfolio in the market's worst 25 months," outperformed it in the next 88 worst performing months, and continued to outperform through the 25 best months. "The value strategy did not expose investors to greater downside risk."

- Historical research confirms that stocks with low price to cash flow outperform and are no more risky.

COOKING THE BOOKS

Before I discuss my results, let me explain why many consider cash flow vital in valuing a company and how they can cook the books.

Back in the late 1970s when I was a hardware design engineer, I went down to the company library and read the magazines every few weeks. I remember the price-to-sales ratio being big at the time along with price to earnings, but not a word did I read about cash flow.

Earnings per share and some of the more popular ratios are subject to manipulation, but cash flow is harder to fudge. It is like eating a bowling ball compared to ice cream: Eating the bowling ball can still be done, but it is more difficult. The more cash a company generates, the stronger the company appears, and the more attractive it looks. Coupled with less manipulation, it is why many analysts prefer cash flow to earnings.

How can a company cook the books? One way is what I call *the cash is in the mail* technique. A company can write checks late while delaying booking accounts payable (money the company owes). Extending payables tends to inflate cash and upsets suppliers who have to wait longer for payment.

Another method is to sell accounts receivable (money owed the company) to another company in exchange for less cash than the accounts are worth. The company selling the receivables gets an influx of cash immediately, but in amounts smaller than if they just waited and collected them directly from their customers in the normal manner. While not illegal, a company using this method probably has a serious liquidity issue. It is a red flag.

Booking revenue today for cash that is not due for more than a year is another manipulation technique. It amounts to a shell game of showing cash increasing from recorded revenue without an offset in accounts receivable. The noncurrent cash settlement is buried in another category like other investments.

I remember channel stuffing was popular years ago. A company provides customers incentives such as a promise to accept unsold merchandise providing they load up on products now. These efforts boost sales one quarter and hurt them the next.

You may have heard the discussions of companies playing with reserves. They inflate charges in one quarter only to say, "Just kidding!" and reverse them in later quarters, giving an added kick to the bottom line.

THE NUMBERS

Value Line defines cash flow per share as "the sum of reported earnings plus depreciation, less any preferred dividends, calculated on a per-share basis, also now including stock option expense." I will use their numbers to determine whether price to cash flow is valuable when picking stocks.

Value Line shows cash flow per share on their newsletter. To simplify the presentation, when you read price to cash flow, I actually mean price to cash flow per share.

The following analysis uses 884 stocks that reported cash flow for a total of 10,198 samples from 1992 to 2007. Not all stocks covered the entire period.

IS INCREASING CASH FLOW GOOD?

Table 5.1 shows the effect on a stock's price of cash flow over time. Many will argue that the more cash a company generates, the more freedom it has to use that cash to make more profit. Perhaps you have heard the phrase, "It takes money to make money."

Many believe that higher profits translate into higher stock prices. Does increasing price to cash flow hurt or help? The table provides an answer. I removed from the analysis all companies not reporting cash flow.

When cash flow increases, the ratio of price to cash flow drops. Thus, a decreasing ratio is good and an increasing one is bad. The results in **Table 5.1** confirm this belief.

TABLE 5.1   Price to Cash Flow over Time

Price to Cash Flow per Share	Year 1	Year 2	Year 3	Year 4	Year 5	$10,000 Invested
Increasing (bad)	10%	11%	10%	10%	8%	$15,958
Decreasing (good)	11%	10%	11%	12%	11%	$16,911

For example, when price to cash flow increased, the stock gained 10 percent a year later compared to a gain of 11 percent when the ratio decreased. Year 5 showed the widest difference, 8 percent versus 11 percent, respectively.

When the price to cash flow dropped from year to year, the stock gain remained relatively constant. However, when the ratio decreased (meaning higher cash per share or a lower stock price), the stock's performance increased over time. In other words, higher cash flow over time was good.

If you invested $10,000 in those stocks reporting cash flow (even minus cash flow), the value would have grown to $15,958 for those companies with increasing price to cash flow and $16,911 for companies with a decreasing ratio. The difference between the two numbers is not exciting in my view.

- Look for decreasing price to cash flow.

Median Performance

I found that the median (mid range) price-to-cash-flow ratio was 9.17. Comparing those stocks with ratios above and below the median provided interesting results. **Table 5.2** shows them.

For example, companies with price-to-cash-flow values above 9.17 showed gains in their stock a year later that averaged 9 percent. Those with ratios below the median had gains averaging 14 percent. A five-year, $10,000 investment in stocks with price to cash flow above the median resulted in the value increasing to $14,931, but the same investment in stocks with below the median ratio had the value rise to $18,694.

This is additional evidence that increasing cash flow helps the company perform and that performance pushes up the stock price.

- Companies with price to cash flow per share below the median 9.17 tended to have their stocks substantially outperform up to five years later.

TABLE 5.2 Average Price Change over Time, Sorted by Median Price to Cash Flow

Condition	Year 1	Year 2	Year 3	Year 4	Year 5	$10,000 Invested
Above median 9.17	9%	8%	8%	8%	9%	$14,931
Below median	14%	13%	13%	13%	13%	$18,694

PERFORMANCE BY MARKET CAP

Table 5.3 shows price to cash flow sorted by market cap. As we have seen with other tables on market cap, small cap stocks show average gains that tower above the other two categories. When you subdivide them into price to cash flow above or below the median, the results are even better.

In fact, small caps below the median 7.50 price to cash flow rank behind book value as the best performing fundamental for one- and three-year hold times. It places fourth for a five-year hold, too.

For example, small-cap stocks below the median 7.50 price-to-cash-flow ratio showed performance averaging 24 percent one year later. Those companies with above-median ratios posted gains in the stock of 15 percent. Values below the median mean rising cash flow, falling stock price, or both—and it is better than the reverse.

Small caps with ratios below the 7.50 median saw an investment of $10,000 over five years grow to $22,706.

When selecting stocks to buy and hold for the long term, stick to small caps.

- The performance of small-cap stocks beats the performance of mid- and large-cap stocks.
- Price-to-cash-flow ratios below their respective median show stocks with better performance up to five years later 73 percent of the time (11 out of 15 contests).

TABLE 5.3 Median Price to Cash Flow by Market Cap

Condition	Year 1	Year 2	Year 3	Year 4	Year 5	$10,000 Invested
Small cap, above median 7.50	15%	13%	11%	8%	10%	$17,003
Below median	24%	18%	15%	16%	16%	$22,706
Mid cap, above median 9.70	9%	9%	7%	10%	11%	$15,618
Below median	9%	9%	12%	10%	10%	$16,192
Large cap, above median 12.10	4%	3%	6%	4%	4%	$12,296
Below median	11%	11%	11%	14%	11%	$17,191

TABLE 5.4   Various Price-to-Cash-Flow Ratios and One-Year Gains

Price/Cash Flow	Gain	Samples
≤1	11%	664
1–2	28%	139
2–3	22%	295
3–4	19%	470
4–5	17%	661
5–6	11%	713
6–7	15%	717
7–8	14%	735
8–9	13%	601
9–10	10%	621

What Is the Best Cash Flow Value?

A frequency distribution of the price-to-cash-flow ratio shows that the 664 companies with ratios below 1 (including negative ratios) posted average gains of 11 percent a year later. Companies with ratios between 1 and 2 performed best: a 28 percent gain a year later, but only 139 samples qualified.

Table 5.4 suggests that the higher the ratio, the smaller the gain a year later.

- The best price-to-cash-flow ratio is between one and two, but few companies qualify. Generally, the higher the ratio, the worse the stock's performance a year later.

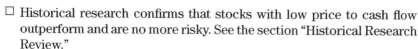

CHAPTER CHECKLIST

Cash flow is important when comparing one company to another, but it can also be handy for selecting stocks for future performance. Here is a checklist of the important findings from this chapter.

☐ Free cash flow is operating cash flow minus capital expenditures. See this chapter's introduction.

☐ Historical research confirms that stocks with low price to cash flow outperform and are no more risky. See the section "Historical Research Review."

☐ Read the section "Cooking the Books" to understand how companies can manipulate financial results.

☐ Look for decreasing price to cash flow. See Table 5.1.

☐ Companies with price to cash flow per share below the median 9.17 tended to have their stocks substantially outperform up to five years later. See Table 5.2.

☐ The performance of small-cap stocks beats the performance of mid- and large-cap stocks. See Table 5.3.

☐ Price-to-cash-flow ratios below their respective median show stocks with better performance up to five years later 73 percent of the time (11 out of 15 contests). See Table 5.3.

☐ The best price-to-cash-flow ratio is between one and two, but few companies qualify. Generally, the higher the ratio, the worse the stock's performance a year later. See Table 5.4.

CHAPTER 6

Dividends

A dividend is a portion of the company's net earnings returned to shareholders. The dividend is often in cash, less often in stock, but according to one source I checked, it could come in the form of property or scrip (which is a certificate for a fractional share of stock or a promise to pay the dividend sometime in the future).

Dividends are like breakfast cereals: They come in many varieties. Here are a few you may come across and many you will not.

- A *cumulative dividend* often refers to preferred stock that, if the company cannot make a dividend payment, must be paid in full before the common stockholders receive their dividend.
- An *extra or special dividend* is a nonrecurring dividend paid (often in cash or stock) in addition to the regular dividend. A company not paying regular dividends might wish to issue a one-time dividend after having a good year, for example. It is similar to winning the lottery and giving your relatives a piece of the action.
- An *interim dividend* is one paid ahead of the regular dividend.
- A company paying a *liquidating dividend* is one that is going out of business and is distributing its net assets on a pro rata basis to its rightful owners.
- A company gives the shareholder the option of choosing either cash or stock in an optional dividend payment, hence the clever name, *optional dividend*.
- A *liability dividend* is one paid with some type of debt, such as a bond, and it often means the company is short of cash.

- A *phony dividend* is an illegal return of principal. In this scheme, when you buy a stock, a portion of your payment is immediately returned to you as a dividend. These phony dividends generate enthusiasm among unsuspecting shareholders and help sell more stock.
- A *property dividend* is most unusual. It happens when a company pays a dividend not in cash, scrip, or the firm's stock, but in shares of another company it owns or even in its own products. Imagine receiving a property dividend from a chocolate company—delicious!
- A *regular dividend* is paid periodically, often quarterly, but sometimes semiannually or even annually.
- A *scrip dividend* is a promise to pay a dividend in the future and it may be interest or noninterest bearing. Often a scrip dividend means the company is short of cash.
- Dividends are a portion of the company's net earnings returned to shareholders. They can come in a variety of forms.

STOCK DIVIDENDS: AN EXPLANATION

A stock dividend is one issued by a company when they pay in stock. A 10 percent stock dividend, for example, gives a shareholder 10 more shares of stock for every 100 shares owned.

I remember buying Essex Chemical Corporation and collecting not only a cash dividend, but a stock dividend as well. I bought 100 shares for $2,250 in July 1983 and the commission on that purchase was a huge $44. Seven months later, I scooped up another 100 shares for about $1,900.

In 1986, I sold both lots, which totaled 288 shares (because of the stock dividend) for about $8,000, again paying a huge commission, but collecting almost $500 in cash dividends. I made 88 percent on the first trade and 123 percent on the second one, including dividends.

What attracted me to Essex Chemical in the first place has long slipped from memory, but I recall being angry about having to sell the stock, probably because of the merger with Rausch Industries.

HISTORICAL RESEARCH REVIEW

A research report by Patel, Yao, and Barefoot (Credit Suisse, 2006), says that investors should search for companies with high yield and a low payout ratio. The payout ratio is dividend divided by earnings.

They assigned their universe of stocks by dividend yield first (three baskets), and then sorted them within each basket according to the payout ratio: high, medium, and low. Finally, at the end of each quarter, they created equally weighted portfolios based on those baskets from January 1990 to June 2006.

They found that low yield, high payout ratio stocks performed worst and the reverse, high yield, low payout ratio performed best. Second place went to low yield, low payout followed by stocks that did not pay a dividend, and then the S&P 500.

- Stocks with high yield and low payout ratio do well.

They also looked at dividend yield alone, but extended the testing dates from January 1980 to July 2006 on the S&P 500, based on equal-weighted decile baskets of dividend yield at the end of each month.

Those companies with high yields tended to outperform those with low yields. However, they found that companies with the highest yields were not the best performing. Rather, those stocks from the eighth (best) and ninth (second best) deciles performed better than decile 10. They concluded that dividend yield alone was not sufficient to select a stock that outperforms.

- Dividend yield alone is not sufficient to select a stock that outperforms.

HIGH YIELD, HIGH PERFORMANCE?

I decided to test the high-yield, high-performance idea that Credit Suisse explored, and **Table 6.1** shows my results.

For those stocks paying a dividend, I separated the list into three bins of equal size, high yield (all stocks yielding equal to or more than 3.123 percent), low yield (stock with yields equal to or below 1.366 percent, but above 0 percent) and medium yield (stocks between those two numbers).

TABLE 6.1 Stock Performance by Yield over Time

Condition	Year 1	Year 2	Year 3	Year 4	Year 5	$10,000 Invested
High Yield (≥ 3.123%)	17%	16%	17%	16%	15%	$21,376
Medium Yield	13%	14%	13%	14%	13%	$18,705
Low Yield (≤ 1.366%)	11%	10%	11%	10%	11%	$16,591
No dividends	11%	10%	10%	10%	11%	$16,399

The bottom row of the table shows the results of companies not paying a dividend.

For example, those stocks with a high yield had gains a year later of 17 percent, including the dividend payment. Medium-yield stocks showed gains of 13 percent and low-yield stocks posted 11 percent gains a year later. Those stocks not paying a dividend scored 11 percent. These results follow the Credit Suisse research.

Stocks with a high yield outperform those with a low yield. An investment of $10,000 makes this clear. After five years, the value climbs to $21,376 for stocks having a high yield compared to $16,591 for stocks with a low yield. Stocks paying no dividends showed the worst performance, $16,399.

- Stocks with a high yield tend to outperform.

TESTING: YIELD AND PAYOUT RATIO

I sorted the stocks based on yield (three bins: high, medium, and low) and within each bin, sorted the payout ratio (high, medium, and low), then evaluated the year-ahead performance of the various combinations. **Table 6.2** shows what I found. The year 1 performance does *not* include dividends. It is only a close to close measure of price from the end of year 0 to year 1.

For example, stocks with a high yield and a high payout ratio had gains a year later that averaged 10.8 percent. The best performance came from stocks with a high yield and low payout ratio. They showed gains of 13.3 percent the following year. This result matches the Credit Suisse research (CS Rank is Credit Suisse rank, derived from their research).

TABLE 6.2 Stock Performance by Yield and Payout Ratio One Year Later

Yield	Payout	Year 1	CS Rank	My Rank
High	High	10.8%		5
High	Medium	11.3%		4
High	Low	13.3%	1	1: Best
Medium	High	10.3%		6
Medium	Medium	10.0%		9
Medium	Low	11.7%		2
Low	High	10.1%	4	8
Low	Medium	9.6%		10: Worst
Low	Low	10.1%	2	7
None	None	11.3%	3	3

The difference between my research method and theirs is I did not rebalance the portfolios each quarter and dividends were not included in the returns.

The worst performance came from stocks with a low yield and medium payout ratio. They gained just 9.6 percent a year later. Stocks not paying a dividend showed gains of 11.3 percent a year later, ranking third.

- The best performance comes from stocks with a high yield and low payout ratio.

WHICH IS BEST: DIVIDENDS OR NO DIVIDENDS?

Do stocks paying dividends perform better than those without dividends? Some believe that a company reinvesting the money in itself would outperform. **Table 6.3** shows the return of dividend versus nondividend paying stocks. The year 1 through year 5 dividends are included in the returns for those years, respectively. If dividend data was not available, the prior year's rate was used.

For example, in the first year after a company pays a dividend the stock climbed an average of 10.6 percent but when you add in the dividend payment for year 1, it boosts the return to 13.1 percent. Those companies not paying a dividend saw their stock price rise by an average of 11.3 percent. At the end of five years, $10,000 invested would have grown to $18,609 for dividend payers compared to $16,397 for those without dividends.

- Owning dividend-paying stocks is better than owning those not paying a dividend.

SURPRISE: DIVIDEND CUTS WORK!

What happens to the stock when a company changes the dividend rate? **Table 6.4** shows the results of my quest to answer that question.

TABLE 6.3 Return of Companies with and without Dividends

Condition	Year 1	Year 2	Year 3	Year 4	Year 5	$10,000 Invested
Dividends	13.1%	13.2%	13.3%	13.2%	13.3%	$18,609
No Dividends	11.3%	9.9%	9.7%	10.1%	11.0%	$16,397

TABLE 6.4 Returns of Companies with Changing Dividend Rates.

Condition	Year 1	Year 2	Year 3	Year 4	Year 5	$10,000 Invested
Increasing dividends	13%	13%	12%	11%	9%	$17,528
Decreasing dividends (samples)	17% (293)	19% (284)	20% (276)	22% (260)	17% (227)	$23,875
Year 0: dividend cut including to zero	−10% (318 samples)					
Year 0: no dividends paid	11% (5,479 samples)					
Year 0: dividend paid, no cut	15% (5,716 samples)					
Year 0: dividend cut to zero	−9% (72 samples)					
Year 0: dividend cut but not to zero	−10% (246 samples)					

When a company increases the dividend rate during the year, price climbs 13 percent the following year, on average, using 3,552 samples (the entire row uses over 2,200 samples). When a company cuts or eliminates the dividend, the stock rises an average of 17 percent the following year. However, that uses only 293 samples.

The trend of stocks with decreasing dividends beating the performance of companies increasing their dividends remains consistent over time. After five years, $10,000 invested in stocks that decreased their dividends would grow to $23,875.

When I discovered these results, I could not believe my eyes. I thought a dividend cut was bad for the stock! I did some investigating. I looked at the price change during the *same* year of the dividend cut (year 0). Table 6.2 shows the results in the bottom portion of the table.

In the year the company cut their dividend, the stock tumbled an average of 10 percent, measured from the closing prices on the starting and ending days of the year, but including any dividends. This compares to a rise of 11 percent for those stocks that did not pay a dividend and a gain of 15 percent for those companies that maintained or raised their dividend. In other words, the difference between cutting a dividend and maintaining it was a swing of 25 percentage points. Wow! The analysis did not look at what happened to the stock immediately after the dividend cut, only at year's end.

Then I looked at those companies that eliminated their dividend. During the year of the elimination, the stock dropped by an average of 9 percent, but the samples are few (72). When a company cuts their dividend, but not to zero (meaning they pay a smaller dividend), the stock closes out the year an average of 10 percent lower than it did on the close of the first trading day of the year (including dividends). Again, samples were few (246).

What does this mean? If a company cuts their dividend and you own the stock, sell it immediately. When it bottoms, if you can tell when that is, then buy the stock and hold it for the long term. If you hold it for five years, you just might double your money. However, this conclusion is based on relatively few samples. A more thorough test is needed to confirm these results.

- Stocks that cut their dividend rates outperform a year later, but samples are few.
- In the year when a company cuts its dividend, expect price to drop substantially.

I have had the misfortune of owning a few stocks that cut their dividends. The result was bloody. If you have a weak stomach or are under 18, you may want to skip the next section that describes one such cut (amputation, really).

WHEN DISASTER STRIKES

Figure 6.1 shows an example of what happens when an electric utility company cuts their dividend. During the economic meltdown of 2007 to 2009, people were cutting their electricity use in their homes, and factories were either cutting production or shutting down entirely. To conserve cash, the utility decided to cut their dividend by 39 percent. They were not the only company or utility to cut their dividend.

Shareholders hated the news. The stock opened almost 16 percent lower and continued plunging like a bungee jumper after the cord breaks.

When the stock went splat at A, price was 39 percent lower (which matches the dividend cut, incidentally). Then investors like me swooped in. I bought a day later at 20.33 to capture the new dividend rate of 7.5 percent. Yum!

Then look what happened. The stock recovered, reaching a peak at B of 27.65 for a paper gain of 36 percent.

Imagine how you would feel if you owned the stock before they cut the dividend. Yes, losing 16 percent overnight was nothing to sneeze at, but if you sold at the open, you could have limited your losses right there. If you decided to hold on, the loss continued to grow, doubling to 32 percent and finally reaching 39 percent.

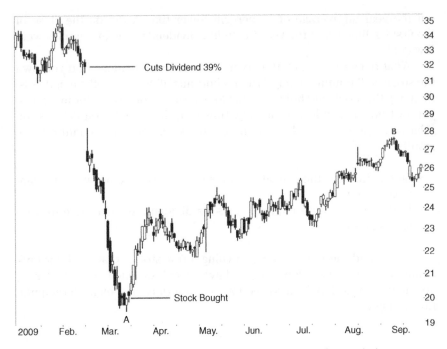

FIGURE 6.1   Ameren cut its dividend almost 40%, forcing the stock down.

The chart teaches us a lesson if we are willing to learn it. When a company cuts the dividend, sell it immediately. Buy back in after the drop has completed to catch the bounce upward.

If you need more proof, then look at Great Plains Energy (GXP) at the same time. The stock closed at 19.55 the day before a dividend cut then opened at 15.94 (18 percent lower), but continued down to a low of 10.20, for a loss of 48 percent. Five months later, the stock had peaked at 18.50 for a gain of 81 percent from the low. I bought this stock four days after it bottomed at a price of 11.58, capturing a dividend of over 7 percent, and riding the price wave upward, too.

- Buy stocks after they cut their dividend and price bottoms.

PERFORMANCE BY MARKET CAP

Table 6.5 shows the performance of dividend paying stocks over time, sorted by their market capitalization. The top half of the table includes the

TABLE 6.5 Dividend and Non-Dividend Paying Stocks by Market Capitalization

Market Cap	Year 1	Year 2	Year 3	Year 4	Year 5	$10,000 Invested
Small	18%	16%	15%	15%	15%	$20,868
Mid	12%	13%	14%	13%	14%	$18,668
Large	12%	12%	11%	11%	11%	$17,135
Dividend Paying Stocks Above, Non-Dividend Paying Below						
Small	23%	17%	13%	12%	14%	$20,860
Mid	9%	9%	7%	9%	9%	$15,097
Large	-2%	-5%	5%	6%	3%	$10,753

dividend payment in the percentages. The bottom half are stocks that do not pay a dividend. Small caps are less than a billion, large caps are over $5 billion, and mid caps are between those two.

The numbers tell a tale similar to what we have seen with other fundamental metrics, with small caps outperforming mid caps that outperform large caps. For example, small caps in year 1 showed gains of 18 percent, mid caps climbed 12.3 percent, and large caps grew 11.6 percent, all of them paying dividends. The right column shows that $10,000 invested in small caps grew to $20,868 but large caps only made it to $17,135, after five years.

The bottom half of the table shows how nondividend paying stocks performed. The small caps beat the mid caps that beat the large caps.

When you compare the lower half of the table with the upper half, we find that dividend-paying stocks outperform those not paying a dividend. Dividend payers win 13 of 15 contests (meaning I compared the five years of small, medium, and large caps for dividend and nondividend results, respectively).

The table suggests that picking small-cap stocks paying a dividend works best for long-term performance (small caps *not* paying a dividend outperform in years 1 and 2 but not after).

- Stocks that pay a dividend outperform for up to five years, with small caps doing best.

CHAPTER CHECKLIST

Dividends can come in a variety of forms, but are usually in cash as a common stock dividend. Based on findings in this chapter, here are some tips to consider when shopping for stocks.

☐ Dividends are a portion of the company's net earnings returned to shareholders. They can come in a variety of forms. See this chapter's introduction.

☐ Stocks with high yield and low payout ratio do well. See the section "Historical Research Review."

☐ Dividend yield alone is not sufficient to select a stock. See the section "Historical Research Review."

☐ Stocks with a high yield tend to outperform. See Table 6.1.

☐ The best performance comes from stocks with a high yield and low payout ratio. See Table 6.2.

☐ Owning dividend-paying stocks is better than owning those not paying a dividend. See Table 6.3

☐ Stocks that cut their dividend rates outperform a year later, but samples are few. See Table 6.4.

☐ In the year when a company cuts its dividend, expect price to drop substantially. See Table 6.4.

☐ Buy stocks after they cut their dividend and price bottoms. See the section "When Disaster Strikes."

☐ Stocks that pay a dividend outperform for up to five years, with small caps doing best. See Table 6.5.

CHAPTER 7

Long-Term Debt

Those who know me understand that I dislike debt. I am talking about personal debt, such as car loans and home mortgages. I use credit cards like everyone else, but pay off the balance each month. By making sensible choices over the years and spending wisely, I have been able to save money. When the lean times came, I dipped into my savings. During plentiful times, I saved and invested.

However, this chapter is about long-term corporate debt, not personal debt. When a company borrows money that is not due within 12 months, it is long-term debt. Let us take a closer look to see what the numbers tell us. I found the results surprising and confusing.

- Long-term debt is borrowed money not due within 12 months.

THE NUMBERS

During my first professional job as a hardware design engineer at Raytheon, every few weeks I visited the small library they had at the plant. I read *Forbes* and *Fortune* magazines and became familiar with fundamental analysis.

I remember thinking that finding a company without debt was like discovering a chocolate candy bar my three brothers had missed. It never dawned on me that a company having a modest amount of debt could use the money to create new products and build wealth. Modest debt was good, not bad, but do the numbers support this theory? Answering that question is where this story becomes weird.

TABLE 7.1 Stock Performance of Companies with and without Long-Term Debt

Condition	Year 1	Year 2	Year 3	Year 4	Year 5	$10,000 Invested
Debt	10%	9%	9%	11%	15%	$16,870
No debt	12%	12%	12%	9%	7%	$16,467

IS DEBT GOOD?

I used my Value Line database and compared the year-ahead performance for companies having no long-term debt versus those with long-term debt. **Table 7.1** shows the results.

For example, companies having long-term debt at the end of year 1 had stocks that gained an average of 10 percent. This compares to gains of 12 percent for stocks in companies without long-term debt (dividends not included). The trend of debt-free companies outperforming those saddled with long-term debt continues through year 3. The last two years show better performance coming from stocks of companies with long-term debt. The sample counts are high, between 3,000 and 5,700.

Presumably, the company used the debt to buy manufacturing plants or equipment in the early years and the investment paid off in later years.

A $10,000 investment grew to $16,870 five years later for companies having debt. That is about $400 larger than from companies with no debt. The results are a wash. However, the first three years favor companies with no debt.

- Companies with no long-term debt outperform for three years.

SINKING SHIP: TAKING ON DEBT

If we look at rising and falling long-term debt levels, what will the performance results show? **Table 7.2** gives the answers for various trend combinations.

TABLE 7.2 Results for Debt Trend and Stock Performance

Debt Condition	Year 1	Year 2	Year 3	Year 4	Year 5	$10,000 Invested
Increasing	8%	7%	11%	13%	13%	$16,313
Decreasing	10%	11%	12%	17%	12%	$17,919
Debt to no debt*	6%	12%	19%	17%	2%	$17,004
No debt to debt	17%	4%	−3%	−9%	34%	$14,394

* As few as 80 samples.

I found that companies with increasing long-term debt from one year to the next had stocks that climbed an average of 8 percent a year later. This compares to a climb of 10 percent for companies cutting their long-term debt. If a company can cut their debt, their interest expense should decline, freeing up money for other corporate purposes. In other words, the results make sense. A $10,000 investment in stocks of companies cutting their debt in year 0 turned into $17,919 five years later. That is the best performance in the table.

- Companies decreasing long-term debt levels outperformed over time. Those eliminating long-term debt also did well.

As few as 80 companies (in year 5 but year 1 had only 161) transitioned from having long-term debt to becoming debt-free. When that happened, their stocks climbed just 6 percent a year later. Surprise! I expected much better performance. Over time, though, the stock responded until year 5. The gain that year was just 2 percent, but it could be due to the low sample count (80). Boosting year 5 results might place this row on top for performance.

The biggest surprise came from companies having no long-term debt to taking on long-term debt the following year. Their stocks gained 17 percent a year later. The performance *after* year 1 is dreadful except for year 5. Then, the 492 stocks gained an average of 34 percent. Even so, the five-year performance of $10,000 grew to only $14,394, the worst of the combinations.

- Companies moving from being debt-free to taking on long-term debt outperform dramatically the first year but suffer in later years.

DEBT BY MARKET CAPITALIZATION

This is my favorite category because I like to see the small caps trounce the other categories with superior performance. **Table 7.3** shows the results when we break down companies by market cap and long-term debt trends.

TABLE 7.3 Debt Trend versus Market Capitalization and Stock Performance

Market Cap	Year 1	Year 2	Year 3	Year 4	Year 5	$10,000 Invested
Small	17%	12%	13%	13%	24%	$20,746
Mid	9%	7%	8%	6%	16%	$15,615
Large	6%	3%	3%	7%	12%	$13,383

(*continued*)

TABLE 7.3 (*continued*)

Market Cap	Year 1	Year 2	Year 3	Year 4	Year 5	$10,000 Invested
Companies with Increasing Debt, Above; Decreasing Debt, Below						
Small	21%	17%	15%	21%	14%	$22,595
Mid	9%	12%	12%	15%	10%	$17,294
Large	4%	6%	9%	13%	10%	$14,900

When long-term debt increased from one year to the next, the following year small-cap stocks showed gains averaging 17 percent. Small caps cutting their long-term debt (but not to zero) showed gains of 21 percent. After five years, $10,000 invested in small caps cutting their debt would have grown to $22,595. That is the best of the various combinations.

You can see how the small caps cream the other cap stocks. Small caps do best when long-term debt is decreasing. Large caps do worst.

Comparing the various market caps on the top of the table with their corresponding reflection on the bottom shows that companies cutting their debt tended to outperform over five years. The "$10,000 invested" column makes this clear.

- Small caps do best with decreasing long-term debt loads and outperform mid- and large-cap stocks.

Debt-Free Market Caps

Table 7.3 discussed market caps with increasing or decreasing debt. How do market caps perform between those with long-term debt and those free of it?

Table 7.4 shows the answer. I split the stocks by market cap and also by their level of long-term debt. Results of those in the top half of the table have long-term debt, but those in the bottom half are debt-free.

TABLE 7.4 Debt Levels and Performance by Market Capitalization

Market Cap	Year 1	Year 2	Year 3	Year 4	Year 5	$10,000 Invested
Small	20%	15%	13%	15 %	19%	$21,448
Mid	9%	9%	10%	10%	14%	$16,382
Large	5%	4%	5%	9%	12%	$14,003
Companies with Debt, Above; No Debt, Below						
Small	17%	16%	13%	9%	8%	$18,055
Mid	10%	10%	9%	11%	8%	$15,728
Large	9%	12%	14%	8%	3%	$15,442

For those with debt, the performance of small-cap stocks beat mid caps that beat large caps. After five years, a $10,000 investment in small-cap stocks more than doubled to $21,448, handily beating mid- and large-cap stocks.

In the bottom half of the table, the performance trend is not as clear. Most of the time, small caps outperform the other two but both mid and large caps win once. After five years of holding stocks of small-cap companies with no long-term debt in year 0, a $10,000 investment grew to $18,055—the best of the trio.

Comparing the top half of the table to the bottom half, we find that stocks from small- and mid-cap companies with long-term debt outperform those that are debt-free. Large caps flip, with debt-free companies slightly outperforming.

- Small-cap stocks with debt outperform over time.

CHAPTER CHECKLIST

This chapter discussed long-term debt and how stocks performed over time with and without debt. Companies with debt marginally outperformed those without debt after five years. Companies decreasing their long-term debt levels in year 0 showed superior results after five years. Small-cap stocks beat the other market caps, regardless of debt levels (increasing, decreasing, or debt-free).

If you need one guideline about selecting stocks and debt, pick small caps with decreasing long-term debt. Table 7.3 shows that they make the most money over five years compared to the other tables.

Below is a checklist of results.

☐ Long-term debt is borrowed money not due within 12 months. See this chapter's introduction.

☐ Companies with no long-term debt outperform for three years. See Table 7.1.

☐ Companies decreasing long-term debt levels outperformed over time. Those eliminating long-term debt also did well. See Table 7.2.

☐ Companies moving from being debt-free to taking on long-term debt outperform dramatically the first year but suffer in later years. See Table 7.2.

☐ Small caps do best with decreasing long-term debt loads and outperform mid and large cap stocks. See Table 7.3.

☐ Small-cap stocks with debt outperform over time. See Table 7.4

CHAPTER 8

Price-to-Earnings Ratio

The price-to-earnings (P/E) ratio is perhaps the most well-known of the financial ratios. If you were to ask anyone walking down a city street what the P/E ratio was, they might say that the nearest store has a bathroom. Those knowing something about finances might even be able to describe the ratio.

The price-to-earnings ratio is the current stock's price divided by a year's worth of earnings. If your crystal ball is especially good, you may want to divide price by future earnings. In one of their P/E numbers, for example, Value Line uses a blend of six months' worth of estimates and six months of reported earnings. However, they base their "Average Annual P/E ratio" on 12 months of actual earnings and the average yearly price. I used their average annual P/E ratio in the studies that follow.

- The price-to-earnings ratio is the current stock's price divided by a year's worth of earnings.

HISTORY LESSON

I learned about P/E ratios in 1979, but people argued about them long before that. According to several sources, S. Francis Nicholson (1960) was an early and significant contributor describing how a low P/E strategy outperformed stocks with high P/Es.

People believed that P/E ratios were a quality measure, that the higher the ratio, the higher the quality of the stock and the higher its price.

67

However, a rising stock price often got ahead of earnings, inflating the ratio and making it soar like a hydrogen balloon. One lightning strike and, well, you can guess the rest.

What confused investors was the wonderful short-term performance of some growth stocks with high P/Es. Investors flocked to them and jumped aboard for rides. They continued to perform, soaring among the clouds, seemingly immune from nearby lightning.

Back on the ground, some doubted the low P/E strategy, throwing around phrases like "survivorship bias" and "higher risk." So researchers included bankrupt firms in their studies and corrected sampling biases. They found that stocks with low P/Es rocked (outperformed those with high P/E ratios). Others adjusted for risk and found the same results and yet the argument continued as to the cause of better performance from low P/E stocks.

I am not going to join the battle because it is a lot like the chicken and egg thing. Which came first? Who cares? I am a vegetarian who is watching his cholesterol. Let us see what my numbers reveal about the P/E ratio.

DO LOW P/E STOCKS OUTPERFORM?

Table 8.1 shows how stocks performed when sorted by the median P/E. The median is the middle one in a sorted list of numbers. In this case, I used 9,175 samples in the study and separated the results by years according to a median P/E of 17.1 for the group.

Those stocks with P/Es above the median performed less well than did those below the median. For example, stocks with P/E ratios above the median climbed 10 percent a year later compared to a gain of 13 percent for those with ratios below the median. At the end of five years, a $10,000 investment would be worth $17,843 for those with below-median P/Es, well above the $15,803 gain for those above the median.

The finding that high P/E stocks perform less well than low P/E ones matches what others have uncovered. What about trends? Does a stock with a rising P/E perform less well than one that is falling? Let us find out.

- For the best performance, select stocks with a P/E ratio below the median 17.1.

TABLE 8.1 Performance of Stocks versus Median P/E

Median P/E 17.1	Year 1	Year 2	Year 3	Year 4	Year 5	$10,000 Invested
Above median	10%	10%	9%	8%	10%	$15,803
Below median	13%	12%	13%	13%	11%	$17,843

TABLE 8.2 Performance of Stocks with Increasing and Decreasing P/Es

Condition	Year 1	Year 2	Year 3	Year 4	Year 5	$10,000 Invested
Increasing P/E	9%	12%	10%	8%	7%	$15,616
Decreasing P/E	13%	10%	11%	13%	11%	$17,215

P/E TRENDS DOWN: GOOD OR BAD?

Table 8.2 shows the performance of stocks with increasing P/E from one year to the next compared to those with declining P/E.

Those stocks with a P/E that increased from the prior year had an average rise of 9 percent compared to a rise of 13 percent for stocks of companies that had a declining P/E. A five-year investment of $10,000 would be worth $17,215 if invested in stocks with a declining P/E at the end of year 0 and held for five years.

- Pick stocks with a decreasing P/E from one year to the next.

PRICE AND EARNINGS COMBINATIONS: YAWN

A decline in the price-to-earnings ratio can come from either a falling stock price or rising earnings, or both (price falling faster than earnings). If we can determine what factor results in better performance, then that will assist in stock selection. **Table 8.3** shows what I discovered.

TABLE 8.3 Lower P/E Ratio and Price-Earnings Combinations versus Performance

Condition	Year 1	Year 2	Year 3	Year 4	Year 5	$10,000 Invested
Falling price, falling earnings	10%	10%	11%	15%	15%	$17,840
Falling price, rising earnings	14%	10%	9%	14%	10%	$17,214
Rising price, falling earnings	10%	9%	11%	11%	17%	$17,383
Rising price, rising earnings	13%	10%	12%	13%	10%	$17,267

All of the results in this table associate with a P/E ratio that is lower than the prior year but above zero. In the first row, stocks with a falling price and falling earnings resulted in a year 1 rise of 10 percent, on average. That means price must have fallen faster than earnings to create a lower P/E.

The rising price, falling earnings row is an unusual combination, but it happens when Value Line uses the average price over the year instead of year-end prices when calculating the P/E ratio. As few as 93 samples qualified.

The best year 1 result comes from the combination of falling price and rising earnings. That makes intuitive sense. In second place are stocks with rising prices and earnings. If earnings rise faster than price then the P/E drops. Stocks qualifying under those conditions climbed an average of 13 percent a year later.

The best performance in the table for a hold time of five years goes to falling price and falling earnings. A $10,000 investment climbs to $17,840. If you look at the right column, the dollar amounts are close to each other, suggesting only a small advantage for the associated combination.

- Stocks from companies with a falling price and rising earnings (year to year) have the best year-ahead performance.

BUY SMALL CAPS WITH LOW P/E

In other chapters, we found that small caps outperformed mid- and large-cap stocks. The results are similar for P/E ratios. I measured the performance over time according to stocks with P/E ratios above and below their respective medians. **Table 8.4** shows the results.

TABLE 8.4   P/E versus Market Capitalization and Stock Performance

Condition	Year 1	Year 2	Year 3	Year 4	Year 5	$10,000 Invested
Small cap, above median 16.0	13%	14%	10%	8%	10%	$16,899
Below median	20%	16%	16%	16%	15%	$21,418
Mid cap, above median 17.3	11%	10%	9%	10%	13%	$16,547
Below median	11%	9%	11%	11%	9%	$16,387
Large cap, above median 18.9	7%	7%	6%	6%	7%	$13,856
Below median	11%	11%	12%	11%	8%	$16,493

For example, small cap stocks below the median 16.0 P/E ratio see price rise an average of 20 percent the following year. Small caps above the median see price climb only 13 percent. The far right column shows a $10,000 investment in below-median P/E, and small-cap stocks would more than double, to $21,418. That is the highest in the table.

Mid caps show little performance difference between above and below the 17.3 median. That is especially true after holding for five years. Large caps show some variation, with stocks below the median 18.9 P/E outperforming.

- Small caps with below median 16.0 P/E ratios outperform mid- and large-cap stocks for up to five years.

HIGH P/E: TIME TO SELL?

An article by Daniel Subach (December 2006) warns that P/E ratios "should be less than or equal to the average highs over the last three years."

Since Value Line reports the average P/E ratio, then all you need do is compare the current ratio with each of the last three years, and make sure the current P/E is below the highest of the prior three.

I tested this and found that he is right. I used 5,880 samples and those with P/Es below the highest of the prior three years saw their stock gain 12 percent the following year. That compares to an average gain of just 8 percent for those with P/Es higher than the highest of the prior three years.

Another way to look at the result is this: If your stock has a high P/E, then year-ahead performance could be below average. It might be time to sell.

- If a stock's P/E ratio is above the average highs of the last three years, then consider selling.

THREE P/E TIPS

Before we move on to the next chapter, let me say a few words about selecting stocks with low P/E ratios. Look at the average annual P/E ratio for your stock. If it was consistently high over several years but has dropped to unusually low heights recently, then it could represent value.

If the stock has a historically low P/E ratio then buying it as a low P/E play may not work as well as hoped. Several industries (auto manufacturers, steel producers) tend to have low P/E ratios that stay low. You are looking for value—a company that used to have a high P/E ratio, but the market has cast it aside like used tissue. The P/E ratio is low because its price has dropped faster than earnings.

Avoid cyclical companies that are sliding downhill toward their cyclical low. Instead, pick companies that have a reason to rise, like a cyclical company beginning to prosper or a company that has invented a low-cost, pollution-free substitute for gasoline. Look for a catalyst for change, one that will power the low P/E into a high one as price climbs along with its prospects.

1. A stock with a historically high P/E that drops to unusually low levels could represent value.
2. Avoid buying stocks with historically low P/Es.
3. Avoid cyclical companies sliding downhill (falling P/Es). Pick them on the rebound (rising P/Es).

CHAPTER CHECKLIST

Based on findings in this chapter, here are some tips to consider when selecting stocks using the price-to-earnings ratio.

☐ The price-to-earnings ratio is the current stock's price divided by a year's worth of earnings. See this chapter's introduction.

☐ For the best performance, select stocks with a P/E ratio below the median 17.1. See Table 8.1.

☐ Pick stocks with a decreasing P/E from one year to the next. See Table 8.2.

☐ Stocks from companies with a falling price and rising earnings (year to year) have the best year-ahead performance. See Table 8.3.

☐ Small caps with below median 16.0 P/E ratios outperform mid- and large-cap stocks for up to 5 years. See Table 8.4.

☐ If a stock's P/E ratio is above the average highs of the last three years, then consider selling. See the section "High P/E: Time to Sell?"

☐ A stock with a historically high P/E that drops to unusually low levels could represent value. See the section "Three P/E Tips."

☐ Avoid buying stocks with historically low P/Es. See "Three P/E Tips."

☐ Avoid cyclical companies sliding downhill (falling P/Es). Pick them on the rebound (rising P/Es). See the section "Three P/E Tips."

CHAPTER 9

Price-to-Sales Ratio

The price-to-sales ratio (PSR) is one of two ratios I grew up with (the other is price to earnings). I remember reading a *Forbes* columnist discuss the PSR in columns back in the late 1970s and early 1980s. So, I added it to my fundamental analysis toolbox.

Depending on whom you ask, PSRs place second only to sliced bread as the greatest invention known to man, or they are as exciting as driving in snow. James O'Shaughnessy (McGraw-Hill, 1997) calls them, "the king of value factors." Others warn that unless you consider debt, the ratio can lead to companies on the verge of bankruptcy. Which is right?

Perhaps the truth lies somewhere between bread and snow, and my numbers should help to clear the confusion. Before we get to that, let us define the ratio and talk about it a bit more.

The price-to-sales ratio compares the stock's current price per share by its annual sales per share. Alternatively, one could compare the market capitalization of the stock by it annual sales or revenue (not per share sales). The ratio describes how much value the market places on each sales dollar.

- The price-to-sales ratio compares the stock's current price per share by its annual sales per share.
- The market capitalization of the stock divided by it annual revenue describes how much value the market places on each sales dollar.

Some claim that it is more difficult for a company to fudge sales numbers, so the PSR is more reliable than are ratios based on earnings (as in the price to earnings ratio). The PSR also gives a valuation when there are no earnings. That can be handy.

But there is a problem with the PSR, too. If a company is in debt up to its eyeballs despite a tiny PSR, how loudly will investors yell when the company declares bankruptcy?

To avoid buying a company that is hanging on by its fingernails, check its debt level and other ratios as well.

- Avoid companies with a low price-to-sales ratio and awful fundamentals, like too much debt.

Another problem with the PSR is that it can vary by industry. For example, the average PSR for companies in the alternate energy field is 57.23 compared to 0.89 for those in the air transport industry.

- The average price-to-sales ratio varies by industry.

Let us look into the numbers to clarify this and other claims.

GOOD BENCHMARK: PSRs BELOW 1.0

Using my database, the *median* PSR for stocks that had sales or revenue was 1.0 compared to an *average* PSR of 4.49. That tells me some companies skew the average by having low sales per share, high stock prices, or both.

I will just use the 1.0 median as the basis for analysis. Fortunately, 1.0 is also the line separating value from froth. I recall that companies with PSRs above 1.0 are inflated while those below 1.0 are where the tasty morsels reside. That may be an oversimplification, but I consider it a good rule of thumb.

Let us discuss performance of stocks above and below the 1.0 median. **Table 9.1** shows the results of a study I conducted using 891 stocks with non-zero PSRs from 1992 to 2007.

TABLE 9.1 Performance of Stocks versus Median PSR

Median: 1.0	Year 1	Year 2	Year 3	Year 4	Year 5	$10,000 Invested
Above	9%	9%	8%	9%	9%	$15,209
Below	14%	13%	13%	12%	13%	$18,405

Companies with PSRs above the median 1.0 saw their stocks climb an average of 9 percent the following year. This compares to a rise of 14 percent for those companies with PSRs below the median. A $10,000 investment in stocks with PSRs below the median would be worth $18,405 after five years. That value handily beats the $15,209 posted by stocks with PSRs above the median.

- Companies with price to sales below 1.0 tend to have stocks outperform for at least five years.

PSR TREND: DOWN IS BEST

If the PSR is climbing from one year to the next, do results get better or worse when compared to stocks with a falling PSR? **Table 9.2** gives an answer.

In year 1, stocks showing an increasing PSR from the prior year climbed 11 percent compared to 10 percent for those with decreasing PSRs. After that, however, stocks that showed decreasing PSRs outperformed for the next four years. At the end of five years, a $10,000 investment was worth $15,999 for stocks with increasing PSRs and $16,951 for those with declining PSRs. The differences are not significant, but it may help to look for stocks with a price-to-sales ratio that drops from one year to the next.

- Companies with a falling price-to-sales ratio from one year to the next have stocks that outperform over time.

SMALL CAPS, SMALL PSRs RULE!

How does the performance of stocks change when we sort them by market capitalization and PSR? **Table 9.3** shows the answer.

If you have been reading the chapters before this one, then you can guess the answer. Small caps beat the other two market capitalizations. The

TABLE 9.2 Performance of Stocks with Increasing and Decreasing PSRs

PSR	Year 1	Year 2	Year 3	Year 4	Year 5	$10,000 Invested
Increasing	11%	10%	10%	11%	8%	$15.999
Decreasing	10%	11%	12%	12%	11%	$16,951

TABLE 9.3　PSR versus Market Capitalization and Stock Performance

Condition	Year 1	Year 2	Year 3	Year 4	Year 5	$10,000 Invested
Small cap, above median 0.76	18%	14%	10%	8%	12%	$17,892
Below median	20%	17%	16%	16%	14%	$21,570
Mid cap, above median 1.07	8%	9%	8%	11%	11%	$15,692
Below median	11%	10%	10%	9%	10%	$16,204
Large cap, above median 1.56	5%	3%	6%	6%	6%	$12,896
Below median	9%	11%	11%	11%	9%	$16,373

trend of small caps beating mid caps that beat large caps is especially true for those stocks with PSRs above their respective median. That trend becomes clear by looking at an investment of $10,000 at the end of year 0 that was held for five years. Small caps show the largest improvement (to $17,892) and large caps show the smallest ($12,896), both using above-median numbers.

Let us discuss a few examples to make the table clear. Small caps in year 0 with PSRs below the 0.76 median gained 20 percent in year 1 compared to a gain of 18 percent for those above the median. Mid caps scored gains averaging 11 percent compared to 8 percent, and large caps gained 9 percent versus 5 percent, respectively.

The best performance in the table comes from small caps with PSRs below the median. The value of $10,000 more than doubles to $21,570 after five years.

- Small-cap stocks beat the other market caps, and those with price-to-sales ratios below 0.76 do even better.

Market Cap versus Sales

In an article, Daniel Subach (December 2006) says that a stock is too expensive if its market cap is greater than annual sales. Is that true? Yes.

I compared the performance of 10,722 samples of market cap and annual sales and found that those stocks with market caps higher than sales showed an average gain of 9 percent a year later. That compares to a 14 percent gain for those stocks with market caps below annual sales. In other words, you can do 56 percent better if you just select stocks with annual sales higher than their market capitalization.

- Select stocks with annual sales higher than their market capitalizations.

CHECKLIST: PSRs BY INDUSTRY

Table 9.4 lists industries in the study and their average and median PSRs. Some are very high due to unusually low sales. Alternate energy (PSR = 57.23), biotechnology (41.85), drugs (30.20), and Internet (13.32) are examples. The high averages show why I prefer to use the median in the tests described in this book.

The list used price and sales information from 1992 to 2007. As a general rule of thumb, I think 1.0 as a PSR still serves as a good benchmark. To be safe, however, check the ratio for other companies in the same industry to determine whether your stock is cheap or not.

- Since the price-to-sales ratio can vary by industry, check the PSR in other industry-related companies to see if your stock is expensive or not.

TABLE 9.4 PSRs by Industry

Industry	Average	Median
Aerospace/Defense	1.16	0.78
Air Transport	0.89	0.57
Alternate Energy	57.23	3.98
Apparel	1.14	0.77
Biotechnology	41.85	12.53
Building Materials	0.88	0.62
Chemical (Basic)	0.76	0.60
Chemical (Diversified)	1.31	1.06
Chemical (Specialty)	1.65	0.81
Computers and Peripherals	3.37	1.23
Diversified Co.	0.79	0.69
Drug	30.20	4.54
Electric Utility (Central)	0.80	0.70
Electric Utility (East)	0.80	0.74
Electric Utility (West)	0.72	0.70
Electrical Equipment	1.55	1.10
Food Processing	1.08	0.79
Furniture/Home Furnishings	0.65	0.51
Homebuilding	0.68	0.46
Household Products	1.35	1.07
Human Resources	0.82	0.55

(continued)

TABLE 9.4 (continued)

Industry	Average	Median
Internet	13.32	3.32
Machinery	1.06	0.75
Medical Supplies	5.82	2.45
Metal Fabricating	0.83	0.64
Metals and Mining (Diversified)	0.94	0.73
Natural Gas (Distributor)	0.58	0.52
Natural Gas (Diversified)	1.99	1.39
Oilfield Services/Equipment	2.49	2.06
Packaging and Container	0.71	0.66
Petroleum (Integrated)	0.52	0.43
Petroleum (Producing)	2.80	2.67
Precision Instrument	2.15	1.64
Retail (Special Lines)	1.06	0.77
Retail Building Supply	1.54	1.00
Retail Store	0.75	0.55
Securities Brokerage	2.90	1.56
Semiconductor	5.22	3.12
Semiconductor Capital Equipment	2.48	2.07
Shoe	0.97	0.82
Telecommunications Equipment	6.97	2.97
Toiletries/Cosmetics	1.19	0.90
Trucking/Transportation Leasing	0.87	0.42

CHAPTER CHECKLIST

Based on findings in this chapter, here are some tips to consider when evaluating stocks on the price to sales ratio.

In the next chapter, I discuss return on equity, which I thought was straightforward until I started testing it.

☐ The price-to-sales ratio compares the stock's current price per share by its annual sales per share. See this chapter's introduction.

☐ The market capitalization of the stock divided by its annual revenue describes how much value the market places on each sales dollar. See this chapter's introduction.

☐ Avoid companies with a low price-to-sales ratio and awful fundamentals, like too much debt. See this chapter's introduction.

☐ The average price-to-sales ratio varies by industry. See this chapter's introduction.

☐ Companies with price to sales below 1.0 tend to have stocks outperform for at least five years. See Table 9.1.

☐ Companies with a falling price-to-sales ratio from one year to the next have stocks that outperform over time. See Table 9.2.

☐ Small cap stocks beat the other market caps, and those with PSRs below 0.76 do even better. See Table 9.3.

☐ Select stocks with annual sales higher than their market capitalization. See the section "Market Cap versus Sales."

☐ Since the price-to-sales ratio can vary by industry, check the PSR in other industry-related companies to see if your stock is expensive or not. See Table 9.4.

CHAPTER 10

Return on Shareholders' Equity

During my quest to discover why my officemate's random stock picks were beating my carefully chosen selections in 1979, I have to admit that I never considered looking at the return on shareholders' equity (ROE). Based on the results in this chapter, it would not have mattered much if I did. That may surprise you.

According to Value Line, return on shareholders' equity is "annual net profit divided by year-end shareholders' equity." Another way of saying it is net profit divided by net worth. If profit rises faster than net worth, the thinking goes, then management is doing a better job running the business. Shareholders are getting a better return on their investment. The belief is that using ROE to compare other stocks in the same industry can help separate purebreds from mongrels. Unfortunately, you are still looking at dogs—stocks that might not perform up to expectations anyway.

- Return on shareholders equity is annual net profit divided by shareholders' equity.

Based on articles I have read, analysts look for 15 to 20 percent return on equity as the minimum for a quality investment. In fact, Ben McClure in his article, "Keep Your Eyes on the ROE," makes a convincing case that ROE can act as a growth rate throttle. He writes, ". . . a firm that now has a 15 percent ROE cannot increase its earnings faster than 15 percent annually without borrowing funds or selling more shares. But raising funds comes at a cost: Servicing additional debt cuts into net income and selling more shares shrinks earnings per share by increasing the total of shares outstanding. So ROE is, in effect, a speed limit on a firm's growth rate, which is why money managers rely on it to gauge growth potential."

Like other financial ratios, ROE should not be used alone. High debt levels could allow a company with a small equity base and proportionately higher net profit to have a high ROE. Despite a high ROE, the company could be at risk of default if their business weakens in the face of a challenging economy.

All of this sounds hunky-dory, right? Find a company with a ROE above 15 percent and little debt, maybe season the broth with a few other ratios, and you are on your way to a winning stock pick. There is just one catch: It does not always work.

After I crunched the numbers and looked at the results, my jaw dropped. I could not believe what I was seeing. Companies with low ROE performed better than did those with high ROE. My first thought was that I could just remove this chapter from the book. Then I did some research and found that I was not the first to discover this anomaly. James O'Shaughnessy (McGraw-Hill, 1997) writes "stocks with high ROE are a good investment only 50 percent of the time." Let us look at the numbers to prove what I am saying.

LOW ROE STOCKS OUTPERFORM: WHY?

I found that the median ROE was 13.4 percent in the 932 companies I looked at from 1992 to 2007. How do stocks with ROE above the median perform in the future compared to those below the median? **Table 10.1** gives the answer.

A $10,000 investment in stocks with ROE above 13.4 percent at the end of year 0 grew to $15,741 by the end of year 5. The same investment in stocks with ROE below 13.4 percent grew more, to $17,432.

Of course, many say that companies with high ROE are higher quality and that should translate into higher stock prices over time. That is not what I found.

Let us look at companies with ROE twice (26.8 percent) and half (6.7 percent) the median to see how they perform.

TABLE 10.1 Performance of Stocks versus Median ROE

Median: 13.4%	Year 1	Year 2	Year 3	Year 4	Year 5	$10,000 Invested
Above	10%	8%	7%	9%	12%	$15,741
Below	10%	10%	11%	12%	16%	$17,432

TABLE 10.2 Performance of Stocks with Increasing and Decreasing ROE

ROE	Year 1	Year 2	Year 3	Year 4	Year 5	$10,000 Invested
Increasing	11%	10%	10%	14%	10%	$16,752
Decreasing	7%	8%	11%	14%	12%	$16,435

Companies with low ROE in year 0 gained 14 percent after one year and 73 percent after five years, on average. Companies with high ROE in year 0 gained 10 percent the first year and 49 percent over five years. In other words, companies with small ROE outperform those with high ROE.

- Stocks with ROE below the median 13.4 percent outperform.
- Stocks with high ROE (over 26.8 percent) underperform those with ROE below 6.7 percent.

ROE TREND OVER TIME: YAWN

Table 10.2 shows the performance of stocks with increasing and decreasing ROE from one year to the next (the year before year 0 to year 0). For example, companies reporting ROE that is less than the prior year (decreasing) see their stocks gain an average of 7 percent a year later. That compares to gains of 11 percent for stocks with increasing ROE.

In dollar terms, the results are tiny: $16,752 versus $16,435 after holding for five years. In other words, whether ROE increases or decreases from one year to the next makes little difference in a stock's long-term performance.

- Whether ROE increases or decreases in one year makes little difference in a stock's long-term performance.

ROE PERFORMANCE BY MARKET CAPITALIZATION

Table 10.3 shows ROE by market capitalization in year 0 and the stock's performance over five years. For example, small caps with ROE below the median 11.4 percent had gains a year later of 15 percent compared to 17 percent for those stocks with ROE above the median.

TABLE 10.3 ROE versus Market Capitalization and Stock Performance

Condition	Year 1	Year 2	Year 3	Year 4	Year 5	$10,000 Invested
Small cap, above median 11.4% ROE	17%	14%	12%	13%	18%	$19,801
Below median	15%	14%	13%	14%	15%	$19,411
Mid cap, above median 13.6% ROE	11%	10%	6%	9%	12%	$15,894
Below median	9%	10%	11%	12%	16%	$17,311
Large cap, above median 17.1% ROE	7%	4%	4%	6%	8%	$13,250
Below median	5%	5%	9%	12%	15%	$15,434

The table shows that small caps beat mid caps and mid caps beat the performance of large caps. Mid- and large-cap stocks do better with ROE below the median (based on $10,000 invested and held for five years) whereas small caps do slightly better when ROE is above the median.

The table confirms what we have seen with other ratios. Small caps give the best performance.

- Sorted by return on equity, small caps outperform mid- and large-cap stocks.

CHAPTER CHECKLIST

This chapter discovered some unusual aspects of return on equity. Here is a checklist.

☐ Return on equity is annual net profit divided by shareholders' equity. See this chapter's introduction.
☐ Stocks with ROE below the median 13.4 percent outperform. See Table 10.1.
☐ Stocks with high ROE (over 26.8 percent) underperform those with ROE below 6.7 percent. See Table 10.1 discussion.
☐ Whether ROE increases or decreases in one year makes little difference in a stock's long-term performance. See Table 10.2.
☐ Sorted by return on equity, small caps outperform mid- and large-cap stocks. See Table 10.3.

CHAPTER 11

Shares Outstanding

A company issues shares to the public and collects money for doing so. What else is there to know? Plenty, it turns out. For example, if a company buys back stock, does it mean performance is likely to improve next year and in following years? What about companies that issue new shares? Does that hurt or help performance? Along with answering those questions and others, I discuss Dutch auction tender offers and the behavior of a stock after a company sells more shares.

- Shares outstanding are shares issued by a company, sold to the public, and still publicly available (not repurchased).

PERFORMANCE VERSUS SHARES OUTSTANDING

When IBM has a successful year, the company may look for other companies to buy. If IBM is growing earnings by 15 percent yearly, buying Podunk Computer whose earnings are growing at 10 percent annually is a nonstarter unless IBM thinks it can turn Podunk around or Podunk has a valuable asset (like patents) that IBM covets.

Buying another firm is an expensive and risky proposition. A company may not get its money's worth and combining the two rarely works well anyway.

Instead, should IBM invest in itself? Since the company is growing 15 percent annually, it can earn a good return by buying its own stock.

Buying back stock also changes financial ratios like earnings per share and book value per share. With fewer shares outstanding, earnings climb. When earnings climb, the stock price tends to follow. Everyone wins. Should the company later decide they want to buy Podunk Computer, they can issue new shares to cover the cost.

Table 11.1 looks at increasing and decreasing shares outstanding. I did not seek the reasons for changes in share totals.

Let us take examples from the table to understand the results. Companies that had between 20 and 25 percent more shares outstanding from one year to the next saw their share price rise by 3 percent the following year. Companies that cut the number of shares outstanding by 5 to 10 percent saw their share price rise by 12 percent the next year. That is a big difference.

A $10,000 investment in stocks that cut their shares outstanding between 10 and 15 percent saw it grow to $24,665 five years later, however, the sample counts are few (55). That means the results will likely not be as rosy when more samples become available. The large increase in price during years 3 to 5 is unusual.

The table shows that as the number of shares outstanding decreases, stock performance improves (compare year 1 results for the bottom three rows with the top three). When a company issues lots of stock, their earnings per share drops because of that additional stock. Holders of that stock find their investment is worth less than what it used to be. It is like splitting your ownership in a company with your brother. You used to own 100 percent of it and then it is down to 50 percent when you cut him in for half of the action. If you owned 1 percent of the company before they issued shares, you would own less after they issued more.

TABLE 11.1   Performance of Stocks versus Shares Outstanding

Change in Shares Outstanding	Year 1	Year 2	Year 3	Year 4	Year 5	$10,000 Invested	Minimum Samples
20% to 25%	3%	7%	14%	15%	10%	$15,936	98
15% to 20%	1%	9%	5%	10%	0%	$12,846	160
10% to 15%	3%	0%	8%	10%	10%	$13,342	208
5% to 10%	8%	13%	9%	11%	11%	$16,524	372
0 to 5%	12%	13%	12%	11%	9%	$17,081	3,029
0 to −5%	11%	10%	9%	10%	9%	$15,834	1,760
−5% to −10%	12%	11%	8%	13%	11%	$16,873	269
−10% to −15%	9%	6%	30%	24%	32%	$24,665	55

Conversely, your ownership rises when a company buys back shares. Of course, the low sample counts make the numbers likely to change, but the overall trend agrees with common sense.

- The larger the share buyback, the better the performance.

EVENT PATTERN: DUTCH AUCTION TENDER OFFERS

A company that wants to buy its own shares frequently does so in the open market, but there is another option (among others) called a Dutch auction tender offer.

Suppose that Podunk Computer thinks its stock is undervalued and it represents a great investment. The company will issue a press release that says something like, "Podunk Computer announced that its Board of Directors approved a modified Dutch auction self-tender offer for up to 1 million shares of its common stock at a price in the range of $20 to $22."

The announcement will provide additional details, but the auction allows stockholders to tender their shares at prices within the stated range, if they desire. The company will use those bids to calculate the lowest price that will allow them to buy back the number of shares they sought (1 million in this example). Once the company settles on a purchase price, they will pay that price to each shareholder that tendered their shares at or below that price.

For example, say you feel that Podunk is worth 21.50, so you offer your shares to the company at that price. Other stockholders offer their shares at different prices. The company tallies the offers and computes the lowest price that will buy 1 million shares.

Suppose the company finds that it has to pay $22 a share to buy back 1 million shares. Even though you bid 21.50, you will receive 22.00 for your shares. If the company finds that $21 will buy 1 million shares, then your bid will be rejected. If more than 1 million shares are tendered at 21, the company will prorate the number of shares bought from each shareholder that bid 21 or less.

- A Dutch auction tender offer is an auction in which the offering price is raised within a range until a fixed number of shares are acquired.

SHOULD YOU SELL?

I analyzed 107 Dutch auctions, and here are some statistics that may help you decide to hold or tender shares. On the last day of the auction,

72 percent of the stocks closed below the final tender price. In 95 percent of the cases, price dropped below the final tender price within three months, declining a median of 13 percent. That suggests you tender shares, and if you feel the company's stock represents value, then buy them back sometime after the auction completes, after price drops.

How quickly do the shares drop? Within a month, 47 percent will have reached their low. Another 24 percent will bottom in month 2, and 29 percent will bottom in month 3.

Sometime within three months after the auction ends, 79 percent of the stocks will close above the tender price. After one month, 38 percent will be higher. At the end of two and three months, 46 percent (for both periods) will close above the tender price. The average rise above the tender price is 15.7 percent. That represents the rise from the tender price to the highest high reached over the following three months.

In 53 percent of the cases, price hits the high before it hits the low after the auction ends. That suggests holding onto your stock through the tender and selling it within a month after the auction ends. Why? Because 48 percent of the stocks posted their three-month post-auction high within a month.

Earlier I said sell during the auction and now I am saying to hold on throughout the auction. Which is best? That is for you to decide. Since the 53 percent number hitting a high post-auction is almost random, it is probably best to tender your shares and then try to buy them back at a lower price after the auction ends. I will discuss how to trade Dutch auctions in *Swing and Day Trading*, Chapter 5, "Event Pattern Setups."

To complete the picture, here is a list of findings from the study. Be aware that I consider 107 samples to be a small number, so the results can change dramatically with additional samples.

- The median buyback is for 14.6 percent of shares outstanding.
- The day before announcement of the auction, the closing price is below the offering range 41 percent of the time.
- On the day the auction ends, the closing price remains below the tender price 72 percent of the time.
- Sometime within 3 months after the auction, price will drop below the tender price 95 percent of the time, dropping a median of 13 percent (or an average of 16 percent). Price hits bottom 47 percent of the time within a month of the auction, 24 percent within the second month, and 29 percent within the third month.
- At one-, two-, and three-month intervals after the auction ends, price is above the tender price 38, 46, and 46 percent of the time, respectively, with 79 percent rising above the tender price sometime with three months.

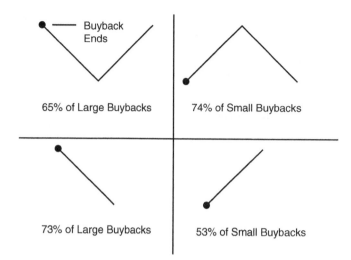

● —— Buyback
　　　　Ends

65% of Large Buybacks

74% of Small Buybacks

73% of Large Buybacks

53% of Small Buybacks

FIGURE 11.1 Price makes four types of moves after an auction ends.

- Of those stocks rising above the tender price (after the auction ends), the rise averages 15.7 percent.

Once the auction completes, price makes four types of movements, as shown in **Figure 11.1**. I split buybacks into large and small with the separator being a median buyback of 14.6 percent of shares outstanding before the auction commenced.

Companies that buy back more than 14.6 percent of shares outstanding tend to have their stocks drop after the auction ends. Of the stocks that made a V-shaped move (a drop followed by a recovery), 65 percent of them were large buybacks and just 35 percent of them were small buybacks.

The percentages are based on the number of stocks showing the associated shape, not as a percentage of all stocks in the study (that is why they do not add up to 100 percent).

The figure shows the other three variations. Price after large buybacks tends to drop, and after small buybacks price tends to rise (at least initially).

Figure 11.2 shows an example of a V-shaped move after Agilent completed an auction to buy back 14.6 percent of shares outstanding (a small buyback). When the auction was announced (buyback range 32 to 37), the stock gapped up then moved in a choppy range between a high of 36.10 and a low of 34.15. After the auction completed at a tender price of 36, the stock dropped to a low of 32.82 before starting a recovery.

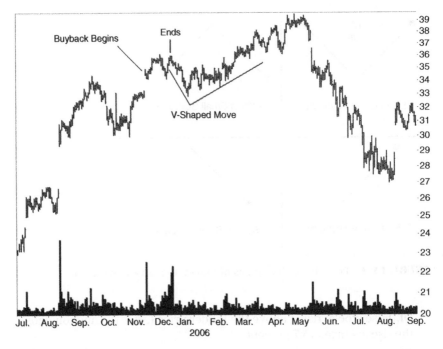

FIGURE 11.2   This is an example of a V-shaped move after the auction ends.

SELL AT WHAT PRICE?

At what price should you tender your shares? To answer that question, I found 107 companies from January 2000 to November 2010 that used a Dutch auction tender offer. I consider 107 to be a small sample, so the results are subject to change. **Table 11.2** shows the results.

TABLE 11.2   Dutch Auction Tender Offers Acceptance

Percentage Below Range High	Percentage Accepted	Percentage Below Range High	Percentage Accepted
Offering high	51%	45%	71%
0% to 10%	54%	50%	75%
15%	56%	55%	76%
20%	59%	60%	77%
25%	65%	65%	77%
30%	65%	70%	81%
35%	67%	75%	83%
40%	70%	Offering low	100%

Using Podunk's $20 to $22 range as an example, a shareholder that offers to sell their shares at 10 percent below the range high (or $21.80) would succeed 54 percent of the time. The range is $2 (22 to 20) and 10 percent of that is 20 cents, so 20 cents below the range high is 22—0.20 or 21.80. An offer 50 percent down from the range high (21) would succeed 75 percent of the time. You can select the percentage below the high range that works for you.

- In a Dutch auction tender offer, tendering shares at a price midway in the offering price range will succeed 75 percent of the time, on average.

EVENT PATTERN: COMMON STOCK OFFERINGS

What happens to price when a company decides to sell shares to the public? The answer should be obvious: It sinks, sometimes like a submarine with a hole in it. Of the 267 events that I looked at, one dropped 45 percent from the prior close to the announcement day's low. That kind of drop hurts more than being stuck overnight in the death zone on Mount Everest. Well, maybe not, but my point is this: Price drops, forming a U- or J-shaped move that often lasts about two weeks.

- When a company sells more shares in a common stock offering, price gaps lower, often making a U- or J-shaped move.

The reason for the violent reaction from stockholders is that their position is diluted by the additional shares, sometimes substantially. Whether the company will use the funds derived from the sale to improve shareholder value is up to management and time. Some banks used the funds to shore up their capital position or repay TARP loans, the so-called, Troubled Asset Relief Program. Other companies use it for general corporate purposes and to reduce debt.

To see if these stock offerings create a tradable event pattern, I studied public offerings of common stock—not preferred stock, and not livestock. They did not include initial public offerings (IPOs) nor did they include private offerings made to selected wealthy investors, mutual funds, hedge funds, or other financial institutions.

Say you own shares of AirTran Holdings. On October 6, 2009, the company announced an offering of 9 million shares of stock. The day before, the stock closed at 6.14 and it closed at 5.08 on the day of the announcement. Congratulations! You are the proud owner of an airline whose stock is worth 21 percent less than it was the day before.

Over the next 10 trading days, the airline gained altitude to a high of 5.57 before crashing. Within three weeks, the stock was trading just above 4.

The severity of the one-day decline is unusual. In 74 percent of the cases I looked at, price dropped between 0 and 12 percent, evenly spread. Of course, the other 26 percent were the declines that killed their owners.

Using the high-low range between the announcement day and the day the company priced the offering to represent an up or down breakout, respectively, then 48 percent of the time price will close above the high (an upward breakout) and 52 percent will breakout downward.

In two weeks or less, 65 percent of those with downward breakouts reach bottom. Two-thirds of the time (66 percent), price drops 15 percent or less and then recovers. If you have a stop-loss order in place, these numbers probably mean your position will be sold just before the stock rebounds.

About three weeks after I bought MannKind, the company announced an offering for 7.4 million shares (see **Figure 11.3**). The stock dropped from a close of 8.13 to a low of 6.80 in seven trading days, for a potential loss of 16 percent.

To say I was upset minimizes how I felt. Fortunately, the stock began to recover, reaching a high of 12.30 about six weeks later. Then the company

FIGURE 11.3 Price makes a U- or J-shaped turn after a Common Stock Offering.

dropped another bombshell by saying that they would delay selecting a partner to help market their inhaled insulin drug. Down the stock went, plunging from a close of 9.21 to a low of 5.02, a drop of 45 percent. Those types of drops *really* hurt. In fact, they represent an event pattern with a special name: dead-cat bounce. I discuss it in *Swing and Day Trading*, Chapter 5: "Event Pattern Setups" along with how to swing trade common stock offerings.

- The day of the common stock offering announcement, price drops an average of 9 percent (prior close to current low), but a frequency distribution shows the range is spread evenly between 0 percent and 12 percent.
- Price closes below the breakout (the price range between the announcement day and the day the company priced the offering) 52 percent of the time.
- Price bottoms or peaks quickly. In two weeks or less, 65 percent reach bottom after a downward breakout and 49 percent peak after an upward breakout.

PERFORMANCE AND MARKET CAPITALIZATION

In prior chapters, we have found that small-cap stocks outperform the other capitalization sizes. **Table 11.3** shows that trend to be true for shares outstanding, too.

Small cap stocks with fewer shares outstanding from one year to the next saw their stock climb an average of 17.9 percent a year later. That compares to an 18.1 percent rise for stocks with an increasing number of shares outstanding.

TABLE 11.3 Shares Outstanding by Market Capitalization and Stock Performance

Market Cap	Year 1	Year 2	Year 3	Year 4	Year 5	$10,000 Invested
Small	18.1%	16%	12%	12%	10%	$18,873
Mid	8%	10%	10%	11%	10%	$15,861
Large	5%	6%	11%	11%	8%	$14,767
Increasing Share Counts (above), Decreasing (below)						
Small	17.9%	15%	14%	18%	16%	$20,983
Mid	10%	8%	11%	10%	9%	$16,003
Large	8%	9%	4%	5%	5%	$13,512

After holding for five years, the dollar difference between small caps and large caps with fewer shares outstanding is big: $20,983 versus $13,512.

In over half of the contests (53 percent of the time), stocks with more shares outstanding beat the performance of those with fewer outstanding. However, stocks with fewer shares outstanding tended to show larger gains over time.

For example, small- and mid-cap stocks with fewer shares outstanding resulted in higher dollar values after five years (but mid caps are close). Large caps perform better with more shares outstanding: $14,767 versus $13,512.

- Small-cap stocks tend to outperform and do especially well if the number of shares outstanding decreases.

CHAPTER CHECKLIST

In this chapter, we learned about the behavior of stocks after offerings and buybacks. Here is a short checklist covering what we found.

☐ Shares outstanding are shares issued by a company, sold to the public, and still publicly available (not repurchased). See this chapter's introduction.

☐ The larger the share buyback, the better the performance. See Table 11.1.

☐ A Dutch auction tender offer is an auction in which the offering price is raised within a range until a fixed number of shares are acquired. See the section "Event Pattern: Dutch Auction Tender Offers."

☐ See the section "Should You Sell?" for a list of findings associated with Dutch auctions.

☐ In a Dutch auction tender offer, tendering shares at a price midway in the offering price range will succeed 75 percent of the time, on average. See Table 11.2.

☐ When a company sells more shares in a common stock offering, price gaps lower, often making a U- or J-shaped move. See the section "Event Pattern: Common Stock Offerings."

☐ See the section "Event Pattern: Common Stock Offerings" for a list of findings that may help you understand the behavior of common stock offerings.

☐ Small-cap stocks tend to outperform and do especially well if the number of shares outstanding decreases. See Table 11.3.

CHAPTER 12

Fundamental Analysis Summary

I n prior chapters, we looked at various fundamental factors to select stocks as value investments. In this chapter, I rank the results. This provides an easy way to value a potential investment based on the discoveries discussed in this book.

PERFORMANCE RANK: ONE-YEAR HOLD

Table 12.1 shows a summary of the results detailed in the associated chapter table. Be careful about depending on anything that has a small sample size.

For example, it is doubtful that the average small-cap stock priced below $15.80 with a falling price to book value and rising return on equity will return 41 percent after one year. That is the first entry in the table and it assumes a $10,000 investment. However, only 77 trades qualify, which is few compared to the thousands of trades that some other items use.

Comparing the second-place rank (which is more reliable than first place) with the last place, we see that the difference of a $10,000 investment is $1,777, or 18 percent. It might be worth an experiment where you select stocks with a variety of fundamental factors. Pick one with a low price to book value. Another might have a low price to cash flow, and so on, to achieve diversity among the fundamental factors. Of course, if you find a stock with a low price to earnings ratio, for example, there is a good chance that it will have other benchmarks that are low (like price to sales or price to book value).

TABLE 12.1 Gain for One-Year Hold Time

Rank	Value	Chapter	Table	Description
1	$14,131	Book Value	3.4	Falling price to book value, rising ROE, small cap, price below $15.80 (only 77 samples).
2	$12,797	Book Value	3.3	Price below $15.80, below median 1.4 price to book.
3	$12,438	Cash Flow	5.3	Small caps below median 7.5 price to cash flow.
4	$12,260	Dividends	6.5	Nondividend paying small caps.
5	$12,221	Book Value	3.2	Small caps below median 1.7 price to book value.
6	$12,087	Debt	7.3	Small caps with decreasing debt.
7	$12,081	Book Value	3.5	Price to book value below 1.0.
8	$12,038	P/E Ratio	8.4	P/E ratio: small caps below the median 16.0.
9	$11,983	Debt	7.4	Small caps with long-term debt.
10	$11,966	PSR	9.3	Small caps below median 0.76 price to sales.
11	$11,848	Capex	4.4	Small caps above median 19.17 price to capital spending.
12	$11,834	Capex	4.2	Decreasing capital spending 2 years in a row.
13	$11,809	Shares Out	11.3	Small-cap stocks with increasing shares out.
14	$11,748	Dividends	6.1	High-yield stocks.
15	$11,695	Debt	7.2	Companies moving from no debt to debt in year 1.
16	$11,686	Dividends	6.4	Companies cutting their dividends (293 samples).
17	$11,664	ROE	10.3	Small-cap stocks above the median 11.4% ROE.
18	$11,569	Capex	4.1	Decreasing capital spending.
19	$11,450	Book Value	3.1	Price to book value below the median 2.11.
20	$11,436	Cash Flow	5.2	Below median 9.17 price to cash flow.
21	$11,430	P/E Ratio	8.3	P/E ratio: Falling price, rising earnings.
22	$11,377	PSR	9.1	Stocks below median 1.0 price to sales.
23	$11,332	P/E Ratio	8.2	Stocks with decreasing price to earnings.
24	$11,314	P/E Ratio	8.1	Stocks below median 17.1 price to earnings.
25	$11,312	Dividends	6.3	Companies paying dividends.

Rank	Value	Chapter	Table	Description
26	$11,293	Book Value	3.4	Falling price to book value, rising ROE.
27	$11,208	Shares Out	11.1	Stocks buying back 5% to 10% of shares.
28	$11,207	Debt	7.1	Companies debt-free.
29	$11,090	ROE	10.2	Stocks with increasing return on equity.
30	$11,075	PSR	9.2	Increasing price to sales.
31	$11,057	Cash Flow	5.1	Decreasing price to cash flow.
32	$11,020	ROE	10.1	Stocks with ROE above the median 13.4%.

PERFORMANCE RANK: THREE-YEAR HOLD

Holding stocks for a longer period means larger potential gains. However, a lot can happen in three years. Even as the reward climbs, so does risk. Table 12.2 shows the list, sorted by the three-year value of a $10,000 investment. The gains measure from the end of year 0 to the end of year 3.

TABLE 12.2 Gain for Three-Year Hold Time

Rank	Value	Chapter	Table	Description
1	$17,040	Book Value	3.3	Price below $15.80, below median 1.4 price to book.
2	$16,911	Cash Flow	5.3	Small caps below median 7.5 price to cash flow.
3	$16,734	Book Value	3.2	Small caps below a median of 1.7 price to book value.
4	$16,704	Dividends	6.4	Companies cutting their dividends (276 samples).
5	$16,534	Book Value	3.4	Falling price to book value, rising ROE, small cap, price below $15.80 (only 62 samples).
6	$16,351	Debt	7.3	Small caps with decreasing debt.
7	$16,329	Dividends	6.5	Non-dividend paying small caps.
8	$16,253	PSR	9.3	Small caps below median 0.76 price to sales.
9	$16,092	P/E Ratio	8.4	P/E ratio: small caps below the median 16.0.
10	$16,045	Book Value	3.5	Price to book value below 1.0.
11	$15,996	Dividends	6.1	High yield stocks.

(continued)

TABLE 12.2 (*continued*)

Rank	Value	Chapter	Table	Description
12	$15,768	Capex	4.4	Small caps below median 19.17 price to capital spending.
13	$15,603	Debt	7.4	Small caps with long-term debt.
14	$15,408	Shares Out	11.3	Small-cap stocks with decreasing shares outstanding.
15	$15,121	Shares Out	11.1	Companies buying back between 10% and 15% of shares outstanding (66 samples).
16	$14,854	ROE	10.3	Small caps above the median 11.4% ROE.
17	$14,797	Book Value	3.1	Price to book value below median 2.11.
18	$14,653	Cash Flow	5.2	Below median 9.17 price to cash flow.
19	$14,527	PSR	9.1	Stocks below median 1.0 price to sales.
20	$14,514	Dividends	6.3	Companies paying dividends.
21	$14,508	Capex	4.2	Decreasing capital spending 2 years in a row.
22	$14,211	Debt	7.2	Long-term debt to no debt.
23	$14,209	P/E Ratio	8.1	Stocks below median 17.1 price to earnings.
24	$14,110	Capex	4.1	Decreasing capital spending.
25	$14,085	Debt	7.1	Companies debt free.
26	$13,871	P/E Ratio	8.3	P/E ratio: Rising price, rising earnings.
27	$13,751	P/E Ratio	8.2	Stocks with decreasing price to earnings.
28	$13,624	PSR	9.2	Decreasing price to sales.
29	$13,549	Cash Flow	5.1	Decreasing price to cash flow.
30	$13,412	Book Value	3.4	Rising price to book value, falling return on equity.
31	$13,366	ROE	10.2	Stocks with increasing return on equity.
32	$13,364	ROE	10.1	Stocks with return equity below median 13.4%.

Be careful to review the chapter discussion when picking a stock based on these tables. For example, rank 4 says to pick stocks that cut their dividends. In the months after a dividend cut, the stock's price gets cut, too. Wait for it to bottom and then go fishing for a stock. You may catch a rebound, especially if the indices come out of a bear market.

PERFORMANCE RANK: FIVE-YEAR HOLD

Slight variations occur between the various tables in this chapter, depending on the hold time. **Table 12.3** shows the most important factors, sorted by the performance over a hold time of five years. Like the other tables, the value is based on a $10,000 investment.

TABLE 12.3 Gain for Five-Year Hold Time

Rank	Value	Chapter	Table	Description
1	$24,665	Shares Out	11.1	Companies buying back between 10% and 15% of shares outstanding (55 samples).
2	$24,080	Book Value	3.4	Falling price to book value, rising ROE, small cap price below $15.80 (only 56 samples).
3	$23,875	Dividends	6.4	Companies cutting their dividends (227 samples).
4	$22,706	Cash Flow	5.3	Small cap below median 7.5 price to cash flow.
5	$22,651	Book Value	3.3	Price below $15.80, below median 1.4 price to book.
6	$22,595	Debt	7.3	Small caps with decreasing debt.
7	$21,856	Book Value	3.2	Small caps below a median of 1.7 price to book value.
8	$21,661	Book Value	3.5	Price to book value below 1.0.
9	$21,570	PSR	9.3	Small caps below median 0.76 price to sales.
10	$21,448	Debt	7.4	Small caps with debt.
11	$21,418	P/E Ratio	8.4	Small caps below the median 16.0 price to earnings.
12	$21,376	Dividends	6.1	High yield stocks.
13	$20,983	Shares Out	11.3	Small caps with decreasing shares outstanding.
14	$20,868	Dividends	6.5	Dividend paying small caps.
15	$20,369	Capex	4.4	Small caps below median 19.17 price to capital spending.
16	$19,801	ROE	10.3	Small caps above median 11.4% return on equity.
17	$18,924	Book Value	3.1	Stocks with price to book value below median 2.11.
18	$18,694	Cash Flow	5.2	Below median 9.17 price to cash flow.
19	$18,609	Dividends	6.3	Companies paying dividends.

(*continued*)

TABLE 12.2   (*continued*)

Rank	Value	Chapter	Table	Description
20	$18,515	Capex	4.2	Decreasing capital spending two years in a row.
21	$18,405	PSR	9.1	Stocks below median 1.0 price to sales.
22	$17,919	Debt	7.2	Companies decreasing debt.
23	$17,916	Capex	4.1	Decreasing capital spending.
24	$17,843	P/E Ratio	8.1	Stocks below median 17.1 price to earnings.
25	$17,840	P/E Ratio	8.3	P/E ratio: Falling price, falling earnings (235 samples).
26	$17,432	ROE	10.1	Stocks with ROE below the median 13.4%.
27	$17,215	P/E Ratio	8.2	Stocks with decreasing price to earnings.
28	$17,131	Book Value	3.4	Rising price to book value, falling return on equity.
29	$16,951	PSR	9.2	Decreasing price to sales.
30	$16,911	Cash Flow	5.1	Decreasing price to cash flow.
31	$16,870	Debt	7.1	Companies with debt.
32	$16,752	ROE	10.2	Stocks with increasing return on equity.

Notice how variations on book value populate the top quarter of the table.

The next chapter discovers the fundamental factors involved in stocks that double in price. Are there common factors among stocks that do well?

CHAPTER 13

How to Double Your Money

One way to double your money is to fold it in half and put it back in your pocket. That is a joke, but trying to double your money is no laughing matter. This chapter looks at fundamental factors that are common to stocks that double in price.

I used split unadjusted data in my analysis. Why? Because in a historical price series, a stock priced at $10 would have a value of $5 after a two-for-one split. Telling readers to shop for stocks priced at $5 would be wrong because they cost $10 pre-split.

I used the same Value Line database, but removed stocks with splits. That left 769 companies with 5,315 samples, or about half the usual number of samples, covering the years from 1992 to 2007. Not all stocks spanned the entire range.

Before you read further, be warned that just because a stock has one, many, or all of the attributes that follow is no reason to believe that it will double within five years. I owned one stock that doubled in a week. Others flat-line like dead animals or worse—go down.

The following is *not* a presentation of a statistics curve fitted to show great results. Rather, the discussion reveals characteristics common to stocks that doubled in price, including dividends.

HOW LONG TO DOUBLE?

In what year did price first double? To answer that, I compared the year 0 price and found that 26 percent of the samples showed price doubling

TABLE 13.1 Frequency Distribution of Gains

Year	Doubled in Five Years	Cumulative
1	20%	20%
2	23%	43%
3	20%	63%
4	22%	85%
5	15%	100%

sometime during the next five years, based on closing prices at year-end with dividends added. I did a frequency distribution, appearing in **Table 13.1**.

The table shows when the samples doubled, providing they had not doubled in prior years. For example, of the 26 percent of stocks that doubled, year 1 contained 20 percent of them. At the end of year 2, excluding those doubling in year 1, an additional 23 percent doubled in price.

Year 2 had the most doubles, but the results are about evenly distributed. Year 5 shows the fewest doublings.

- Of those stocks that doubled in five years, 63 percent took less than three years.

WHAT IS THE BEST BUY PRICE?

From what price did the stock double? Did they start below a dollar or above $100 or perhaps somewhere in between? I sorted the year 0 numbers to find the answer, shown in **Table 13.2**.

TABLE 13.2 Stock Price of Stocks That Double

Price	Double	Cumulative	Benchmark	Cumulative
$0–5	**13%**	13%	1%	1%
6–10	**26%**	39%	7%	8%
11–15	**22%**	61%	**13%**	21%
16–20	**15%**	76%	**16%**	37%
21–25	9%	85%	**14%**	51%
26–30	5%	91%	**12%**	62%
31–35	3%	94%	**10%**	73%
36–40	2%	96%	8%	80%
41–45	1%	97%	5%	86%
>45	3%	100%	14%	100%

The most common price range is more than $5 but less than or equal to $10 (from the Double column). That range accounts for 26 percent of the samples. On a cumulative basis, stocks priced $20 or less doubled 76 percent of the time. Those priced over $20 showed fewer doublings.

Compare the results to the Benchmark column. This column is for all those stock that did *not* double within five years. I bolded the ranges with the highest numbers to help show how the range has slid downward. The double digits begin at $15 and end at $35. That compares to a $0 to $20 range for those stocks that doubled.

As a personal choice, I would avoid stocks priced below a dollar. They tend to teeter on the edge of bankruptcy or go nowhere for years. Mutual funds tend to avoid picking stocks priced below $5, too.

- Most doubles (63 percent) begin with a price between $5 and $20.

WHICH MARKET CAPS DO BEST?

Unless you have been asleep for the prior chapters, you know the answer to this question: Which market cap shows the most stocks doubling?

The answer is small caps (worth up to $1 billion). **Table 13.3** shows the results. Of the samples that doubled within five years, 65 percent of them were small caps, 27 percent were mid caps, and the rest were large caps.

- Small-cap stocks, those worth less than $1 billion, double most often.

Compare the Double column to Benchmark. Thirty-six percent were small caps, 42 percent were mid caps, and the remainder were large caps. The distribution is more uniform between the three caps. Stocks that double show a pronounced shift to small caps.

TABLE 13.3 Market Capitalization

Market Cap	Double	Benchmark
Small	65%	36%
Mid	27%	42%
Large	8%	21%

TABLE 13.4   Price to Book Value

Price/Book Value	Double	Cumulative	Benchmark	Cumulative
≤ 0.5	9%	9%	2%	2%
0.6–1.0	**18%**	26%	7%	9%
1.1–1.5	**23%**	50%	**19%**	28%
1.6–2.0	**14%**	63%	**18%**	46%
2.1–2.5	**10%**	74%	**12%**	59%
2.6–3.0	6%	79%	**10%**	68%
3.1–3.5	4%	84%	7%	75%
3.6–4.0	3%	87%	5%	80%
4.1–4.5	3%	90%	4%	84%
>4.5	10%	100%	16%	100%

FOCUS ON FUNDAMENTALS: WHICH ARE BEST?

This section looks at fundamental factors covered in this book to see which are important toward doubling your money. Let us begin with one that has shown its worth in picking stocks that perform well: book value.

Price to Book Value

I sorted the samples according to their price to book value and found what I expected. Most samples had price to book values residing in the low ranges. See **Table 13.4**.

Frequencies with double-digits had ratios in the range of 0.6 to 2.5. In fact, 74 percent of the samples I looked at had price to book value ratios on or below 2.5. The highest frequency (23 percent) occupies the range from 1.1 to 1.5.

Stocks that failed to double (Benchmark column) had price to book values in a higher range. At 2.5 price to book value, the doublers had 74 percent of samples below 2.5 (from the Cumulative column), but the nondoublers had only 59 percent.

The two-digit range for the nondoublers (Benchmark) moved higher by a row as the bold numbers show. Stocks that doubled tended to have lower price to book values than those that did not double.

- Stocks that doubled started with low price to book values (half the time below 1.5).

Capital Spending

Did spending on plant and equipment increase, decrease, or hold steady? **Table 13.5** shows half the samples (50 percent) that doubled within five

TABLE 13.5 Capital Spending

Cap Ex	Double	Benchmark
Increase	37%	50%
Decrease	50%	35%
No Change	13%	15%

years posted a *decrease* in capital spending. That compares to the nondoublers (Benchmark) that saw 50 percent of samples with *increased* capital spending.

The chapter on capital spending suggested that decreased capex leaves more money for other endeavors. After building a plant, the company can decrease capital spending and watch the profit tumble in (in theory).

One company I worked for moved to a new manufacturing plant just before the recession hit. They had their first layoffs ever and eventually moved back to the old plant to survive.

- Capital spending decreased from the prior year in stocks that doubled.

Price to Cash Flow

Table 13.6 shows a frequency distribution of price to cash flow for stocks that doubled within five years. Those companies with a ratio on or below 2 had the highest frequency of doubling, 21 percent. That compares to a 7 percent rate for stocks that failed to double (Benchmark).

Double-digit frequencies for stocks that doubled continued through 8 and tapered off thereafter. That compares to a higher price to cash flow range of 6 to 12 for those stocks that failed to double.

TABLE 13.6 Price to Cash Flow

Price/Cash Flow	Double	Cumulative	Benchmark	Cumulative
≤2	**21%**	21%	7%	7%
3–4	**15%**	36%	5%	12%
5–6	**15%**	51%	**12%**	24%
7–8	**12%**	63%	**13%**	37%
9–10	9%	72%	**12%**	49%
11–12	6%	78%	**11%**	61%
13–14	5%	83%	9%	70%
15–16	3%	87%	7%	77%
17–18	2%	88%	5%	81%
>18	12%	100%	19%	100%

The cumulative column shows that 63 percent of stocks that doubled had price to cash flow of 8 or less compared to just 37 percent for stocks that did not double.

- Stocks that double have low price to cash flow values (63 percent below 8).

Dividends

Dividends are a double-edged sword. On one side, shareowners get the benefit of a periodic dividend check (in the case of regular dividends) and that boosts profits. On the other side, the cost of the dividend means there is less cash for the company to invest in products or services it sells. If they cannot use the money to reinvest in their business, that could affect future growth.

Of the stocks that doubled, 59 percent of them did not pay a dividend. The dividend payment *was* included in the tabulation of whether or not price doubled, but it did not make much difference. That compares to 44 percent of stocks that failed to double and did not pay a dividend.

Companies that see their stock double use the cash for general corporate purposes instead of paying dividends.

- To double your money, avoid stocks that pay dividends.

Long-Term Debt

Debt is a lot like paying a dividend only the payment goes to someone other than the common stockholder. If a company has a modest amount of long-term debt, then it provides additional capital to build new plants, products, or services, enhancing shareholder value in the long term. The downside of debt is that the company has to pay interest on that debt. Too much debt, and the cost of servicing it harms the company's health.

A company having no debt often has a better chance of weathering difficult business environments (like recessions). They can always borrow money in a pinch. But having no debt could mean that they cannot afford to build a new plant, develop a new product, or peddle their wares like the suits in marketing demand. That could harm the business especially if their competitors are using debt to fund growth.

Of the samples that doubled in price within five years, 65 percent had long-term debt compared to 64 percent of stocks that failed to double. In other words, debt is not a factor in deciding whether a stock doubles. However, make sure that the debt level is reasonable. You do not want to buy a stock only to find that the company is in debt up to its eyeballs. As

TABLE 13.7 Various Long-Term Debt Measures

Debt	Double	Benchmark
Increase	27%	28%
Decrease	39%	35%
No Change	3%	3%

a helpful gauge, compare your stock to others in the same industry to see what level of debt they carry.

- Long-term debt is not a factor in stocks doubling.
- Check other stocks in the same industry to see what level of long-term debt they carry and compare it to the stock you want to buy.

Table 13.7 slices the debt pie differently and shows what I found.

Of those stocks that doubled, 27 percent increased their long-term debt, 39 percent showed it decreasing from the prior year, and 3 percent held it steady (but had debt). The numbers for stocks that failed to double (Benchmark) are nearly the same, 28, 35, and 3 percent respectively. The remainder had no long-term debt.

The totals for this pie are different from the 65/64 percent slice because of having to check the prior year.

Price-to-Earnings Ratio

Table 13.8 shows the price-to-earnings ratio of samples that doubled within five years. Just 1 percent had price-to-earnings ratios below 5, but double

TABLE 13.8 Price to Earnings

Price/ Earnings	Double	Cumulative	Benchmark	Cumulative
≤5	1%	1%	0%	0%
5.1–10	**13%**	15%	4%	5%
10.1–15	**31%**	46%	**26%**	31%
15.1–20	**20%**	66%	**31%**	62%
20.1–25	**13%**	79%	**16%**	78%
25.1–30	5%	84%	8%	86%
30.1–35	4%	88%	4%	90%
35.1–40	4%	92%	3%	92%
40.1–45	2%	94%	2%	95%
>45	6%	100%	5%	100%

digits begin after that. The most common range is 10.1 to 15, representing 31 percent of the samples, with another 20 percent having PEs of 15.1 to 20. PEs of 25 or below cover 79 percent of the samples. In other words, the stocks do not appear to have excessive valuations.

PE ratios will vary from industry to industry, so keep that in mind.

For stocks that failed to double (Benchmark), the PE ratio is similar, but shifted down the table one row as the bold numbers suggest. The high frequency range is for companies with PEs from 15.1 to 20, with 10.1 to 15 placing second.

Comparing the Double and Benchmark columns shows stocks that double have lower price to earnings. This is most evident in the 10.1 to 15 PE row. Stocks that double have a 13 percent frequency versus just 4 percent for stocks that failed to double.

When you look at the Cumulative columns, the two are similar at PEs of 20.1 and above.

- The most popular P/E ratio for stocks that double is between 10 and 15 with 20 coming in second.
- Stocks that double tend to have a lower PE ratio in year 0 than do those failing to double.

Price-to-Sales Ratio

At least one financial analyst touts the price-to-sales ratio as a reliable benchmark for selecting value stocks. But what PSR ratio do stocks have that double in price? **Table 13.9** shows a range of them.

The most frequent ratio is between 0.26 and 0.50, representing 21 percent of the samples in the study. The range up to 1.0 covers 63 percent of

TABLE 13.9   Price to Sales

Price/Sales	Double	Cumulative	Benchmark	Cumulative
≤0.25	17%	17%	4%	4%
0.26–0.50	21%	38%	13%	17%
0.51–0.75	15%	53%	14%	31%
0.76–1.00	10%	63%	14%	45%
1.01–1.25	5%	68%	9%	54%
1.26–1.50	5%	73%	7%	62%
1.51–1.75	4%	77%	5%	66%
1.76–2.00	2%	80%	4%	71%
2.01–2.25	2%	82%	4%	74%
>2.25	18%	100%	26%	100%

the samples, and the 1.0 value is often mentioned as a good separator between value and froth. I also think that 1.0 is a good upper limit to set when looking for stocks that will double in the future.

Compare the Double column with Benchmark. The ≤0.25 row for stocks that double shows 17 percent of samples compared to just 4 percent for nondoublers (Benchmark). In other words, stocks that doubled tended to have lower price-to-sales ratios when they started out. Over half of stocks (53 percent) that doubled had PSRs of 0.75 or less compared to just 31 percent for non-doublers.

- Stocks that double have low price-to-sales ratios, most below 0.75.

Return on Equity

I am not a big fan of return on equity, but **Table 13.10** shows the range that most samples occupied. Double-digit frequencies occur from 6.1 to 14 percent of return on equity (shown in bold), representing 48 percent of samples. The other 52 percent occurs outside of that range. The >18 row covers a lot of territory, so do not attach much significance to the high frequency.

Compare the double column with nondoublers (Benchmark). Stocks that double tend to have a smaller return on equity as the bold numbers show. Higher frequencies appear starting from the 6.1 percent row for doublers compared to 8.1 percent for nondoublers. The cumulate columns show the contrast more clearly, but there is not much separation between doublers and the benchmark.

- Return on equity often ranges between 6 and 14 percent in stocks that double. The return on equity is lower than for stocks that fail to double.

TABLE 13.10 Return on Equity

ROE	Double	Cumulative	Benchmark	Cumulative
≤2%	5%	5%	3%	3%
2.1–4	8%	13%	5%	7%
4.1–6	8%	21%	6%	14%
6.1–8	**10%**	31%	9%	23%
8.1–10	**12%**	43%	**12%**	35%
10.1–12	**14%**	56%	**12%**	47%
12.1–14	**12%**	69%	**11%**	58%
14.1–16	6%	75%	9%	67%
16.1–18	5%	80%	7%	75%
>18	20%	100%	25%	100%

Shares Outstanding

A company issuing more shares can use that money to fuel its growth, but existing shareholders see their holdings diluted. That dilution often means the stock nosedives when the company announces a stock offering.

The flipside of that situation is a company that buys back shares could see its price skyrocket. One example comes to mind: Savient Pharmaceuticals. In August 2006, the company offered to buy back 10 million shares, representing 16 percent of shares outstanding. When the Dutch auction tender offer completed, the stock eased lower, bottoming just below 6, and then it took off. In five months, the stock reached a high of 15.75, almost triple the 5.93 low. I watched it all from the sidelines, too afraid that their new gout drug could flop.

In 2008, news of the gout drug having possible nasty side effects dropped the stock from a close of 11.58 to a low of 2.80, or 76 percent, in *one* session. I was right to be cautious, but my timing was wrong.

Table 13.11 shows a frequency distribution of changes in shares outstanding. Stocks that doubled in price showed increasing share counts of 70 percent in year 0 compared to the prior year. That is almost the same rate as nondoublers (Benchmark), 67 percent.

The table suggests that the number of shares outstanding is not important to whether price doubles.

- Shares outstanding is not a significant contributor to a stock doubling in price.

WARNING: LOSSES AHEAD. WHAT YOU NEED TO KNOW

How many stocks declined in price from one year to the next over the five-year holding period? The Loss Year-to-Year column in **Table 13.12** shows that it ranges between 18 percent in year 1 to 26 percent in year 5 with dividends excluded. For example, in 23 percent of the cases in year 3, price was lower at the end of that year than at the end of the prior year.

TABLE 13.11   Shares Outstanding

Shares Out	Double	Benchmark
Increase	70%	67%
Decrease	25%	30%
No Change	6%	3%

TABLE 13.12 Frequency Distribution of Losses

Year	Loss Year to Year: Double	Benchmark
1	18%	48%
2	23%	37%
3	23%	29%
4	23%	23%
5	26%	16%

Year	Lost Half Year to Year: Double	Benchmark
1	2%	6%
2	2%	4%
3	2%	3%
4	3%	2%
5	3%	1%

Year	Lost Half Original: Double	Benchmark
1	2%	6%
2	2%	7%
3	1%	7%
4	1%	6%
5	1%	5%

Those results compare to 48 percent (year 1) to 16 percent (year 5) for stocks that failed to double (Benchmark).

It appears that year 1 is a strong year for stocks that double. They only lose value 18 percent of the time (end year 1 below the price at the end of year 0).

- Stocks that double show strong first-year performance.

The Lost Half Year to Year column represents the number of samples in which price lost at least half of its value from the prior year using year-end prices. For example, at the end of year 4, 3 percent of the samples lost at least half their value posted at the end of year 3.

Notice that the Benchmark column shows higher rates, up to 6 percent of stocks losing half their value.

- Stocks that double in price have a lower than normal chance of seeing price drop in half until year 4.

How often does price drop far enough over five years such that it is half the original investment? The table shows the answer to that question in the

Lost Half Original column. Since the period studied (1992 to 2007) did not include the 2007 to 2009 bear market (but did include the bear market from 2000 to 2002), the results could change.

Out of 1,353 samples that doubled in five years, just nine (1 percent) were worth less than half of their original value at the end of year 5. That compares to 5 percent (or 198 of 3,921) for stocks that failed to double (Benchmark). You are twice as likely to lose half the original value in the first two years (for stocks that double) than in the last three. The nondouble column shows catastrophic losses peaking in years 2 and 3.

TESTING THE SETUP

This chapter began by finding stocks that doubled in price within five years and then looked to see what attributes they shared. Now that we have a laundry list of common elements, how do they perform when applied to all stocks in the database?

Here are the assumptions I used, most of them selected from the tables showing the end of double-digit frequencies (typically near 66 percent).

- Price the stock between $1 and $20.
- Pick small cap stocks, those worth less than $1 billion.
- Price to book value ≤ 2.5.
- Capital spending this year should be less than last year.
- Price to cash flow ≤ 8.
- No dividends paid.
- P/E ratio ≤ 25.
- Price to sales ratio ≤ 1.0.
- Return on equity ≤ 14 percent.

Assuming a purchase price using the close of year 0 and a sale at the highest year-end closing price of years 1 through 5 (because I wanted to find those that doubled *within* five years), the 89 samples would have made an average of 254 percent. Sixty-seven percent of them would have at least doubled in price and only 11 or 12 percent would have lost money (losing an average of 23 percent).

If you ignore those stocks that qualified using the above selection guidelines, you would find that 26 percent of them doubled sometime during the year 1 to year 5 period. That compares to 67 percent doubling over the same period for those stocks following the criteria.

- Using the nine selection criteria boosts the chance of finding stocks that double from 26 percent to 67 percent.

This setup uses in-sample, but not curve-fit data. However, since only year-end closing prices are used, it is expected that the results would improve if I used the highest price over the five years.

CHAPTER CHECKLIST

The following is a checklist based on the above discussion. Refer to the table or section for more information. Please keep in mind that using these values is no guarantee that price will double within five years.

☐ Of those stocks that doubled in five years, 63 percent took less than three years. See Table 13.1.

☐ Most doubles (63 percent) begin with a price between $5 and $20. See Table 13.2.

☐ Small-cap stocks, those worth less than $1 billion, double most often. See Table 13.3.

☐ Stocks that doubled started with low price to book values (half the time below 1.5). See Table 13.4.

☐ Capital spending decreased from the prior year in stocks that doubled. See Table 13.5.

☐ Stocks that double have low price-to-cash-flow values (63 percent below 8). See Table 13.6.

☐ To double your money, avoid stocks paying dividends. See the section "Dividends."

☐ Long-term debt is not a factor for stocks that double. See Table 13.7.

☐ Check other stocks in the same industry to see what level of long-term debt they carry and compare it to the stock you want to buy. See the section "Long-Term Debt."

☐ The most popular P/E ratio for stocks that double is between 10 and 15 with 20 coming in second. See Table 13.8.

☐ Stocks that double tend to have a lower P/E ratio in year 0 than do those failing to double. See Table 13.8.

☐ Stocks that double have low price-to-sales ratios, most below 0.75. See Table 13.9.

☐ Return on equity often ranges between 6 and 14 percent in stocks that double. The return on equity is lower for stocks that fail to double. See Table 13.10.

☐ Shares Outstanding is not a significant contributor to a stock doubling in price. See Table 13.11.

☐ Stocks that double show strong first-year performance. See Table 13.12.

☐ Stocks that double in price have a lower than normal chance of seeing price drop in half until year 4. See Table 13.12.

☐ Using the nine selection criteria boosts the chance of finding stocks that double from 26 to 67 percent. See the section "Testing the Setup."

CHAPTER 14

Finding
10-Baggers

1 0-baggers—stocks that move up by at least 10 times their original value—are easy to spot. "I should have bought right there," I will say and point to a chart of a stock that became a moon shot. Trying to find 10-baggers *before* they make their move is more challenging.

This chapter looks at traits common to stocks that climb at least 900 percent (10-baggers) in five years or less. Since such stocks are as rare as snow flurries in Florida, I added more samples to my Value Line database. After I finished typing in the information, I had unearthed only 163 nonoverlapping 10-baggers covering the years from 1992 to 2007. By nonoverlapping, I mean a stock can have two 10-baggers providing one ends before the next begins. I found only 11 stocks that had more than one 10-bagger and the separation between where one ended and the next began averaged 3.3 years.

I used split-unadjusted data to get an accurate price representation. If price is cut in half by a two-for-one split, for example, price to book value, price to sales, and other ratios change. I eliminated that possibility by removing quote data that had a split during or after price began its 10-bagger run.

To find the start of a 10-bagger, I located where price made a large move and then measured from the highest price backward in time and stopped if price qualified as a 10-bagger in five years or less. This method of looking backward in time means I did not have to guess about where a 10-bagger began, only where it ended.

HOW LONG TO 10X?

How long does it take a stock to climb to 10 times its original value?
Table 14.1 shows a frequency distribution to answer the question. For example, 8 percent of the stocks finished the move within one year, another
17 percent completed the move in two years, and so on. Five years has the
highest completion rate: 41 percent.

Please note: This table shows how long it takes a stock to reach 10-
bagger status, counting from the start to end of the entire price move.
Table14.4 shows the move over time using end-of-year closing prices for
year 0, year 1, and so on). Thus, 8 percent of stocks reached 10-bagger
status in 365 days (Table 14.1) but none made it in year 0 (in Table 14.4 they
made their move by starting in year 0 and completing their move in year 1).
That is why the two tables show different results over time.

- 41 percent of 10-baggers take five years to complete the move.

WHAT IS HIGHEST STARTING PRICE?

At what price do stocks begin their journey to 10-bagger status? To find
the answer, I worked backward in time from the end of the pattern to the
start until price dropped to one-tenth its ending price. Price could continue
lower, changing a 10-bagger into a 20-bagger or more, but that did not concern me. It had to make the 10-bagger move in five years or less.

You can think of this method as the last opportunity to buy a 10-
bagger—the highest starting price.

Table 14.2 shows the results. The most frequent starting price is
between $3 and $4, representing 19 percent of the samples. Over half
(55 percent) of the samples had a starting price of $5 or less.

Be cautious about buying stocks below $1. They tend to go bankrupt
or stay flat for years. The median (mid-range) starting price is $4.19 and the
average is $6.38.

TABLE 14.1 10-Bagger Completion Time

Years	Frequency	Cumulative
1	8%	8%
2	17%	25%
3	13%	37%
4	21%	59%
5	41%	100%

TABLE 14.2 Starting Price of 10-Baggers

Price	Frequency	Cumulative
$0–1	2%	2%
1–2	13%	15%
2–3	14%	29%
3–4	19%	48%
4–5	7%	55%
5–6	12%	67%
6–7	10%	77%
7–8	7%	83%
8–9	2%	86%
9–10	3%	89%
>10	11%	100%

- Most 10-baggers (55 percent) begin their move at prices below $5.

WHAT HAPPENS THE FIRST YEAR?

What happens to the stock price in the first year? That may sound like a question best answered by, "Who cares?" but all 10-baggers begin by doubling in price. How many doubles happen the first year?

Table 14.3 shows a frequency distribution of gains in year 0. Although a stock can double in a day, it often takes months for it to occur. A stock that doubles rises by 100 percent, and the table shows that 42 percent of the 10-baggers fail to achieve that in year 0. That means 58 percent of the stocks *do* double.

TABLE 14.3 10-Bagger Gains in Year 0

Gain	Frequency	Cumulative
0–25%	8%	8%
25%–50%	11%	19%
50%–75%	11%	30%
75%–100%	12%	42%
100%–125%	12%	54%
125%–150%	11%	65%
150%–175%	6%	71%
175%–200%	3%	75%
200%–225%	3%	78%
>225%	22%	100%

Look at the bottom of the table that shows 22 percent of 10-baggers more than tripled the first year. That is the highest frequency in the table.

The median move in year 0 is 116 percent, by the way, and the average is 149 percent. The difference between the two numbers suggests that several stocks posted large gains, pulling the average upward.

- Most 10-baggers (59 percent) double in price during year 0 with a median rise of 116 percent.

RISING OVER TIME: HOW FAST?

Table 14.4 shows the first time that price reached the percentage gain, using closing prices from the end of year 0, end of year 1, and so on as the cutoff.

For example, 59 percent of the samples first doubled in price during year 0; 36 percent did not double in year 0, but *did* double sometime in year 1; and so on. The next row down shows that 26 percent of samples first tripled (200 percent gain) by the end of year 0.

Although six columns are shown (year 0 through year 5), each 10-bagger had a duration of five years or less. The longest duration 10-baggers ended life sometime in year 5 and began life five years earlier.

Why is Table 14.4 important? The Totals row shows that year 1 tends to be significant since the most samples rise by large amounts during that year.

As the percentage gain increases, the highest frequency totals shift to the right. That makes sense since it usually takes years for price to rise by large amounts. For example, year 1 sees the most samples (49 percent) climb at least 200 percent. In year 2, the highest frequency (36 percent) is

TABLE 14.4 10-Baggers Rise Over Time

Gain	Year 0	Year 1	Year 2	Year 3	Year 4	Year 5
100%	59%	36%	4%	1%	1%	1%
200%	26%	49%	18%	6%	1%	0%
300%	13%	38%	32%	12%	5%	1%
400%	5%	25%	36%	24%	8%	2%
500%	2%	16%	29%	29%	21%	3%
900%	0%	11%	0%	22%	33%	33%
Totals	105%	175%	119%	94%	69%	40%

at 400 percent, and the 900 percent row shows that years 4 and 5 have the most samples (33 percent) achieve 10-bagger status.

* Year 1 is when price often moves up the most.

10-BAGGERS BY MARKET CAP

A frequency distribution shows that 77 percent of the stocks that moved up by 10 times were small caps, 21 percent were mid caps, and 2 percent were large caps.

If you want to pick stocks that have the best chance of moving up a great deal, start your search with small-cap stocks.

* 77 percent of 10-baggers are small caps.

FUNDAMENTAL RATIOS COMMON TO 10-BAGGERS

Let us turn to financial ratios common to 10-baggers. What makes them tick? In the tables that follow, remember that the sample counts are few. Doing a frequency distribution on few samples splits them even more, making the results subject to change and perhaps unreliable. That is why I compare them against companies that failed to see price rise to 10-bagger status (Benchmark in the tables). Contrasting the two provides hints to 10-bagger behavior.

Price to Book Value

You can probably guess what the range of book value is for most 10-baggers, but it varies depending on when a 10-bagger starts life.

Recall that I found the *end* of the 10-bagger first and worked backward in time to find the first price where it became a 10-bagger (within a five-year window, too). The 10-bagger I uncovered was the *last* one in the price move. The beginning of the identified 10-bagger was *not* the start of the up-move.

This is an important point, so let me give you another example to clarify it using a window not five years wide, but one. Imagine price rising for two years, but the window you are looking through can only see one year's worth of action. I placed the window such that it looked at the final year's move, not the first year.

In the tables that follow, I discuss what happened the year *before* the 10-bagger (shown in the tables as Year − 1, not to be confused with Year 1).

TABLE 14.5 Price to Book Value for 10-Baggers, One Year Before

Price/Book Value	10-Baggers Year − 1	10-Baggers Cumulative	Benchmark Year − 1	Benchmark Cumulative
≤0.5	**18%**	18%	4%	4%
0.6–1.0	**18%**	35%	**11%**	15%
1.1–1.5	**15%**	50%	**20%**	35%
1.6–2.0	**11%**	61%	**16%**	51%
2.1–2.5	7%	69%	**11%**	63%
2.6–3.0	6%	75%	8%	71%
3.1–3.5	5%	80%	6%	77%
3.6–4.0	5%	84%	4%	81%
4.1–4.5	4%	88%	4%	85%
>4.5	12%	100%	15%	100%

I am assuming that the 10-bagger began life during the prior year. It may not have, but the results will help uncover what to look for when hunting for 10-baggers in the future.

Table 14.5 shows a frequency distribution of price to book value for 10-baggers and stocks not qualifying as 10-baggers (Benchmark).

Half (50 percent) have a price to book value at or below 1.5 compared to a benchmark of 2.0. Over a third (35 percent) of 10-baggers have price to book values below 1.0, but non-10-baggers show the same 35 percent in the next row down. In other words, 10-baggers tend to have a lower price to book value than stocks that failed to qualify as 10-baggers.

Since we want to catch a 10-bagger when it begins life, look for low price to book values.

- The year before a 10-bagger shows that half the samples have a price to book value below 1.5.

Capital Spending

Capital spending on plant and equipment decreases in 10-baggers 59 percent of the time (measured from the year before year 0 to year 0). That is the highest percentage among increasing (32 percent), decreasing (59 percent), and no change (9 percent). In other words, in year 0, capital spending was less than the prior year 59 percent of the time. **Table 14.6** shows this.

TABLE 14.6 Capital Spending for 10-Baggers, One Year Before

Cap Ex	10-Baggers Year – 1	Benchmark Year – 1
Increase	32%	47%
Decrease	59%	39%
No Change	9%	14%

When searching for 10-baggers, look for stocks that show a decrease in capital spending.

Notice that the benchmark shows an increase in capital spending (47 percent of samples) among non-10-baggers most of the time, not a decrease. In fact, capex decreases only 39 percent of the time compared to 10-bagger's 59 percent.

- 10-baggers show decreasing capital spending in year 0 from the prior year 59 percent of the time.

Price to Cash Flow

Analysts have emphasized cash flow as key to determining the current and future prospects of a company. Is cash flow important to 10-baggers? Maybe, and **Table 14.7** shows the reason why.

In the year before I found the 10-bagger, 40 percent had price to cash flow on or below 1.0. That is huge! It compares to 10 percent for non-10-baggers (Benchmark).

TABLE 14.7 Price to Cash Flow of 10-Baggers

Price/Cash Flow	10-Baggers Year – 1	10-Baggers Cumulative	Benchmark Year – 1	Benchmark Cumulative
≤1	40%	40%	10%	10%
1.1–2	7%	47%	2%	11%
2.1–3	3%	50%	3%	14%
3.1–4	4%	54%	5%	20%
4.1–5	7%	61%	7%	27%
5.1–6	5%	66%	7%	34%
6.1–7	2%	68%	7%	41%
7.1–8	3%	72%	6%	47%
8.1–9	3%	75%	5%	52%
>9	25%	100%	48%	100%

The over-nine row (>9) is a catchall that shows another huge group of 10-baggers: 25 percent of samples reside there, but look at the benchmark. Forty-eight percent cower in the over-nine row.

Drilling into the 40 percent number, I found that 38 percent had negative cash flow in the year before I logged them as 10-baggers. That compares to just 10 percent for the benchmark (the same as that shown, oddly, due to rounding).

- 40 percent of 10-baggers had price to cash flow below 1.0.

Dividends

Do stocks that move up by ten times their original value within five years pay dividends? No. Just 13 percent of the samples paid dividends in the year before their official birth. Non-10-baggers showed 43 percent paying dividends during the same period.

- 10-baggers do not pay dividends at birth; only 13 percent did.

Long-Term Debt

Do 10-baggers have debt? You might think that the answer would be no, but 72 percent of the samples showed companies carried at least a splash of long-term debt in the year before year 0. I did not measure how large the debt was, just whether a company had debt. See **Table 14.8**.

The 72 percent debt number compares to 63 percent for non-10-baggers (Benchmark) holding long-term debt. Based on those two numbers, it appears that there is not a significant difference between 10-baggers and non 10-baggers. Let us dig deeper.

Is the amount of debt growing, shrinking, or holding steady? The debt load of 10-baggers increased in 29 percent of the cases, decreased in 37 percent, and held steady in 6 percent. The benchmark numbers are similar: 28, 33, and 3 percent, respectively.

TABLE 14.8   Various Long-Term Debt Measures for 10-Baggers

Debt	10-Baggers Year – 1	Benchmark Year – 1
Debt	72%	63%
Increase	29%	28%
Decrease	37%	33%
No change	6%	3%

TABLE 14.9 Are 10-Baggers Profitable?

Net Profit	10-Baggers Year – 1	Benchmark Year – 1
Profit	36%	62%
Loss	64%	38%

Since the numbers are close, I do not view the change in long-term debt as significant to finding 10-baggers. However, it *is* important that the potential 10-bagger not be overloaded with debt.

- 72 percent of 10-baggers hold long-term debt.

Net Profit

Are companies that qualify for 10-bagger status profitable before year 0? No. Just 36 percent made money. In year 0, that rises to 46 percent, meaning that most are still losing money.

For the benchmark companies, 62 percent of them posted a profit in the year before year 0. **Table 14.9** contrasts the numbers.

- Most 10-baggers (64 percent) lose money in the year before birth.

Price to Earnings

With 64 percent of the companies losing money, the price-to-earnings ratio cannot be calculated for those companies. **Table 14.10** shows the results for the 56 profitable companies. The rows typically have only four or five samples. That means the results could be unreliable.

TABLE 14.10 Price to Earnings

Price/Earnings	10-Baggers Year – 1	10-Baggers Year 0	Benchmark Year – 1
≤5	7%	3%	0%
5.1–10	**20%**	**25%**	7%
10.1–15	**16%**	**21%**	**28%**
15.1–20	9%	**13%**	**27%**
20.1–25	9%	**14%**	**15%**
25.1–30	7%	**10%**	7%
30.1–35	7%	2%	4%
35.1–40	7%	0%	3%
40.1–45	9%	2%	2%
>45	9%	11%	6%

However, the trend of lower P/E ratios for 10-baggers is clear even in this table. That matches the trend we saw for stocks that doubled in price (see Chapter 8, "Price to Earnings Ratio").

To explain the table, look at the 5.1 to 10 row. It shows 20 percent of 10-baggers had a price to earnings ratio within the 5.1 to 10 range for the year before year 0. The year 0 tally (using 63 samples) showed 25 percent in the same range. For the benchmark companies, those stocks not qualifying for 10-bagger status, only 7 percent fell into the same P/E ratio.

If we have a rule to include only money-losing operations (from the prior section, Net Profit), then the P/E ratio is moot. Otherwise, the year 0 column shows a migration from high ratios to lower ones, with the 5.1 to 10 row being the most popular.

However, a consistent number of samples appear in the higher P/E ratio cells, considerably more than the Benchmark column. Thus, using a rule to qualify 10-baggers based on their P/E ratio could be a mistake. It may remove too many 10-baggers.

What is a solution to this problem? Answer: price to sales, which I discuss in a moment.

- As profits increase, the P/E ratio for 10-baggers drops leading to year 0.

Sales

Do sales explode before a 10-bagger begins? No. I looked at the change in sales that year and the prior year, which I show in **Table 14.11**.

In the prior year, sales climbed a median of 0.5 percent and an average of 2.9 percent compared to the benchmark's 6.4 and 10.4 percent respectively. In other words, sales of non-10-baggers are considerably higher than 10-baggers.

During year 0, the same sales underperformance remains with 10-baggers posting a median sales increase of 3.6 percent, which is almost half the benchmark rate of 7.0 percent. It seems clear that booming sales do not ignite 10-baggers.

TABLE 14.11   10-Bagger Sales

Sales	10-Baggers Year − 1	Benchmark Year − 1	10-Baggers Year 0	Benchmark Year 0
Median	0.5%	6.4%	3.6%	7.0%
Average	2.9%	10.4%	7.7%	11.0%

- In the year preceding a 10-bagger, sales are considerably weaker than non-10-baggers. However, 10-baggers see a dramatic improvement in sales during year 0 but remain about half the rate of non-10-baggers.

Price-to-Sales Ratio

One of the benefits of the price-to-sales ratio is it does not depend on earnings. If a company has sales and a stock heartbeat, then one can calculate the price-to-sales ratio (PSR).

Table 14.12 shows a frequency distribution of the ratio for 10-baggers. For samples with a PSR on or below 0.25, in the year before year 0, 26 percent of 10-baggers fell within that range. That compares to just 7 percent for non-10-baggers.

Over half (56 percent) had a PSR below 1.0. When looking at the Benchmark columns, we see that after a PSR of 1.0, the two cumulative columns are similar. Below 1.0 and 10-baggers have a higher cluster toward the low PSR numbers, especially below 0.50.

- In the year before year 0, over half (56 percent) of 10-baggers had price-to-sales ratios of 1.0 or lower.

Return on Equity

Table 14.13 shows a frequency distribution of 57 samples of 10-baggers, sorted by their return on equity (ROE).

TABLE 14.12 Price to Sales of 10-Baggers

Price/Sales	10-Baggers Year – 1	10-Baggers Cumulative	Benchmark Year – 1	Benchmark Cumulative
≤0.25	26%	26%	7%	7%
0.26–0.50	15%	41%	16%	23%
0.51–0.75	6%	47%	15%	38%
0.76–1.00	9%	56%	12%	50%
1.01–1.25	5%	61%	8%	59%
1.26–1.50	5%	66%	6%	65%
1.51–1.75	2%	68%	4%	69%
1.76–2.00	4%	72%	3%	73%
2.01–2.25	3%	76%	3%	76%
>2.25	24%	100%	24%	100%

TABLE 14.13 Return on Equity of 10-Baggers

ROE	10-Baggers Year − 1	10-Baggers Cumulative	Benchmark Year − 1	Benchmark Cumulative
≤2%	7%	7%	3%	3%
2.1–4%	12%	19%	6%	9%
4.16%	14%	33%	7%	16%
6.1–8%	18%	51%	9%	25%
8.1–10%	4%	54%	12%	37%
10.1–12%	2%	56%	13%	50%
12.1–14%	16%	72%	11%	61%
14.1–16%	4%	75%	8%	70%
16.1–18%	4%	79%	6%	76%
>18%	21%	100%	24%	100%

Half the samples (51 percent) had a ROE at or below 8 percent, and the other half had a higher return. Some analysts consider 15 percent as the minimum ROE for quality performers. A full 75 percent have a ROE below 15, leaving just 25 percent to satisfy the quality minimum. Before you laugh at the analysts, remember that I was only able to find 57 samples, which I consider a small number.

The benchmark shows that ROE is much higher for non-10-baggers. Half of 10 baggers (51 percent) have a ROE below 8 percent, but just a quarter (25 percent) of non-10-baggers squeeze into the same range.

- High return on equity is not a good measure for selecting 10-baggers since 51 percent of them had ROE below 8 percent.

Shares Outstanding

Do 10-baggers issue more shares in the year before year 0? Yes, but it is not much different from non-10-baggers: 71 percent to 69 percent, as **Table 14.14** shows. About the same number of companies also decrease their shares outstanding, 21 percent to 28 percent, respectively.

However, look at year 0. Eighty-four percent of 10-baggers issue more shares compared to 68 percent for the benchmark companies (non-10-baggers).

TABLE 14.14 Shares Outstanding for 10-Baggers

Shares Out	10-Baggers Year − 1	Benchmark Year − 1	10-Bagger Year 0	Benchmark Year 0
Increase	71%	69%	84%	68%
Decrease	21%	28%	11%	28%
No Change	8%	4%	5%	4%

I assume that the money received from issuing shares goes into products or services that help power the stock upward during the next 5 years. It may not, of course. In the weeks immediately after a company issues more shares, the stock tends to dive because shareholders hate the dilution to their holdings.

- 84 percent of the time, 10-baggers had more shares outstanding at the end of year 0 than the prior year compared to 68 percent for non 10-baggers.

INDUSTRIES MOST LIKELY TO MAKE 10-BAGGERS

I counted the number of times an industry with 10-baggers appeared. **Table 14.15** shows the results for industries with more than nine stocks. Not all industries known to man were analyzed, either. I looked at only 60.

The most frequent industry with big movers was semiconductor makers. There were 29 10-baggers out of 35 stocks in that industry. The remainder of the table shows where 10-baggers hide most often.

- Of the 60 industries included in the study, the semiconductor industry and homebuilders had the most 10-baggers from 1992 to 2007.

TABLE 14.15   10-Baggers by Industry

Industry	Percentage
Semiconductor	83%
Homebuilding	77%
Internet	77%
Semiconductor Capital Equipment	73%
Alternate Energy	67%
Biotechnology	67%
Computers and Peripherals	60%
Telecommunications Equipment	59%
Drug	52%
Retail (Special Lines)	43%
Precision Instrument	42%
Medical Supplies	35%
Machinery	25%

THE MOST POPULAR YEARS FOR 10-BAGGERS

Table 14.16 shows a frequency distribution of *starting dates* for 10-baggers. As explained earlier, this is not when the stock began rising. Rather, it is the highest price in which the stock still qualified as a 10-bagger within five years.

In 1998, 10-baggers started to participate in the raging bull market in a big way when their frequency soared to 13 from 1 the prior year. The number of 10-baggers peaked in 2003, hitting 50 (31 percent of the total). That makes sense since October 2002 marked the end of a bear market that began in March 2000. The bear market lows represented the seeds that would germinate into large gains during the next five years.

To put it another way, 50 stocks achieved 10-bagger status some time between 2003 and 2007, the highest in the table.

The end of the table shows diminished samples because it can take five years for a 10-bagger to reach its peak price. If a 10-bagger was born after 2003, there was probably not enough time for it to move up before the end of the study.

- Most 10-baggers begin their move up just after a bear market ends.

TABLE 14.16 10-Bagger Birth by Year

Year	Frequency	Samples
1992	0%	0
1993	0%	0
1994	1%	1
1995	2%	3
1996	0%	0
1997	1%	1
1998	8%	13
1999	10%	17
2000	7%	11
2001	12%	19
2002	13%	21
2003	31%	50
2004	12%	19
2005	3%	5
2006	2%	3
2007	0%	0

	TABLE 14.17	Frequency Distribution of Gains and Losses	
Year	**Loss Year to Year**	**Lost Half Year to Year**	
1	18%	0%	
2	31%	5%	
3	34%	7%	
4	31%	9%	
5	38%	8%	

SURPRISING FINDING ABOUT 10-BAGGER LOSSES

Let us talk about losses since every stock has them. If you buy at the high for the year and price drops the following year, then you have a paper loss bleeding all over your brokerage statements.

You might think that a stock achieving 10-bagger status would show price rising from year to year. Unfortunately, that is not true about a third of the time.

Table 14.17 shows the breakdown. All of the results use end of year closing prices. For example, at the end of year 1, 18 percent of the samples had a lower price compared to the end of year 0; 31 percent had a lower price in year 2 compared to year 1; and so on.

How many samples lost half their value from one year to the next? It ranges between 0 percent in year 1 to 9 percent in year 4. Imagine achieving 10-bagger status in year 4 only to see your gains drop by half the next year!

Since the table uses year-end values only, the results could be worse if stocks made lower lows during the year.

- 10-baggers are not immune to price drops.

BACKWARD TESTING

This chapter listed elements common to most 10-baggers. Now that we know those attributes, how do the numbers work when applied to the entire database?

Here are the parameters based on the Year − 1 column in the various tables and cutting off the numbers to include 66 percent of the samples.

- The year 0 closing price should be below $6.
- The company must be a small cap (those worth less than $1 billion).

- Price to book value at or below 2.5.
- Decrease in capital spending from the prior year.
- Price to cash flow at or below 6.
- The stock does not pay a dividend.
- The amount of long-term debt is not important: Exclude.
- Companies should show a loss (exclude) or have a price-to-earnings ratio below 30 (include).
- Price-to-sales ratio at or below 1.5.
- Return on equity below 14 percent.
- Shares outstanding. Exclude since there is not much difference between 10-baggers and non-10-baggers.

The ten stocks that qualified made an average of 605 percent (measured from the year 0 to year 5 closing prices), and three of them (30 percent) were 10-baggers. None lost money over the five-year holding period, but the test period was 16 years long. That means finding a stock that qualifies about once every two years.

I prefer a different list of components. Here they are, but be warned: These are curve fitted. That means I saw how little some of the above rules affected results (or negatively impacted results) and discarded them.

- The year 0 closing price should be below $5.
- The company must be a small cap, those worth less than $1 billion.
- Price to book value below 2.5.
- The stock does not pay a dividend.
- Price to sales ratio below 1.5.

Using these guidelines on split-unadjusted stocks finds 108 samples with gains averaging 649 percent. Thirty-five of them, or 32 percent, were 10-baggers. Five lost an average of 32 percent. You take more risk (loss), but have more stocks to choose from with a slightly higher average gain.

CHAPTER CHECKLIST

The following checklist is based on the above discussion. Refer to the table or section for more information.

Please keep in mind that using these results is no guarantee that price will rise by 900 percent or more within five years.

☐ Fully 41 percent of 10-baggers take five years to complete the move. See Table 14.1.

☐ Most 10-baggers (55 percent) begin their move at prices below $5. See Table 14.2.

☐ Most 10-baggers (59 percent) double in price during year 0 with a median rise of 116 percent. See Table 14.3.

☐ Year 1 is when price often moves up the most. See Table 14.4.

☐ Small caps represent 77 percent of 10-baggers. See the section "10-Baggers by Market Cap."

☐ The year before a 10-bagger starts shows that half the samples have a price to book value below 1.5. See Table 14.5.

☐ 10-baggers show decreasing capital spending in year 0 from the prior year 59 percent of the time. See Table 14.6.

☐ Many 10-baggers (40 percent) had price to cash flow below 1.0. See Table 14.7.

☐ 10-baggers do not pay dividends at birth; only 13 percent did. See the section "Dividends."

☐ Most 10-baggers (72 percent) hold long-term debt. See Table 14.8.

☐ Most 10-baggers (64 percent) lose money in the year before they achieve 10-bagger status. See Table 14.9.

☐ As profits increase, the P/E ratio for 10-baggers drops leading to year 0. See Table 14.10.

☐ In the year preceding a 10-bagger, sales are considerably weaker than non-10-baggers. However, 10-baggers see a dramatic improvement in sales during year 0 but remain about half the rate of non-10-baggers. See Table 14.11.

☐ In the year before year 0, over half (56 percent) of 10-baggers had price-to-sales ratios of 1.0 or lower. See Table 14.12.

☐ High return on equity is not a good measure for selecting 10-baggers since 51 percent of them had ROE below 8 percent. See Table 14.13.

☐ Most of the time (84 percent), 10-baggers had more shares outstanding at the end of year 0 than the prior year compared to 68 percent for non-10-baggers. See Table 14.14.

☐ Of the 60 industries included in the study, the semiconductor industry and homebuilders had the most 10-baggers from 1992 to 2007. See Table 14.15.

☐ Most 10-baggers begin their move up just after a bear market ends. See Table 14.16.

☐ 10-baggers are not immune to price drops. See Table 14.17.

☐ See the section "Backward Testing" for ideas on parameter selection choices.

CHAPTER 15

Trading 10-Baggers

Trading 10-baggers sounds like an oxymoron. Why consider trading stocks intended to be held for up to five years or longer? The answer is simple: to make money. A review of the charts gives hints how 10-baggers are born, live, and die, and using those hints can save time and money. Follow along as I explore the visual world of 10-baggers.

10-BAGGER BIRTH

Based on fundamental factors discussed in prior chapters, use the screening tools available on the Internet to pick a potential 10-bagger. After finding one, should you buy the stock? No. Why not? Because price may not rise for months or even years. That is where technical analysis helps by timing the entry. Let us look at a few charts to discover common elements that 10-baggers share during the birthing process.

Figure 15.1 shows a 10-bagger in BJ's Restaurants. If you bought the stock in April 1997 at about $1 per share, the stock would have peaked about a year later at 2.47. By June 2000, it would have been priced about $1.50. For a three-year hold time, 50 percent is not much of a gain for a 10-bagger, is it?

A doctor slapping the stock on the backside gives life to it, and price begins moving up. It pierces a trendline (cleverly labeled Trendline A) drawn along the price peaks, signaling a buy at about $2.

FIGURE 15.1   A 10-bagger in BJ's Restaurants, drawn on the monthly scale.

In the bear market of 2000 to 2002, the stock stumbles and throws back to B before making a robust climb to nearly $6 in just three months (point F). Price retraces some of the gains before continuing the climb up to C. At C, price hits 10.45, which is more than 10 times the low at G in December 1999.

Those investors not selling at C would see their investment drop almost in half to a low of 5.30 in March 2003 (D) before another up-leg begins. The journey takes price up to E at 15.50 and then onward to peak at 27.50 in June 2006.

Why do I spend so much time reviewing the chart? Let me give you some reasons. First, the chart is on the linear scale. That means each ladder rung up the price scale has the same distance as the prior rung. The linear scale tends to compress price when large moves are involved. In other words, the three-year run from 1997 to 2000 has price moving from a low of $0.81 to a high of $2.47—a triple, but it does not look like the stock moved much at all.

Second, the chart shows two patterns. The first is a flat base. That is the horizontal-looking run that begins in 1997 and stretches to 2000. Trendlines are effective tools to highlight price breaking out of a flat base.

Another phrase for a flat base is a trading range. Price is range bound, bouncing up from the bottom only to fall back again, but remaining between the high and low for years, in this case. Only when price closes above the top of this range does the stock become interesting for traders and investors. That is the time to buy.

Finally, the chart shows a measured move-up chart pattern. Price bottoms at B, rises to C where it forms the corrective phase CD before continuing up to E.

The theory behind the measured move is that leg BC will equal leg DE in both price and time. I discuss the weekly measured move-up pattern later in this chapter.

10-Baggers Start from a Flat Base

Let us tear apart the flat-base pattern to see how we can use it to buy 10-baggers. I used the linear chart on the monthly scale to review more than 400 10-baggers and found that 46 percent of them started from a flat base.

- 46 percent of 10-baggers start from a flat base.

Figure 15.2 shows another example of a flat base on the monthly and weekly (inset) logarithmic price scale. The flat base began in September 2003 and lasted until October 2004. Had you invested in the stock during September 2003, you would have had little to show for it a year later. In November 2004, the stock blasted off from a low of 1.73 to a high of 8.64— all in one month! But the moon shot was just beginning. Price eventually peaked at 66 in November 2007.

When prospecting for a flat base, what should you look for? As I mentioned, use the linear scale instead of the log one. That is an important step because the linear scale compresses price and helps with finding a flat base. Then look for price moving horizontally for months, forming waves that bounce between the top and bottom of the flat base. Do not be that concerned if price pokes outside of the range now and again.

The price movement will resemble an ocean beach composed of rocks and pebbles instead of sand. Close up (the daily scale), the beach will not look smooth at all, but from a distance (weekly scale), you will see that it is quite even. So, too, will be the flat base. Like that shown in the inset, it will look jagged but price remains between upper and lower boundaries. Price moving above the top of the range signals a buy.

- Switch to the linear scale and look for a flat-base pattern.
- Buy when price closes above the top of the flat base.

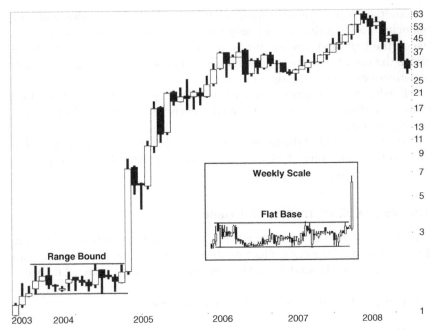

FIGURE 15.2 A flat base on the monthly, semi-log scale, inset on the weekly scale, leading to a 10-bagger.

Figure 15.2 uses the log scale because I wanted to show price moving in the low ranges on a historical basis. Had I used a linear scale, you would see a flat line and little more until price took off.

Some 10-Baggers Prefer a V-Shaped Start

Contrast the flat base with the V-shaped turn shown in **Figure 15.3**. If the flat base represents the easy way to make money, the V-shaped turn is like racing cars for a living. It takes courage to buy a stock near the bottom when accidents abound.

The V-shaped turn occurs 54 percent of the time in 10-baggers. On the linear scale, price trends down and then it does not. Surprise! The rebound may look like just another upward retrace in a downward price trend, but something has changed. Price becomes a helium balloon released by tiny fingers. I show the V-shaped turn at point A on the monthly chart.

Look at the inset on the weekly scale. The stock peaked in March 2000 at 55.50 (not shown), finally hitting bottom in October 2002, matching the bear market drop in the Standard & Poor's 500 index exactly.

FIGURE 15.3 The V-shaped turn at A happens most often in 10-baggers, but it is difficult to trade.

After seeing price drop for two years, would points B, C, or D look like bottoms to you? The move after B is a steep rise that quits in a few weeks and the pattern repeats at C. At D, the takeoff is a bit shallower, but does explode upward at E. Do you think the rise would end soon because the climb at E is too steep? Only you can answer that, but my guess is you would not have bought the stock until it became clear that the rise is a lasting one. And by that time, price will have doubled or more from the low.

Let us zoom in on the price action using the daily chart (**Figure 15.4**), but keeping the linear scale. This is the kind of price movement that chartists love to see, like having your wife or husband return from overseas deployment!

What pops out when I look at this chart is the head-and-shoulders bottom chart pattern. The two shoulders are not symmetrical in distance from the head, but the valley prices are similar. If you were to invert this figure, it would look like a person's head-and-shoulders. The chart pattern suggests higher prices ahead.

Look at trend line D. I drew this line along the peaks and let it slice through the right shoulder. When price closes above this line, it suggests the move up has begun. Of course, if you bought the day after price reached

FIGURE 15.4   A Head-And-Shoulders Bottom Marks The Turn On The Daily Chart, Linear Scale.

E and then saw it drop over the next two weeks, you would be pissed. But price cooperated thereafter by blasting upward in a burst of frenetic energy.

I do not show the traditional neckline of the head-and-shoulders bottom. The neckline joins the armpit peak at F with the one at E. A close above the neckline is the buy signal.

- Most 10-baggers begin life with a V-shaped start.

Moving Up: A Higher Valley Turn

If you do not see a reversal pattern such as a head-and-shoulders bottom, then look for a turn like that shown at ABC. Price bottoms at A, forms a higher valley at B, and closes above peak C—the highest peak between A and B. When that happens, price is moving higher.

In an *upward* trend, price will close above C. If it does not then price is still trending downward. Unfortunately, as good as this technique is to detecting a trend change, it does not always work. Price peaks at G and in a strong *downtrend*, price at H will just continue lower, eventually dropping below A, and making you feel like an idiot for buying the stock.

The key ingredient is that price will always make a higher valley and then close above the peak between the two valleys. If it fails to do that, then price is still falling. This chart pattern I call an ugly double bottom. Bottom B should be at least 5 percent higher than bottom A. When price closes above the peak between the two bottoms, it confirms the trend change.

Another example of this pattern is the head and right shoulder valleys. Price bottoms at the head, makes a higher valley at the right shoulder, and then closes above the high at E. When that happens, it signals a buy.

- Look for a confirmed ugly double bottom to signal a trend change.

LIFE OF A 10-BAGGER

Now that we know what to look for on the price charts to detect the birth of a 10-bagger, what can we expect during its life? To answer that question, I looked at 396 10-baggers to determine common shapes. I found four. Before I discuss those shapes, let us discuss the weekly measured move-up chart pattern.

Weekly Measured Move Up

The measured move up and down are two aptly named chart patterns. Using them can help predict where price will reverse. Since we are dealing with 10-baggers in which price climbs to the upper reaches of the stratosphere, I will discuss only the measured move up on the weekly scale.

I cataloged 455 measured move-up chart patterns in 10-baggers, and **Figure 15.5** shows four of them. The first is the ABCD move. Price begins the move up from turning point A in a straight-line run to B. This is the first leg. The corrective phase, BC, retraces a portion of the AB move. After C, the second leg begins and takes price up to D in another near-straight-line run. The other measured moves are CDEF, EFGH, and GHIJ.

The theory behind the measured move is that leg one will equal leg two in both price and time.

Each of the measured moves begins from a turning point—a minor low—and end at a minor high, making a straight or nearly straight-line run along the way. Between the two up-legs is the corrective phase where price turns at a minor high at the start and ends before the second leg begins moving up. The corrective phase is where price stalls by moving horizontally to down.

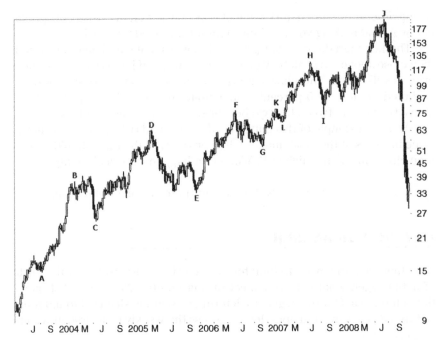

FIGURE 15.5 The Measured Move Up Chart Pattern Occurs Frequently in 10-Baggers (Weekly, Log Scale).

The size of the three components of the measured move, namely the two legs and the corrective phase, should be proportional. Proportionality is hard to explain, but it is like pornography: You will know it when you see it.

The four measured moves in Figure 15.5 are proportional. The corrective phase looks properly sized for the length of the two legs, and the two legs look similar in size, duration, and angle of climb.

The corrective phase should not retrace too far into the AB move, nor should the CD move be significantly shorter or longer than the AB move, but be flexible.

The angle and appearance of AB and CD should be similar, but the corrective phase will displace the two legs on the time scale. Trend lines drawn below AB and CD will be almost parallel, but with CD often rising at a shallower angle.

Measured moves are fractal. In other words, they sometimes appear embedded within a larger measured move. The move from G to H has a measured move-up pattern buried within it (GKLM). I did not catalog these smaller measured moves, only the major turning points in 10-baggers where an investor might entail significant loss during the corretive phase.

TABLE 15.1 Frequency Distribution of Corrective Phase Retrace by Extent

Retrace	20%	25%	30%	35%	40%	45%
Frequency	6%	9%	15%	18%	17%	10%

Retrace	50%	55%	60%	65%	70%	75%
Frequency	9%	5%	3%	3%	3%	2%

- Use the weekly measured move-up chart pattern to predict the ending price and time.

In studying measured moves in 10-baggers, at first I did not care much about the length of the two legs. What concerned me was the retrace an investor suffers during the corrective phase. **Table 15.1** shows a frequency distribution of the retrace of the measured move as a percentage of the highest price found in the corrective phase BC (for the ABCD pattern). In other words, the formula was $(B - C) \div B$ expressed as a percentage, where B is the highest high and C is the lowest low in the corrective phase.

The table shows that the most frequent retrace is between 25 and 45 percent, with a tendency for many to appear near 35 percent. The median retrace is 35.4 percent: Half the samples retraced less than 35.4 percent, and half retraced more.

How often does a measured move-up (MMU) pattern appear in 10-baggers? I found 396 10-baggers and 455 MMUs, suggesting just over one (1.15) measured move up per 10-bagger, on average. A number of stocks did not have measured moves whereas Figure 15.5 shows that some had many.

While we are on Figure 15.5, look at how the 10-bagger ends. Price peaked at 196 in June 2008 (note: weekly, log scale) and reached a low of 20.71 in November before retracing and then falling to 16.66 in March 2009. Although I like buy and hold, the figure shows that holding on too long can be detrimental to your wealth.

- The most frequent retrace in a weekly measured move up is between 25 and 45 percent with a 35 percent median.

TABLE 15.2 Frequency Distribution of Corrective Phase High Price in 10-Baggers

Bags	1	2	3	4	5	6	7	8	9
Frequency	6%	19%	16%	15%	12%	10%	10%	8%	3%

Table 15.2 shows where in the price scale measured moves appear, based on the highest price found in the corrective phase.

For example, 6 percent of the measured moves appear on the weekly scale when price first doubles (1 bag). The most frequent appearance is between price doubling (bag 1) and tripling (bag 2), with 19 percent of samples appearing there. As price nears 10-bagger status, fewer corrections appear probably because any correction turns into a full-fledged drop, ending the 10-bagger.

- Weekly measured moves appear most often between price doubling and tripling, but the frequency distribution is quite wide.

Table 15.3 shows where the corrective phase starts along the time scale. For example, 12 percent of measured moves appear within the first 10 percent of the 10-bagger move. The most frequent position is between 20 and 40 percent (at 13 percent each), but the range is comparatively smooth from 0 to 80 percent. Only as the 10-bagger nears its end do measured moves disappear. That makes sense (cents, too) since I am looking at where the corrective phase starts, not where leg two ends.

- The corrective phase starts where the measured move appears on the time scale spreads almost evenly between 0 percent to 80 percent from start to end of the 10-bagger.

MMU Measure Rule

Although I confined the analysis of measured moves to the corrective phase so far, it is helpful to know where price is going to turn. If we know the length of the first leg, we can project that move in both price and time to the second leg. We use the measure rule (the first leg will approximate the length of the second leg) to accomplish that. How well does the measure rule work for weekly measured moves?

Using the length of the first leg of the measured move—from the low at the start (C in Figure 15.5) to the highest high found in the corrective phase (D) and projecting it upward from the lowest low found in the corrective

TABLE 15.3 Time Distribution of Corrective Phase in 10-Baggers

Location	10%	20%	30%	40%	50%
Frequency	12%	12%	13%	13%	10%

Location	60%	70%	80%	90%	100%
Frequency	9%	11%	9%	7%	2%

phase (E)—gives the price target where the second leg is supposed to end (F). Price reaches or exceeds the target an average of 79 percent of the time. Expressed another way, the first leg is shorter than the second one 79 percent of the time.

- The first leg of a weekly measured move up is shorter than the second leg 79 percent of the time.

On a calendar basis, from the day the first leg starts to the beginning of the corrective phase added to the end of the corrective phase gives us a prediction of when the second leg will end. Unfortunately, price only meets the prediction an average of 48 percent of the time.

For a more accurate projection, multiply the price length by 79 percent and the duration by 48 percent (before adding it to the corrective phase low or end, respectively) to get closer targets. That boosts the success rate to 93 percent for price and 88 percent for time. In other words, price will reach or exceed the target in 93 percent of the cases and will meet or take less time to get there in 88 percent of the cases.

- The measure rule on the calendar scale for weekly measured moves works only 48 percent of the time.

Of course, those projections do not tell when price will reverse, only that it will reach or exceed the target. Price could continue rising for months.

Recognizing that a measured move might be forming will help you predict at what price and when a turn might happen. That is valuable information.

Two-Hump Shape

Figure 15.6 shows the appearance of a two-hump 10-bagger on the weekly chart, logarithmic scale. The log scale shows price better over a taller price range. Notice how the price scale divisions are not equally spaced as they are on a linear chart.

Price begins its climb in early 2005 from 6.35 (point A) to 7.25 (point B), depending on where you start. Since I found the 10-bagger by finding the highest hump first (E) and working backward, B is my starting price. That later starting point gives investors several weeks to find and buy the stock. Notice that the AB pattern resembles a higher valley turn (ugly double bottom) that I already discussed.

Price climbs in a near straight-line run until it has a major tumble in the shape of a corrective phase of a measured move-up chart pattern, circled on the chart.

FIGURE 15.6   This is the Hump Shape of a 10-bagger on the weekly logarithmic scale.

The price expedition continues moving higher up the slope until reaching C, at 17.05, a gain of 135 percent. Upon reaching the peak and congratulating each other, the summit party turns around and the weather clears to reveal a much larger price mountain (E).

Unfortunately, between humps 1 and 2 is a drop almost back to base camp, bottoming at 7.99 (D). The large drop represents the bad news for these hump-shaped 10-baggers. After D, price moves up in a nice run to finally peak at E.

Notice that the hump 2 summit is not a gentle rounded turn, but a pointed one. It reminds me of the hypodermic needle the nurse used a few weeks ago for my H1N1 flu shot. Investors not selling near E find their gains disappearing with each passing week.

The hump-shaped 10-bagger is a twin-peak construction (rarely does it have more than two peaks). On the log scale, the first hump is often a large one, but the second dwarfs the first. The draw down (from C to D) is a painful one. After seeing their investment double (the move from B to C), investors dump the stock on the way down to D, probably quite close to D, and then the real up-move begins without them.

- The hump-shaped 10-bagger is a twin peak pattern with the second peak taller than the first.

Of the four 10-bagger shapes, the hump variety is rarest, occurring 16 percent of the time. The average time to reach 10-bagger status is 3.3 years, with a median of 3.5 years. Measured moves, like the BC pattern on the chart, appear next to last in terms of frequency among the four 10-bagger shapes. The ratio of measured move-up patterns to 10-baggers is 1.2, meaning the average 10-bagger has at least one measured move-up pattern. For a 10-bagger that investors would love to hate, having few measured move-up chart patterns along the way is good news (because price drops in the corrective phase). Just remember, the stats apply to the weekly scale only.

- Humped 10-baggers are rare, occurring 16 percent of the time and lasting an average of 3.3 years.

Trading Humps

I show five trend lines drawn along peaks or valleys on the chart, beginning with TL1. Since fundamentals may have qualified this 10-bagger as a value play, investors need only time the entry. TL1 shows how entry (at 8.62) could have been made when price *closed* above the trend line drawn on the weekly chart. Since this is a long-term investment, use the weekly or monthly chart for entry and exit timing, not the daily chart.

If you sold the stock when price closed below TL2 (exit at 13.75), you would have captured most of the profit, at least more than selling as price approached D. Since D would have represented a value almost as good as B (in terms of price, anyway), another trend line (not shown) drawn along the move from C to D would have gotten you back into the stock when price crossed the line at about 12.

From there, it is just a matter of having the courage to ride the stock upward. TL3 (exit price at 40) shows a trend line that an investor could use to exit with most of his winnings intact. TL4 (exit price 50), connecting higher valleys, allows the investor to capture more profit, but risks a premature exit.

I show TL5 as an example of a premature exit. TL5 is a steep trend line drawn along the bottoms. This trend line is similar to TL4, but it takes an investor out of the stock at 25 when E peaks at 73.

One last tip is to recognize the measured move-up pattern from D to E. If the first leg is supposed to equal the price and duration of the second leg, you can predict where price may peak. Switch to the linear scale so that vertical distances are the same, not the log scale, if you do this visually.

The first leg begins at 7.99 and ends at the corrective phase high price of 32.57 for a height of 24.58. The second leg begins at a corrective phase low of 19.77, suggesting a target price of 44.35. Price actually peaks at 73, so the prediction missed it by a mile.

On a time basis, the first leg begins the week of 7/14/06 and ends 12/8/06 (the start of the corrective phase, not the date of the corrective phase high), for a duration of 147 days. The second leg begins on 6/29/07 and 147 days later would be 11/23/07, about three weeks short of the actual peak the week of 12/14/07. That is not a bad prediction considering the measured move is 17 months long.

- Trend lines can be invaluable when trading humped 10-baggers.

Line Shape

The next 10-bagger shape is what I call the line shape, and I show an example of it on the weekly scale in **Figure 15.7**. The 10-bagger ends at B (near the top of the chart), and dividing the price by 10 says it begins at A. Of course, we can see that price actually bottomed a few weeks before A.

Price climbs the chart following a straight trend line, hence the name *line shape* for the pattern it makes on the chart.

FIGURE 15.7 A 10-bagger follows a straight-line upward.

- A line-shaped 10-bagger follows a straight line upward until the end.

The line shape is the type of 10-bagger investors dream of finding. Buy and hold the stock until it stops climbing and then dump the turkey.

Price peaked at 64.20 and a close below the trend line would have signaled an exit at 51.95, assuming a sale at the open the next week. That is a bit of a give back (19 percent) from the peak, but it is not bad.

One significant measured move-up chart pattern appears along the trend, which I show as CDEB, highlighting the major turning points and keeping proportionality in mind. Since this is a measured move up, you can use the same measuring technique described earlier to make a prediction of where price will peak. Running through the computations, I found that the peak was supposed to end on 10/22/2004 at 44.78, but the 10-bagger actually ended on 11/26/2004 at 64.20.

Since price followed a straight line or nearly so, a trend line makes a good exit tool. Connect the valleys with a line drawn upward. When price closes below the line, consider selling. Make sure to use the weekly (or longer) chart. The intent is to sell after price reaches a major turning point, not on a normal retrace of the upward price trend.

The line-shaped 10-bagger has the lowest time to reach 10-bagger status of the four shapes: an average of 2.3 years. The median is 1.9 years with one sample taking just two weeks! The line shape also occurs most often, 42 percent of the time. That is delicious news.

The appearance of measured moves as a ratio to 10-baggers has the lowest score of the four shapes: 0.9. That means slightly less than one measured move appears in each line-shaped 10-bagger, and that suggests less worry about the corrective phase taking price down by huge amounts.

If you see a stock trending higher following a straight line then maybe it is a 10-bagger beginning life.

- The line-shaped 10-bagger has an average duration of 2.3 years, occurs 42 percent of the time, and has the fewest appearances of measured moves (0.9) of the four shapes.

Rounded-Turn Shape

Figure 15.8 shows a rounded-turn 10-bagger on the monthly scale. I chose the monthly scale so that I could fit the turn into the figure without crowding, although I prefer the weekly scale.

Price peaks at A, at a high price of 17.15. That means a 10-bagger begins when price is one-tenth of that, namely below 1.72, which happens at C. Point B is slightly lower, showing that you had about 8 months to buy the stock before price began a sustained move up.

FIGURE 15.8   A rounded turn 10-bagger on the monthly scale.

As price climbed, the peaks followed a rounded shape, which I show as following the curved trend line D. Another trend line connecting the lows follows a straighter trajectory, from E to F. When price closes below the trend line, sell.

Since price curves, the sell trend line may be curved also, such that it hugs the price valleys. Do not be afraid to use curved lines as sell signals. The D curve can also be bowed downward and not upward like that shown. Those types of curves tend to follow an exponential trajectory and the breakdown from those is often a quick decline.

Notice that the rounded shape continues after A, bottoming at 4.92 at G. That is a huge drop from 17.15, so it pays to sell your 10-bagger in a timely fashion.

The rounded-shaped 10-bagger occurs just 19 percent of the time in the samples I looked at. It takes an average of 3.5 years to reach the peak price, which ties with the stair-step shape for the longest average duration. The median rise is 3.8 years. Rounded 10-baggers also tie with the stair-step shape for the highest ratio of measured moves to 10-baggers: 1.4.

- The rounded-turn 10-bagger is just as it sounds, a long slow turn. It only happens 19 percent of the time and takes an average of 3.5 years to reach 10-bagger status.

Stair-Step Shape

Figure 15.9 shows what a stair-step 10-bagger looks like. In this example, price rises and pauses numerous times along the way up the price ladder. Each horizontal step is the corrective phase of a measured move-up chart pattern.

If you ignore the individual steps and look at the contour, this one resembles a rounded turn or even a line shape. Trend line AB shows how the valleys follow a line upward in this example. When price closes below the trend line then that is the sell signal.

As I mentioned, the stair-step shape ties with the rounded turn for the number of measured moves encountered on the weekly charts: 1.4. That is the highest of the four shapes. The stair-step pattern occurs 23 percent of the time, which is second to the line shape in terms of frequency. The stair-step 10-bagger takes an average of 3.5 years to complete with a median of 3.9 years.

Trading the stair step can pose a challenge if a trend line is used. Sometimes the shape is so irregular that it does not follow a straight or even a curved trend line. Looking at the fundamentals may not do any good since the reports can be delayed by up to three months (quarterly) or more. The stock will tend to lead fundamentals anyway. Thus, earnings may still be exploding, but the stock will start its downhill run.

FIGURE 15.9   A stair-step-shaped 10-bagger on the weekly scale.

- The stair-step 10-bagger happens 23 percent of the time, but takes an average of 3.5 years to complete.

10-BAGGER DEATH

How do 10-baggers end? They die in two ways: a rounded turn or an inverted V-shaped turn. The difference between the two is a matter of degrees and the screen you are looking at. Stretched out, a turn can look rounded, but if the screen is narrow, it might look like an inverted V-shape.

Figure 15.10 shows what an inverted V-shaped top looks like. This 10-bagger ends at B and begins at A. Of course, the actual 10-bagger begins to the left of A when price makes a lower low in November 2004.

Look at B, how narrow the turn looks. This type of decline makes skydivers nervous! The peak is needle sharp, lasting just one week. If you miss the peak by selling too early or too late, you give up big bucks.

Most inverted V-shaped turns are not this pretty. They tend to be wider, about a month long, perhaps more, but the drop is precipitous nonetheless. The underside of the inverted *V* tends to be a better gauge of the

FIGURE 15.10 These inverted V-shaped tops help predict the shape of the 10-bagger's end

shape. The three insets marked ECOL, AVID, and IN show three inverted V-shaped turns in American Ecology (July 2008), Avid Technology (March 2005), and Intermec (January 2006), respectively. Pull them up on your computer and see what they look like on your screen, then contrast them with Jones Soda.

Figure 15.11 shows another 10-bagger, but this one has a rounded ending. The climb ends at A and the 10-bagger begins in the fall of 2004. An investor had eight months from the low at C to discover this stock and still qualify for 10-bagger status.

Turn A is a wonderful example of a rounded ending to a 10-bagger. Price hovers near the highest high for months, reluctantly sliding lower. The turn is tall, too, from about 45 to almost 60.

Turn B is another example of a rounded top (it is a head-and-shoulders top, really). When trying to imagine what the 10-bagger's end will look like, scan the chart for prior peaks or turns. Figure 15.10 shows several that are narrow, spike-shaped needles. Figure 15.11 shows rounded turns.

- Use prior price action that forms shapes to help determine what the 10-bagger's end will look like.

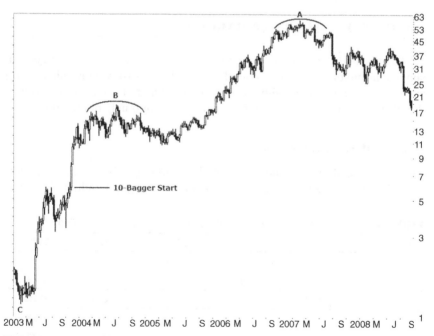

FIGURE 15.11   A rounded end to a 10-bagger.

The Numbers

How often does a 10-bagger end with an inverted *V* shape? Answer: 42 percent of the time leaving the other 58 percent to rounded turns.

- 10-baggers have two shapes at the end, a rounded turn or an inverted *V*.

After the 10-bagger ends, what is the decline to the lowest low over the next year? Answer: price drops an average of 66 percent and a median of 63 percent. If you do not sell your 10-bagger in a timely way, you could lose more than half your money!

- In the year after a 10-bagger ends, the average decline is 66 percent.

Table 15.4 shows a frequency distribution of the declines up to a year after the 10-bagger ends. For example, just 1 percent of the stocks dropped about 10 percent within the following year. The most frequent drop is between 60 and 70 percent. That happens 18 percent of the time. Just 29 percent drop less than 50 percent and that means 71 percent drop more.

If you own a 10-bagger, then look for signs that it is time to sell. What do you look for? Answering that is the subject of the next section.

CHART PATTERNS IN 10-BAGGERS

We have already identified the end of the 10-bagger as having two general shapes: an inverted *V* and rounded turn. Within those general shapes are six variations: head-and-shoulders top (including the complex variety), double top, triple top, rounded turn, inverted *V*, and ugly double top.

Head-and-Shoulders Top

Figure 15.12 shows a head-and-shoulders top (top of the chart). The left shoulder (LS) is near the same price level as the right shoulder (RS), and

TABLE 15.4 Frequency Distribution of Declines after a 10-Bagger Ends

Decline	10%	20%	30%	40%	50%
Frequency	1%	2%	5%	7%	14%
Cumulative	1%	3%	8%	15%	29%
Decline	**60%**	**70%**	**80%**	**90%**	**100%**
Frequency	15%	18%	17%	15%	6%
Cumulative	44%	62%	79%	94%	100%

both are near the same distance from the head. The head towers above the other two peaks just as it does on a person's body. The neckline joins the two armpits. When price closes below the neckline, sell.

In some cases, the shoulders will not look as symmetrical in time or price, so allow variations. Sometimes, many months can span between the two shoulders. A head-and-shoulders top occurs 16 percent of the time in the 396 10-baggers I looked at.

- A head-and-shoulders top ends a 10-bagger 16 percent of the time.

Double Top and the 2B Rule

The left inset of Figure 15.12 shows a double top in Quanta Services (PWR in 2007). Peaks A and B are near the same price level. When price closes below a confirmation line drawn at the low between the two peaks, sell. Unfortunately, waiting for price to drop that far can take months, and the distance from the peak at A or B to the confirmation line can be huge.

One solution to the potential drop is to trade on the 2B rule, which I discussed in *Trading Basics*, Chapter 5, in the section "Timing the Exit: The 2B Rule." Victor Sperandeo writes, "In an uptrend, if a higher high is

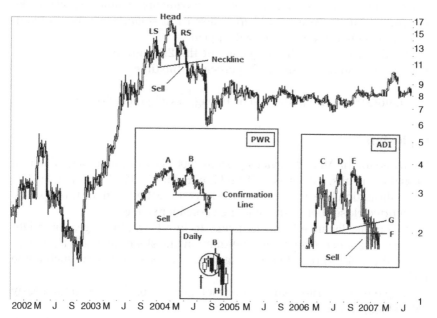

FIGURE 15.12 The end of 10-baggers form several types of chart patterns, including head-and-shoulders, double, and triple tops

made but fails to carry through, and then prices drop below the previous high, then the trend is apt to reverse."

For example, say you owned PWR and price reached a high at A of 32.58 before dropping back to a low of 23.36 (at the confirmation line). Seeing such a large drop is not pleasant, and you vow to sell the stock if it rises back to the old high.

Luck is on your side and price cooperates. The stock rises again and peaks at 33.42, at B. Then the stock begins sliding. Since you do not want to give back your profit and you vowed to sell it anyway, you switch to the daily chart (a portion of it appears below the PWR chart) and suffer through the large drop at H, closing at 30.71, below the congestion area circled. Price is going down. You sell at the open the next day and receive a fill at 30.75. Selling was the correct decision since price dropped to a low of 18.38 in January 2008.

I have used the 2B rule many times to capture profits before the trend changed, sometimes exiting before breathtaking drops and sometimes seeing price dip briefly before moving higher.

If you use the 2B rule to sell a stock and then price reverses again to climb above the recent top (peak B in this example), it could be another 2B in the form of a triple top or it could be the start of another up-leg. If price continues rising on high volume, then you can buy back in to ride the stock higher or just look elsewhere for another buying opportunity. If you are like me, you will throw your hands up in disgust at selling too soon and look elsewhere. Other opportunities will appear.

I did not measure the frequency of the 2B pattern, but double tops occur at the end of 10-baggers 22 percent of the time.

- Double tops form at the end of 10-baggers 22 percent of the time.

Triple Top

The triple top of Analog Devices (ADI in 2000) is a variant of a double top. It has three peaks, shown as C, D, and E in Figure 15.12. Horizontal line F is the confirmation line drawn below the lowest low between the three peaks. When price closes below the line, then consider selling.

Since the distance from the peaks to line F can be large, you might want to sell sooner. Also, if the confirmation line slopes upward (if you join two of the valleys) then that can signal an earlier exit. I show such a line at G.

Triple tops are rare, happening just 9 percent of the time in the nearly 400 10-baggers I checked.

- Rarely (9 percent of the time) will a triple top end a 10-bagger.

Inverted *V*

Figure 15.13 shows an example of an inverted V-shaped turn at B, the end of the 10-bagger, on the weekly chart. The 10-bagger starts at A (11.12), which is one-tenth the price at B (113). That is what I used for statistical purposes, but an investor had over a year to find the stock before price made its move.

Price zips up to B, turns on a dime, and then zips right back down like a mouse coming out of his hiding place and scurrying back in when you flick on the kitchen lights.

The left shoulder (LS?) and the right shoulder (RS?) are too far apart in price—56.00 to 77.56 to form a valid head-and-shoulders top. If this pattern were a person, you would want to take them to a chiropractor for some serious work. Nevertheless, the three-peak pattern issues a warning of a coming trend change.

Notice that peak C is also narrow, suggesting that later peaks might form the same shape. The inverted V-shaped end to 10-baggers occurs 29 percent of the time, making it the most frequent shape found.

- Inverted *V* shapes end 10-baggers most often: 29 percent of the time.

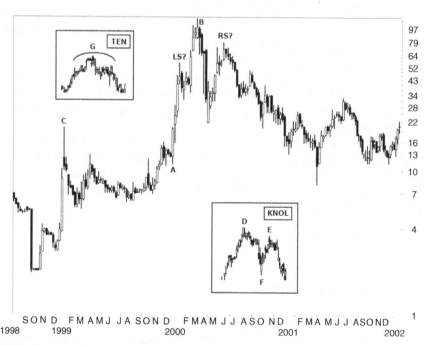

FIGURE 15.13 An inverted V-shaped turn at B, an ugly double top, and round turns complete these 10-baggers.

Rounded Turn

Figure 15.13 also shows the rounded turn at G in Tenneco (TEN) during 2007. This might look like a head and shoulders, but the left shoulder is not well defined. Those versed in chart patterns would probably call this a *V* top with an extension on the right, which it is, but the wide, rounded turn is similar to the type of gradual turns that compose 16 percent of 10-baggers.

When searching for rounded turns, look at other major turning points (peaks) in the same chart. If they are wide, lumbering turns, then that increases the chance that the 10-bagger will end with a rounded turn.

- Look for similar-shaped peaks to help predict the ending shape of a 10-bagger.

Ugly Double Top

The last 10-bagger shape is an ugly double top, and I show an example of that from Knology (KNOL) in 2007, pictured in Figure 15.13. It looks like a double top with peaks D and E, but peak E is too far below D. Thus, it is a double top, but an ugly one, hence the name.

The ugly double top functions the same as a regular one. When price closes below the low between the two peaks (F), it confirms the pattern as valid and shouts the coming of lower prices.

Every top will have a second peak below the first. That is true regardless of whether the peak is wide or narrow, tall or short. However, the second, lower peak can be months away. Nevertheless, if you see a second peak below the first, then get nervous. The uptrend might not be over, but it is signaling weakness.

Ugly double tops are rare, happening just 6 percent of the time. Many times, if you see a peak on the left, the pattern will be a head-and-shoulders top. If the two peaks are close together in price, then it will be a classic double top. Add a third peak and you have a triple top. These patterns tend to occur before an ugly double top.

- Ugly double tops end 10-baggers just 6 percent of the time.

CHAPTER CHECKLIST

Table 15.5 shows a summary of the chart patterns that appear in 10-baggers.

Based on findings in this chapter, here are some tips to consider when trading stocks showing 10-baggers.

TABLE 15.5 Summary of 10-Bagger Patterns

10-Bagger Start Shape	Frequency
V shape	54%
Flat base	46%

10-Bagger Life	Details
Measured move up	Median retrace is 35%.
Measured move up	First leg is shorter than second leg 79% of the time.
Line shape	Frequency: 42%, averages 2.3 years long.
Stair step	Frequency: 23%, averages 3.5 years long.
Rounded turn	Frequency: 19%, averages 3.5 years long.
Two hump 10-bagger	Frequency: 16%, averages 3.3 years long.

10-Bagger End Shape	Frequency
Rounded turn	58%
Inverted V	42%

End Shape Variations	Frequency
Inverted V	29%
Double tops	22%
Head-and-shoulders top	16%
Rounded turn	16%
Triple tops	9%
Ugly double top	6%
Average decline	66% one year after 10-bagger peaks

☐ Many 10-baggers (46 percent) start from a flat base. See the section "10-Baggers Start from a Flat Base."

☐ Switch to the linear scale and look for a flat base pattern. See the section "10-Baggers Start from a Flat Base."

☐ Buy when price closes above the top of the flat base. See the section "10-Baggers Start from a Flat Base."

☐ Most 10-baggers begin life with a V-shaped start. See the section "Some 10-Baggers Prefer a V-Shaped Start."

☐ Look for a confirmed ugly double bottom to signal a trend change. See the section "Moving Up: A Higher Valley Turn."

☐ Use the weekly measured move-up chart pattern to predict the ending price and time. See the section "Weekly Measured Move Up."

☐ The most frequent retrace in a weekly measured move up is between 25 percent and 45 percent with a 35 percent median. See Table 15.1.

☐ Weekly measured moves appear most often between price doubling and tripling, but the frequency distribution is quite wide. See Table 15.2.

☐ The corrective phase starts where the measured move appears on the time scale spreads almost evenly between 0 percent to 80 percent from start to end of the 10-bagger. See Table 15.3.

☐ The first leg of a weekly measured move up is shorter than the second 79 percent of the time. See the section "MMU Measure Rule."

☐ The measure rule on the calendar scale for weekly measured moves works only 48 percent of the time. See the section "MMU Measure Rule."

☐ The hump-shaped 10-bagger is a twin-peak pattern with the second peak taller than the first. See the section "Two Hump Shape."

☐ Humped 10-baggers are rare, occurring 16 percent of the time and lasting an average of 3.3 years. See the section "Two Hump Shape."

☐ Trend lines can be invaluable when trading humped 10-baggers. See the section "Trading Humps."

☐ The line-shaped 10-bagger has an average duration of 2.3 years, occurs 42 percent of the time, and has the fewest appearances of measured moves (0.9) of the four shapes. See the section "Line Shape."

☐ The rounded turn 10-bagger is just as it sounds, a long slow turn. It only happens 19 percent of the time and takes an average of 3.5 years to reach 10-bagger status. See the section "Rounded Turn Shape."

☐ The stair-step 10-bagger happens 23 percent of the time, but takes an average of 3.5 years to complete. See the section "Stair-Step Shape."

☐ Use prior price action that forms shapes to help determine what the 10-bagger's end will look like. See the section "10-Bagger Death."

☐ 10-baggers have two shapes at the end, a rounded turn or an inverted V. See the section "10-Bagger Death."

☐ In the year after a 10-bagger ends, the average decline is 66 percent. See the section "The Numbers" and Table 15.4.

☐ A head-and-shoulders top ends a 10-bagger 16 percent of the time. See the section "Head-and-Shoulders Top."

☐ Double tops form at the end of 10-baggers 22 percent of the time. See the section " Double Top and the 2B Rule."

☐ Rarely (9 percent of the time) will a triple top end a 10-bagger. See the section "Triple Top."

☐ Inverted *V* shapes end 10-baggers most often: 29 percent of the time. See the section "Inverted *V*."

☐ Look for similar-shaped peaks to help predict the ending shape of a 10-bagger. See the section "Rounded Turn."

☐ Ugly double tops end 10-baggers just 6 percent of the time. See the section "Ugly Double Top."

CHAPTER 16

Selling Buy
and Hold

O ne owner of a school franchise that teaches people how to day-trade stocks says that the flaw with buy and hold is that no one knows when to sell. Does buy and hold really mean hold forever, or does it really mean buy and wait?

The complaint of not knowing when to sell applies to position trading, swing trading, and day trading as well. This chapter provides several techniques that help an investor decide when it is time to sell a long-term holding.

THE WEINSTEIN SETUP

Stan Weinstein (McGraw-Hill, 1988) describes four stages that price takes during its lifetime. The book provides an excellent tutorial on how to use the four stages along with a 30-week simple moving average to time the trades.

I show an example of the various stages labeled 1 through 4 in **Figure 16.1**, including an idealized pattern of the stages in the inset.

Weinstein calls stage 1 the basing area. The ideal setup comes in two flavors. The first is when price moves horizontally and volume shrinks until late in the stage. The 30-week simple moving average flattens out with price bobbing above and below the moving average like a cork on water. This sideways movement can last from months to years, according to Weinstein.

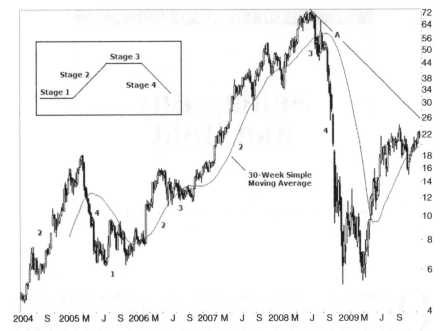

FIGURE 16.1 A 30-week moving average helps determine trend, entry, and exit points as price moves along the four stages.

Look for stocks with little overhead resistance so any breakout from the congestion area will have less chance of pausing on its way to the stars.

The second buying flavor is after a strong stage 4 decline. Price pulls out of the stage 4 dive and goes horizontal (or nearly so), while the 30-week moving average is still dropping. Price rises above the moving average and above the top of the trading range that it has been in, preferably on high volume. That is the time to buy. Figure 16.2 at point C shows this setup, which I will discuss later.

Stage 2

Stage 2 is the advancing phase. The countdown hits zero and the stock blasts off, rising above the moving average on impressive volume, signaling a breakout from a congestion area. That is the buy signal. Weinstein warns that most breakouts experience at least one dip that returns the stock back to the breakout price, so do not be surprised if that happens as the rocket ship struggles to gain altitude.

"The less it pulls back, the more strength it actually is showing," he writes. Although I did not measure this phenomenon for stage 2 breakouts, I did measure it for various types of chart patterns. I found that 97 percent of chart pattern types with upward breakouts performed better if a retrace did not occur (what I term a throwback) after the breakout. Weinstein is right.

In another test of 3,167 chart patterns with throwbacks from July 1991 to March 2005, I found patterns with stocks remaining equal to or above the breakout price gaining an average of 40 percent. If the throwback dropped the stock below the breakout price, the gain averaged just 29 percent. In other words, those stocks with large retraces will have less powerful moves upward than those with smaller retraces, on average. The tests measured the move from the breakout to the highest high before price dropped at least 20 percent, and they represent hundreds of *perfect* trades unlikely to be duplicated in actual trading.

The start of the explosive stage 2 rally is when you want to be in the stock. Getting in late can result in diminished profits or even large losses. The moving average turns upward, chasing price higher. Price continues soaring in a stair-step rise with the stock making higher peaks and higher valleys, but price usually remains above the moving average throughout the stage.

Stage 3

Stage 3 is the top area. Price begins to trend sideways, allowing the moving average to catch up. Volume is high as buyers and sellers fight it out for dominance. The moving average flattens out and price begins bobbing up and down around the average just as it did in stage 1. Weinstein recommends that investors sell only half of their position (or all of the position if you are a trader) since stage 3 can become stage 2 if the advance resumes.

Stage 4

Stage 4 happens when the last drop of propellant burns, ceasing to power the rocket ship upward. The craft rounds over and price drops below support. The moving average that was flat in stage 3 begins heading lower in stage 4.

Volume can be heavy, but need not be during the decline. Price may pull back to the bottom of the prior support area (now overhead resistance) but usually continues lower. If you have not sold already, then do so as soon as price pierces support, heading back to earth. Let me repeat: You have to sell here or risk being flattened when the rocket ship crashes.

The price chart (Figure 16.1) begins with a stage 2 advance on the far left, skips stage 3, and goes directly to stage 4. During 2005, stage 1 begins as price plays tag with the moving average. A brief stage 2 takes price higher, but hesitates during stage 3 in mid-2006. Then a long and tasty stage 2 begins. Notice how price remains above the moving average throughout most of the climb.

To the left of A, price drops below the moving average, which is rounding over, and that combination is a warning of a coming trend change.

Stage 3 sees price move horizontally for a time, allowing investors and traders to dump the stock at a good price.

After stage 3 comes stage 4 with a massive decline that takes just weeks to return the stock back almost to where it began.

Testing

How often do the four stages work? I tested this method on my own trades and found that it adds value. I removed trades that made or lost a bundle of money, which would have skewed the results, and excluded day trades and stocks or ETFs sold short. **Table 16.1** shows the results.

For example, if I bought in stage 1 (regardless of when I sold), I gained an average of 13.2 percent on the trade, and over 69 percent of the stage 1 buys were profitable. If I bought in stage 2, the gain dropped to just 4.1 percent with just over half making a profit. If I sold a stock in stage 1 (regardless of when I bought), I lost an average of 5.8 percent and just 23.1 percent of sales were profitable. And so on.

TABLE 16.1 Buying and Selling the Four Stages

Stage	Gain	Profitable Trades
Buy 1	13.2%	69.3%
Buy 2	4.1%	56.9%
Buy 3	−5.9%	14.5%
Buy 4	−8.3%	24.4%
Sell 1	−5.8%	23.1%
Sell 2	13.6%	81.5%
Sell 3	3.4%	46.3%
Sell 4	−10.8%	11.8%

I tested the various combinations of stage buying and selling and found that buying in stage 1 and selling in stage 2 resulted in an average 25.9 percent gain from 62 trades, followed in second place by buying in stage 1 and selling in stage 3 with a 21.5 percent average gain from 15 trades. Complete results are on my website at http://thepatternsite.com/Stages.html.

In another test, I used the 30-week moving average, price, and 179 of my trades from August 2000 to March 2010. If price was dropping and I bought below the 30-week moving average instead of waiting for price to rise above the moving average, how did I do?

I found that I did better than waiting 21 percent of the time. That means I would have had a winning trade or a better trade 79 percent of the time had I waited for price to rise above the 30-week simple moving average before buying. In short, if the stock is in a strong downward price trend, then wait for price to recover enough that it rises above the 30-week simple moving average before buying. That way, you avoid buying during stage 4. It *will* save you money, but test it yourself and decide.

- Buying a stock in stage 1 and selling in stage 2 often results in profitable trades.

EXAMPLE: THE SOUTHWEST AIRLINES TRADE

The Weinstein method is good for warning that you may be buying too early, especially when you are anticipating the bottom in a bear market. It is a lot like trying to guess how deep a muddy pond is when you cannot see the bottom.

During the 2007 to 2009 bear market, I had difficulty with my bottom fishing skills. **Figure 16.2** shows a trade in Southwest Airlines on the weekly scale as an example. My trading notebook says that I bought the

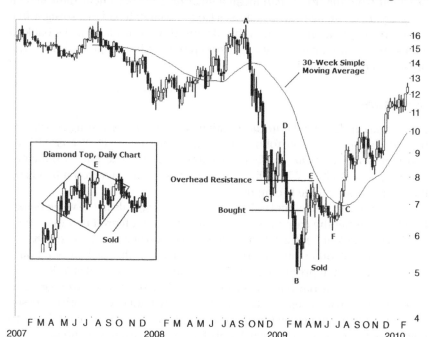

FIGURE 16.2 Waiting until price closed above the 30-week moving average would have improved the trade.

stock at 6.80 on April 3 with the belief that oil prices would continue dropping. The stock broke out of a small congestion zone (not shown on the weekly scale), along with a rising market, and an economy that I figured would recover in 6 to 9 months—it was time to buy.

Unfortunately, the price of oil continued to move up, putting pressure on the cost of jet fuel. Overhead resistance setup by valleys in late 2008 would begin at 8, potentially halting the move higher.

On May 13, the day I sold the stock, I feared a measured move down chart pattern would take the stock lower. The measured move begins at D, drops to B in the first leg, corrects to E, and then completes at F in the second leg.

Of course, at the time I sold, I had no idea how far down F would be. What I did not see is the existing measured move down, from A to B with the corrective phase between G and D. As you know, price often returns to the corrective phase (84 percent of the time on the daily charts) before deciding on a new direction. That is what happened here. Price climbed from B to E, reached the price level of the corrective phase G and then reversed.

A diamond top chart pattern on the daily scale, which I show in the inset, corresponds to point E on the larger, weekly chart. Diamonds are not pretty patterns because their shape often skews to one side. A downward breakout from diamonds can mean a swift drop back to near their launch price. By that, I mean price often rises from the launch pad in a straight-line run up to the diamond and then breaks out downward and drops back to almost where it started. That suggested price could plunge to 5 from 7, a prospect I did not relish.

Indicators

I saw bearish divergence in the relative strength index during April, and by mid-May, price began following the indicator lower (I discussed how poorly it works in *Trading Basics*, Chapter 5, in the section "Is Indicator Divergence a Dud?"). When divergence works, it can give you a heads-up that a direction change is coming.

The commodity channel index issued two sell signals in the week before I sold, bolstering the case of weakness in the stock. I feared that the airline would land back at 5 rather than push through overhead resistance at 8.

A check of other airline stocks did not clear the technical picture, either. With a small profit, I decided to sell and received a fill at 7.06.

Now look at the buy point in relation to the 30-week moving average. Price is below the moving average. Had I waited to buy until C when price crossed the moving average heading upward, I would have had more confidence to hold onto the stock. I could have doubled my money in a few months.

Even though this trade was supposed to be a long-term holding, the prospect of seeing the stock drop 41 percent (from 7.06 to 5) was enough to scare me out of the position. I took the safe route and locked in a small profit.

EXAMPLE: SAVIENT PHARMACEUTICALS

Sometimes it is best to walk away from a trade when the risk is too high. **Figure 16.3** shows an example, on the weekly scale.

I became interested in the company due to its Dutch auction tender offer for up to 10 million shares, priced between 5.80 and 6.80 per share. In Chapter 11, "Event Pattern: Dutch Auction Tender Offers," we learned that price would drop after the offer ended (a median of 10 percent below the tender price), but then rise. Within three months after a tender ends, 79 percent of the stocks close above the tender price, peaking an average of 15.7 percent higher.

On September 18, 2006, the company announced that they would pay $6.80 for 10 million shares. That meant the company would swallow over 16 percent of the shares outstanding.

FIGURE 16.3 A Dutch auction tender offer set the stage for an extended climb.

The technical picture looked promising. An ascending triangle formed during the summer of 2006, and price staged an upward breakout with the announcement of the tender offer. Once the offer ended, the stock threw back to the top of the triangle and then continued moving up, just as the pattern predicted.

Other patterns formed as price climbed, such as a rectangle top and a double top. The double top predicted a decline in price, but the stock did not cooperate. It busted the pattern when it made a new high.

In 2006, of course, I had no idea about those two chart patterns. I began looking into the fundamentals of the company and read that they faced possible generic competition to their Oxandrin drug. That drug represented 52 percent of sales in 2005. Some of the patents protecting the drug had already expired and Barr Pharmaceuticals was angling to market their own generic version. Savient sued Barr over possible patent infringement.

I felt that a lengthy court case would sap cash and, if Savient lost, the stock would plummet. I walked away from the trade because of that risk.

The chart shows what happened to the stock. From the tender price of 6.80, it climbed to a high of 15.75 in less than five months, and moved sideways for almost a year before beginning a second leg up to peak at 28.42, or more than four times the offering price.

Then news came out about safety concerns for their new gout drug. The stock tanked 76 percent in one session from the close at 11.58 to a low of 2.80. Revenue dropped from 113 million in 2004 to just 3 million in 2008. It took eight months, but the stock recovered in June 2009. That is when the FDA accepted an accelerated review of their gout drug.

Did I make the right decision to avoid buying the stock? The answer depends on whether you trust technicals or fundamentals more. If you base the answer on the chart and providing I sold the stock before it began its plunge to 2.80, then I made the wrong decision. On a fundamental side, yes, I was smart to walk away. Having half of the revenue coming from one drug is just too risky, especially with another company threatening that revenue stream.

Always remember that another opportunity will come along soon enough.

- Technicals are more timely than fundamentals. Evaluate the risk of both and trade accordingly.

1-2-3 TREND CHANGE FOR DOWNTRENDS

The phrase *1-2-3 trend change* is my name for a method described by Victor Sperandeo (John Wiley & Sons, 1991). The method helps detect trend changes.

Figure 16.4 shows the 1-2-3 trend change method for downward price trends. There are three rules to using this approach. Here they are.

1. Draw a trendline from the highest high to the lowest low on the chart such that price does not cross the trendline until after the lowest low. When price closes above the trendline, that is the first sign of a trend change.
2. Price should attempt a new low.
3. Price must rise above the peak between the two lows.

I drew a trendline from the highest high on the chart, A, to the lowest low at B such that price did not cross the trendline until after B. Notice that at C, price touches but does not cross the trendline. Price closes above the trendline at the white candle below 1.

The second rule says that price should attempt a new low. That happens at 2. By *attempt*, I mean that price tries to make another lower low, but either fails to do so, or reverses soon after. In this example, price fails to make a lower low.

FIGURE 16.4 The 1-2-3 trend change method helps determine when price changes from trending down to up.

The final test is when price closes above the peak between lows B and 2. That occurs at 3. After all three conditions are satisfied, the trend has changed from down to up.

The 1-2-3 trend change method is not as easy to apply as it seems. When selecting the highest high, how much of the chart do you look at? Consult Figure 16.1. I drew trendline A from the highest high to the lowest low such that price did not cross the trendline until after the lowest low.

Guess what? Price has not crossed the trendline, and yet the stock has climbed from a low of 5.20 to almost 25. Can we say that the trend has changed from down to up yet? It certainly looks as though it has. The answer is to use the method with a dose of common sense. If it does not look right then adjust the method to fit the situation. In this example, I would draw a steeper trendline to get a more timely reading.

1-2-3 TREND CHANGE FOR UPTRENDS

Similar rules apply to upward price trends, and here they are.

- Draw a trendline from the lowest low to the highest high such that price does not cross the trendline until after the highest high. A close below the trendline completes step 1.
- Price should attempt a new high.
- Price must close below the valley formed between the two peaks.

Once all three conditions are met, the trend has changed from up to down. **Figure 16.5** shows an example of the method.

I drew the trendline from the low at A to the highest high at B such that price did not cross the trendline until after B. Price closed below the trendline at 1.

Step 2 says price has to attempt a new high. I show the attempt at spike C. Notice how far away C is from the high. Can that be right?

What if peak 2 is the highest high and peak B is the attempt at a new high? When price drops to 3, the low between the two peaks, rule 3 is satisfied. All we have to do is wait for price to close below the trendline at 1 to satisfy the three rules. That results in a much better application of the rules to this situation.

1-2-3 Testing

I tested the 1-2-3 trend change method for both up and downward sloping trendlines in my book, *Trading Classic Chart Patterns* (John Wiley & Sons, 2002).

FIGURE 16.5 The 1-2-3 trend change method as applied to upward price trends.

For down-sloping trendlines, I found that the method resulted in rises of at least 20 percent in 74 out of 101 cases or 73 percent of the time, compared to a 69 percent success rate for the other 109 trendlines I tested that did not use the 1-2-3 trend change method.

I used the 20 percent benchmark as the separator between bull and bear markets. In other words, when price rises by at least 20 percent, then analysts say we are in a bull market. A drop of at least 20 percent represents a bear market. I applied that logic to stocks and trendlines. The 20 percent benchmark is the minimum needed to signal a trend change from up to down or the reverse, and that is what the 1-2-3 method is supposed to detect.

For up-sloping trendlines, I found that 29 out of 67 trendlines, or 43 percent, showed declines of at least 20 percent. The method is an improvement over 50 of 132 trendlines, or 38 percent, which showed drops of at least 20 percent. In short, the 1-2-3 method helps predict changes in the price trend.

- Use the 1-2-3 trend change method to determine a change in trend.

THE CLOUDBANK SETUP

Figure 16.6 shows what I call a cloudbank chart pattern on the monthly scale, in XL Capital. The theory behind the pattern is that the cloudbank represents the normal price for the stock (since it has been trading above 56 for years). The swift decline is due to the bear market and poor economic conditions. When the economy recovers, the stock should rise back into the clouds. If that happens, then investors buying stocks showing cloudbanks can make a lot of money. Cloudbanks also provide a convenient selling target, and selling is what this chapter is all about. Let us take a closer look at that cloudbank pattern.

- The cloudbank pattern is an easy way to determine when to sell.

Identification

To find and catalog cloudbanks, I looked at 574 stocks with data ranging from January 1990 to February 2010, but not all stocks covered the entire period. The monthly scale was the easiest to use to spot these long chart

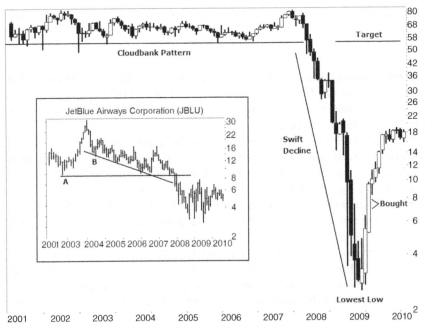

FIGURE 16.6 A cloudbank representing overhead resistance becomes a price target.

patterns. I looked for an extended period (preferably years) in which price rested upon a horizontal trendline. The horizontal trendline represents the bottom of the cloudbank. The top of the cloudbank can be any shape, because it is not important. The bottom of the cloudbank represents the target price—a price at which to consider selling.

Following the cloudbank, I require a swift decline that takes price down dramatically. The larger the drop, the larger the recovery potential. If a large decline did not follow a cloudbank, then I discarded the chart pattern. A bear market often caused the large decline, and the recent 2007 to 2009 plunge was a good source for many cloudbank patterns.

The Shape of Bottoms

Once price hits bottom, it bounces, and that bounce makes one of four shapes, which I show in **Figure 16.7**. If you know about chart patterns, you will recognize these, but I did not include more complex varieties, such as head-and-shoulders bottoms, in the analysis.

The first shape is a double bottom. Price touches down, bounces up, and then touches down again near the same price but separated in time, often two to five months or so. The price variation between the two bottoms should be trivial, say 5 percent or less, but be flexible. The double-bottom variation happens 17 percent of the time after a cloudbank. Figure 16.1 shows a double-bottom example (but unrelated to a cloudbank) near point 1 and starting in the fall of 2008.

- A double bottom happens 17 percent of the time after a cloudbank.

The next shape is an ugly double bottom. In this shape, the second bottom is higher than the first, making it an ugly version of the classic double bottom. In this variety, the second bottom is higher than the first by at least 5 percent but again, be flexible. If the second bottom is too far above the first bottom, then the shape is a V-turn and not an ugly double bottom.

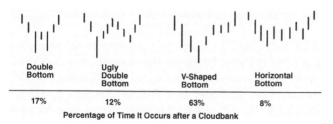

Double Bottom	Ugly Double Bottom	V-Shaped Bottom	Horizontal Bottom
17%	12%	63%	8%

Percentage of Time It Occurs after a Cloudbank

FIGURE 16.7 When price bottoms, it usually forms one of four shapes.

I did not set an upper limit on where the second bottom should occur, so just use your best judgment. If you are unsure, then scan several charts and look at how the bottoms occur. Figure 16.4 shows an ugly double bottom at points B and 2. An ugly double bottom occurs after a cloudbank 12 percent of the time.

- An ugly double bottom occurs after a cloudbank 12 percent of the time.

The V-shaped turn occurs most often—63 percent of the time. The turn in XL Capital, shown in Figure 16.6, is V-shaped. Price drops into the pattern and then rebounds, often following a mirror image of the descent (meaning the angles are similar). The V-shaped turn does not mean price will return to the cloudbank without any horizontal consolidation regions (although that does occur when the drop to the lowest low is modest). In fact, there is a variation of the V shape called an extended V. The extension is a horizontal price movement after the stock bottoms in the v shape. Figure 16.2 shows an example of a V bottom at B followed by an extension at F. The BF turn also qualifies as an ugly double bottom.

- The V-shaped turn occurs most often—63 percent of the time—after a cloudbank.

The horizontal bottom is the rarest of the four types of turns. It happens 8 percent of the time after a cloudbank. Price hits the lowest low and recovers somewhat, but then tends to move horizontally for a period. The lowest low is often not a pronounced spike like you see at double bottoms, but it is marginally lower than the surrounding price action. Eventually, price will drift higher on its way to the cloudbank.

- The horizontal bottom is the rarest of the four types of turns. It happens 8 percent of the time after a cloudbank.

Investing in Cloudbanks

Before I discuss the numbers, let us talk about using cloudbanks as investment tools.

I looked for stocks with a solid pattern of overhead resistance (the cloudbank) that was at least twice as far above the current price, but preferably three times or more. If the stock was selling at $5, for example, I wanted to see the cloudbank no closer than $10 but preferably $15 or higher. Figure 16.6 shows XL Capital, a stock I bought at less than $8 with a cloudbank starting at $56. That difference represents a tasty recovery potential. Even if the stock makes it only halfway to the clouds, I will have done well.

Next, I looked for a swift decline. I wanted to see stocks that held up well until the very end as the economy deteriorated and the bear market clawed stocks lower. I discarded stocks as potential buy candidates that were sliding lower for years.

The inset of Figure 16.6 shows an example of JetBlue Airways (JBLU) on the monthly scale. Looking at horizontal trendline A, I thought the stock might be an investment since it had a cloudbank that I was looking for (but the cloudbank did not touch the trendline as often as I like to see). Then I noticed that price peaked in October 2003 and had been sliding lower ever since.

Why is a horizontal price trend (the cloudbank) leading to the decline important? The cloudbank pattern provides another method for determining a selling price for buy-and-hold investments. My belief is that the bear market performance is an outlier, an anomaly that took price down well below its normal value. I am *not* looking for the stock to soar to Mount Everest heights, but I do expect it to return to normal. The bottom of the cloudbank represents the minimum normal price. Some call this behavior regression or reversion to the mean, and the cloudbank pattern is just a visual representation of that.

The cloudbank makes it easy to pick a selling price, such as $56 for XL Capital. When the stock reaches the bottom of the cloudbank, then it is time to consider a sale. It might not be an automatic sell, but it does provide a price target that is easy to spot.

With JetBlue, the downward price movement shown by trendline B suggests the company was having problems for years. Recovery would likely take longer than just waiting for the economy or business conditions to improve.

From an investor's perspective, there are two ways to look at the JetBlue chart. The first is an optimistic one. If the company can fix its problems, the stock should achieve liftoff and soar into the clouds. The second way is to recognize that the company has been trying to fix its problems for over five years without success. What suggests a turnaround anytime soon? I chose to look elsewhere for a more promising opportunity with less risk.

I bought XL Capital twice in April 2009, once at 6.52 and the second at 7.93. I sold most of it at 17.73 in May 2010.

A trade in Conseco (CNO) is an example of how cloudbanks can work in the short term. The stock shows a cloudbank from September 2003 to July 2007 with an irregular-shaped base at 15 to 17. I was planning to hold the stock for years when I bought it on May 5, 2009 at 1.64, but six days later, I sold it at 3.47, more than doubling my money. I sold on the day it peaked, representing the highest high as price slid lower for the next several months.

- A cloudbank can represent a short-term bonanza, too.

The Numbers

Let us talk about the statistics behind the cloudbank pattern. As I mentioned, I used 574 stocks with data from January 1990 to February 2010. I found 184 cloudbanks, but only 59 percent have seen price climb high enough to pierce the base of the cloudbank, and 24 percent have moved to the top of the cloud, or higher.

The reason I studied this pattern is to find how long it takes price to return to the cloudbank. **Table 16.2** provides an answer. It shows recovery times measured from the lowest low after the cloudbank until price returned to the cloud, for all cloudbank patterns that made it back to the cloud.

For example, 34 percent of the cloudbanks took less than half a year to return to the bottom of the cloudbank, and 9 percent made it to the top of the cloud (or higher). For the recovery to the cloud low, it shows that 82 percent of stocks that returned to the cloudbank did so within 1.5 years of finding the lowest low. For the stock to reach the top of the cloudbank, it takes longer, of course. For example, 73 percent made it to the cloud top within three years after finding the lowest low.

- 82 percent of stocks with cloudbanks returned to the cloud within 1.5 years.

The median time to return to the cloudbank is 0.7 years with an average of 1.1 years. The maximum time was 7 years. To reach the cloudbank

TABLE 16.2 Recovery Time for All Stocks in Which Price Returned to the Cloudbank

Years:	0.5	1	1.5	2	2.5	3	3.5	4	4.5	5
Recovery to cloud low	34%	34%	14%	4%	3%	5%	0%	0%	4%	3%
Cumulative	34%	69%	82%	86%	89%	94%	94%	94%	97%	100%
Recovery to cloud high	9%	18%	16%	7%	13%	11%	4%	4%	0%	18%
Cumulative	9%	27%	42%	49%	62%	73%	78%	82%	82%	100%

top, the duration took a median of 2.0 years, an average of 2.4 years, and a maximum of 7.2 years. All of these times measure from the lowest low (not the cloudbank low).

The lowest low is just as it sounds, but the definition I used is complicated. It is the lowest valley that occurs after the cloudbank ends and before price rises above the 30-week simple moving average providing the crossover of price and the moving average represents a worthwhile decline (I used about 50 percent as a minimum). This definition helped prevent buying too soon and buying when the profit potential was not worth the risk.

The drop from the cloudbank to the lowest low averaged 56 percent for those stocks that returned to the cloudbank and 81 percent for those that have not made it back yet. For those stocks before January 1, 2007, the decline averaged 59 percent, but for those after January 1, 2007, (which includes the 2007 to 2009 bear market) the decline averaged 73 percent. Those are important numbers. Why? Because it will take longer for price to return to the cloudbank this time than last since the drop was further.

- It takes longer for price to return to the cloudbank after a large decline than a short one.

Buying Cloudbanks

If you were to buy a cloudbank stock after it climbed above the 30-week simple moving average, you would make an average of 41 percent. That compares to a gain of just 16 percent by the S&P 500 index over the same holding periods. Both numbers measure from the opening price the day after the moving average crossover to the cloudbank base or the most recent closing price if the stock has not made it back to the cloud.

Table 16.3 shows a frequency distribution of the largest drop below the buy price. For example, I found that 20 percent of the stocks dropped no more than 5 percent below the purchase price on their way to the cloudbank. The median drop is 13 percent and the average is 19 percent. As good as those numbers seem, the largest was a plunge of 95 percent. That trade is part of the 18 percent of stocks that dropped more than 35 percent after buying. In other words, the drop can be huge.

TABLE 16.3 Potential Drop below Buy Price.

Drop	5%	10%	15%	20%	25%	30%	35%
Frequency	20%	22%	16%	9%	8%	7%	18%
Cumulative	20%	42%	58%	68%	76%	82%	100%

The results suggest that you either close your eyes when trading cloud-banks or have some way to limit losses.

- Over half the stocks (58 percent) with cloudbanks dropped less than 15 percent below the buy price, but 18 percent plunged more than 35 percent.

Selling Cloudbanks

When should you sell an investment using a cloudbank pattern? Answer: when price returns to the base of the cloud. Here is why. I measured the time from the lowest low to the base of the cloud and found the average rise was 129 percent and it took 1.1 years. However, it took nearly the same amount of time (1.0 years) to move through the cloud, but the rise averaged only 64 percent. In other words, price took the same amount of time to go half as far (from cloud base to cloud top). Momentum must have declined, so it makes more sense to sell when price reaches the cloud base and then search for another cloudbank to buy.

- Sell a cloudbank stock when it returns to the bottom of the cloud.

USING TRAILING STOPS TO SELL

In *Trading Basics*, Chapter 3, I discussed the trailing stop as a way to make selling a stock easy. It is time for a review of that tactic, but this time using the 30-week simple moving average as the tool.

Figure 16.8 shows a trade we all would welcome in our portfolios. A trendline connecting peaks 1 and 2, with price rising at point E, sug-gests the 30-week moving average will follow. When price closes above the trendline, that is the buy signal. Where do you place a stop loss order in case the trade does not work as expected?

To answer that, draw a line vertically from the day of entry to the value of the 30-week moving average, then place a stop a few pennies below the intersection. I show that as E, at about 16, so I would place a stop at 15.93 to avoid the round number 16. That is not too far from the entry price of 18.21 (assuming the opening price the following week).

- Place a trailing stop below the 30-week moving average.

As price climbs, raise the stop, trailing it below the moving average. Unfortunately, as price climbs at a brisk pace, the moving average falls

FIGURE 16.8 Various stop locations can help traders and investors limit down-side risk.

further behind. At F, the drop represents 26 percent, and at G, the gap is 34 percent or about $10 per share. Huge!

In situations when price makes a straight-line run up, or at least a brisk trot, use a volatility stop instead of tucking it beneath the moving average. That would have shaved the loss to 6 and 5 percent, respectively.

- If price rises in a straight-line run, use a volatility stop.

Once price pauses along the uptrend, then you can hide your stop beneath the minor low or beneath the moving average. Once price rises up to A, matching a prior minor high, raise the stop to just below B. If that stop location represents too much distance then use a volatility stop instead.

When price rises to C, raise the stop to D, a few pennies below the moving average at the point. You can place the stop a few pennies below the minor low that D points to, below the moving average at D, or use a volatility stop.

The reason for placing the stop below the moving average is that many times price will drop back to the moving average before continuing higher.

A stop placed too close will take you out. Unfortunately, if price continues down, then you will have given up a boatload of profit.

- When price breaks out to a new high, find the most recent minor low. Raise the stop to below the 30-week moving average at the time of the minor low.

Let us use L as an example. When price climbs to the price level of L on the rise to H, find the nearest minor low and set a stop below the moving average at that point (I in this case).

At H, price reaches a high of 173, but a stop placed at I would be at 112. Do you really want to give back 61 points of profit? Placing a stop beneath the minor low (not below the moving average) at I would raise the stop to 121.

Seeing that, a potential head-and-shoulders top (L is the left shoulder, S is the right, and H is the head) would take you out at about 125. I get that value by connecting the two armpits with a neckline, NL. When price closes below the line, sell the stock at the open the next day.

A volatility stop based on H would be 150. That is closest to the peak, but it almost guarantees that the position will be stopped out. If you suspect you will be stopped out, then just sell the stock immediately and walk away. I have done that many times and saved myself the difference between where I actually sold and the drop to the stop.

- If you think you are going to be stopped out, then just sell the stock.

TIMELY TREND-LINE EXITS

I discussed trend lines previously, so there is little need to explore them at length. However, sometimes a trend line can offer clearer and timelier exit signals than the moving average. **Figure 16.9** shows such a situation. This is a weekly chart of Northrop Grumman (NOC) showing a 30-week moving average. Since the average is slicing through price frequently, a longer moving average would work better (such as a 50-week moving average).

Look at TL1, constructed by connecting touches 1, 2, and 3. A close below the trendline is the exit signal, which occurs at Sell 1. Sell 2 is where price crosses the 30-week moving average. Sell 1 would take you out at the next day's opening price of 70.25, but the moving average exit at Sell 2 would close out the position at 64.00.

A timely exit is not always the case, and TL2 shows such a situation. The trendline begins at point 1, and then touches points 4 and 5 before

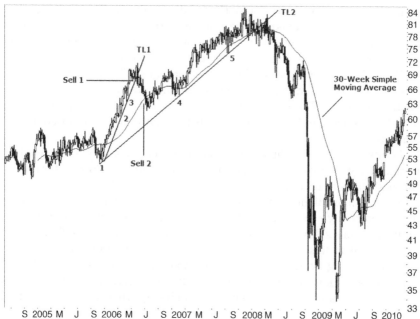

FIGURE 16.9 A trendline can offer a clearer sell signal than a moving average.

exiting somewhere in the mass of price bars as the stock rounds over. The 30-week moving average is right there, too, fighting it out among the price bars. It looks as if the moving average and the trendline cross each other, signaling an exit near the same time when price closes below each one.

Perhaps the answer to the should-I-sell-now question involves a combination of a trendline and an appropriate moving average, one that skirts price instead of plowing through it like a bulldozer. Since a moving average introduces lag (price turns first and then the moving average turns later), it is less timely than a trendline.

- Trendlines can signal a sale earlier than other methods.

CAN MOVING AVERAGES HELP?

If you want to know when to be in the market and when not to, here is a simple technique for timing the market using a 10-month simple moving average.

Figure 16.10 shows the Standard and Poor's 500 index on the monthly scale *using closing prices* only. A 10-month simple moving average of the closing prices appears as the smoother of the two lines. This moving average is a simple way of making sure you are on the right side of the market. By that, I mean go long when the index is above the moving average and go into cash when it is not. Let us look at a few examples.

Point C is near the start of the bear market in 2000. A few months after the index heads lower, it falls below the moving average, telling you that it is time to leave. The same situation occurs at D in 2007, just after the market turns bearish. Moving into cash is the smart move for both of these situations.

Points E and F highlight when the index crosses above the moving average. They are signals to reenter the market and they do so after it bottoms and starts to recover.

There is a problem with the moving average, of course. Point A signals a buy even though the bear market is only half waythrough. Point B prematurely signals sell when the index is moving sideways in a bull market.

To eliminate false signals, you can choose a longer moving average. A 12-month moving average removes both A and B crossover signals, but it delays entry back into the markets when the bear turns into a bull. It also increases the drawdown or the profits you give up while waiting for a sell

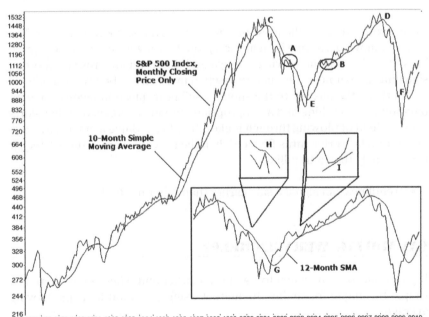

FIGURE 16.10 This shows how a 10-month simple moving average would have avoided the two most recent bear markets.

signal. Price has to drop a bit further to trigger a sell. However, I think it works better than the 10-month moving average.

I show the 12-month simple moving average in the inset. Points H and I are the same as A and B, only zoomed in. Notice that a crossover does not occur. However, point G is higher than E, so expect a late entry back into a rising market.

- A 12-month simple moving average of closing prices on the S&P 500 index can help determine when you should be in or out of the market.

In mid 2010, the S&P index closed below the moving average, so I sold half of my portfolio. The market turned higher a few months later. That is the danger you face when using moving averages.

Another way to reduce the number of false signals is to add a filter, such as a rule that says price must close at least 1 percent beyond the moving average. You can pick any value you wish for the filter, of course. The larger the value, the more price can drop before you act on the signal.

The key to using the monthly moving average is that it is based on closing prices and not the high or low reached during the month. If you charted the moving average against an open-high-low-close bar chart, you would see many crossovers since the highs and lows cross the average. However, a line chart based on closing prices makes the crossovers clearer and fewer.

- When using a monthly moving average, plot prices using a line chart, not a bar chart.

FOLLOW INSIDER TRANSACTIONS

Insider buying and selling are tools that help gauge what the smart money thinks about a stock. If an insider is buying and has done so before at well-timed prices (meaning he bought just before the stock moved higher), that information can provide a trader with the confidence needed to enter a trade. If numerous insiders buy the stock and none have sold within the past six months, then they consider the stock a good value.

The same logic applies to insider selling, although it is not as reliable. If numerous insiders are selling and none are buying, then beware. They could be wrong, so check prior years to see how well their timing has worked.

Two articles by Volker Knapp (*Active Trader*, October and November 2008) explore systems for trying to profit from insider transactions. He concluded that insider sell signals did not have much value, but "combining insider buying with other tools to identify severely depressed stocks proved useful."

In fact, Gary S. Glass's thesis (Ohio State University, 1966) concluded that "an investor who diversified his holdings over a number of securities selected by this criterion in the recent past would probably have obtained an average price performance over the near-term significantly superior to that achieved by the Dow-Jones Industrial Average." He goes on to say that, "it seems reasonable to conclude that extensive insider purchase decisions have provided a useful indicator of near-term stock price performance."

Before I buy a stock, I always check insider transactions. If XYZ climbs to 50 and each time it does so, the CEO, CFO, and other three-letter insiders dump the stock, then it is clear that 50 is overvalued. If numerous insiders buy at 15 and none sell, and price rises from there, then 15 represents a good value.

I like to see several different insiders buying thousands of shares, not hundreds. If there is selling, I want to see few shares sold in comparison to the number of shares bought. These transactions should not include stock given to the insider as part of the company's compensation plan.

I do not check insider transactions when I consider selling a stock. An insider can sell for any number of reasons (a new jet, house, college expenses, and so on) but buys because the stock represents value.

- If insiders buy the stock, it could represent value, but they can sell for any number of reasons.

SELLING: TWO RATIO TIPS

A few ratios are worth repeating here. The first is market cap versus annual sales, discussed in Chapter 9 (see the section "Market Cap versus Sales"). Market cap is shares outstanding times the current price. If market cap exceeds annual sales, then the stock is overpriced. Consider selling. Tests showed that stocks with market caps higher than sales scored year-ahead gains of 9 percent compared to 14 percent gains for those with market cap below sales.

If the price-to-earnings ratio is higher than the maximum of the prior three years, then consider selling. Stocks with high P/Es gained an average of 8 percent compared to gains of 12 percent when the P/E was below the three-year maximum.

- If market cap exceeds annual sales, then consider selling.
- If the P/E ratio is higher than the three-year maximum, consider selling.

SELLING DOWN FROM A HIGH

I asked a financial consultant how she decides to sell a long-term holding. "If it's a blue chip stock, then warning bells go off at 5 percent down," she said. "And I may or may not sell it. If the stock drops 10 percent, then I sell it." In her mind, blue chips are any member of the Dow Jones industrial average and prominent large-cap stocks.

What about nonblue chips, the runts of the litter? She could not give me a good answer. Each situation was different. For example, if a biotech stock had a promising drug awaiting FDA approval, she would hold the stock providing she believed in the company's ability to make the drug, and if the drug had a large potential audience.

Does the selling-down-from-a-high approach have value? I decided to find out.

- If a blue chip drops 10 percent from a high, consider selling it.

Selling Methodology

I programmed my computer to find every 20 percent change in the stock's trend. If price reached a high and dropped by 20 percent, the top became what I called the ultimate high. If price bottomed and then rose by 20 percent, the bottom became the ultimate low. This 20 percent trend-change behavior distinguishes bull and bear markets, which is why I use it in tests on individual stocks.

Once I found every ultimate high and low in the stock, I looked at the peak-to-valley retrace in an uptrend. This method is like measuring the height of each wave, but only during incoming tides.

To identify a peak or valley, I looked for the highest peak or lowest valley within five price bars (days). That means a peak was the highest high within 5 days before to 5 days after the peak, or 11 days total. I used the same method for valleys. I found the lowest valley between two peaks (providing the second peak was higher than the first). Yes, it sounds complicated.

For up trends, looking from the ultimate low to the ultimate high (the tide), I measured every peak-to-valley drop (the waves) as a percentage of the high price until reaching the ultimate high. The result is the average retrace size as price climbs.

Why is this important? If we can find the average retrace size, then any unusually large retrace can be the start of a bear market in the stock.

Selling Results

Table 16.4 shows a frequency distribution of the results for 1,745 stocks (regardless of market cap) ending April 2012 and beginning from January 1990 or when their data began, providing price remained above $3. The table shows the average drop of a retrace.

TABLE 16.4   Frequency Distribution of Percentage Down from a High.

Drop	Frequency	Cumulative	Drop	Frequency	Cumulative
0%	0%	0%	8%	9%	60%
1%	0%	0%	9%	8%	68%
2%	2%	2%	10%	7%	75%
3%	6%	8%	11%	6%	80%
4%	9%	18%	12%	5%	85%
5%	11%	29%	13%	4%	89%
6%	12%	40%	14%	3%	92%
7%	10%	51%	15%	2%	94%

The Drop column is the percentage down from a peak. The Frequency column is a count of each drop as a percentage of all samples. The Cumulative column is a running total of the Frequency column.

The 10 percent row, for example, shows how often each wave retraced 10 percent from a peak in a rising price trend (the tide). In this case, there were 3,218 hits out of 48,272 samples, or 7 percent of the total number of retraces. Seventy-five percent of the samples (the Cumulative column) showed declines of 10 percent or less on their way to a trend change. The financial consultant is comfortable selling at a 10 percent drop.

Think of each drop as the height of the typical stock wave. How much profit are you willing to relinquish (the height of the wave) to participate in a long-term up trend?

If you use this method, instead of telling yourself, "Look at how much money I have given up from the peak!" remind yourself that if the stock continues to drop 30, 50 percent, or even more, how good selling at 10 percent down would have looked.

Focus not on the money, but on technique. This technique will help you time the exit on long-term investments. It might not always work, but it can save a lot of money when it does work.

Look at bins 5 to 7. Those three represent 33 percent of the samples. It means that a third of the samples retrace between 5 and 7 percent from a high. They are the three most common drops of any in the table. Over half of the samples will see declines in the 4 to 8 percent range. If you want to set a stop, then do so outside of this range.

- The most common retrace is between 5 and 7 percent. Over half of the samples retraced between 4 and 8 percent.

CHAPTER CHECKLIST

Here is a checklist of methods for trading investments.

☐ Buying a stock in stage 1 and selling in stage 2 often results in profitable trades. See Table 16.1.

☐ Technicals are more timely than fundamentals. Evaluate the risk of both and trade accordingly. See the section "Example: Savient Pharmaceuticals."

☐ Use the 1-2-3 trend change method to determine a change in trend. See the section "1-2-3 Testing."

☐ The cloudbank pattern is an easy way to determine when to sell. See the section "The Cloudbank Pattern."

☐ A double bottom happens 17 percent of the time after a cloudbank. See the section "The Shape of Bottoms."

☐ An ugly double bottom occurs after a cloudbank 12 percent of the time. See the section "The Shape of Bottoms."

☐ The V-shaped turn occurs most often—63 percent of the time—after a cloudbank. See the section "The Shape of Bottoms."

☐ The horizontal bottom is the rarest of the four types of turns. It happens 8 percent of the time after a cloudbank. See the section "The Shape of Bottoms."

☐ A cloudbank can represent a short-term bonanza, too. See the section "Investing in Cloudbanks."

☐ 82 percent of stocks with cloudbanks returned to the cloud within 1.5 years. See Table 16.2.

☐ It takes longer for price to return to the cloudbank after a large decline than a short one. See Table 16.2.

☐ Over half the stocks with cloudbanks (58 percent) dropped less than 15 percent below the buy price, but 18 percent plunged more than 35 percent. See Table 16.3.

☐ Sell a cloudbank stock when it returns to the bottom of the cloud. See the section "Selling Cloudbanks."

☐ Place a trailing stop below the 30-week moving average. See the section "Using Trailing Stops to Sell."

☐ If price rises in a straight-line run, use a volatility stop. See the section "Using Trailing Stops to Sell."

☐ When price breaks out to a new high, find the most recent minor low. Raise the stop to below the 30-week moving average at the time of the minor low. See the section "Using Trailing Stops to Sell."

☐ If you think you are going to be stopped out, then just sell the stock. See the section "Using Trailing Stops to Sell."

☐ Trendlines can signal a sale earlier than other methods. See the section "Timely Trend-Line Exits."

☐ A 12-month simple moving average of closing prices on the S&P 500 index can help determine when you should be in or out of the market. See the section "Can Moving Averages Help?"

☐ When using a monthly moving average, plot prices using a line chart, not a bar chart. See the section "Can Moving Averages Help?"

☐ If insiders buy the stock, it could represent value, but they can sell for any number of reasons. See the section "Follow Insider Transactions."

☐ If market cap exceeds annual sales, then consider selling. See the section "Selling: Two Ratio Tips."

☐ If the P/E ratio is higher than the three-year maximum, consider selling. See the section "Selling: Two Ratio Tips."

☐ If a blue chip drops 10 percent from a high, consider selling it. See the section "Selling Down from a High."

☐ The most common retrace is between 5 and 7 percent. Over half of the samples retraced between 4 and 8 percent. See the section "Selling Results."

CHAPTER 17

Fundamentals: What I Use

One day, when I lived in Lowell, Massachusetts, I sat on a park bench beside the Merrimack River, trying to solve a Rubik's cube. A man walking by, stopped, and asked me about tips on solving the puzzle. He said that he was an accountant and was looking to buy Hewlett Packard stock by crunching the numbers in its annual report.

A few weeks later, I met him again and he was still shredding the annual report.

Fundamental analysis can be as complicated as you want it to be. You can become a forensic accountant by taking a microscope to the annual report and comparing it to others in the same industry. I prefer a simpler approach. This chapter describes how I tear apart the annual report to check on fundamentals, but you may want to dig deeper.

None of the fundamentals discussed below will force me to throw away a stock. Rather, they serve as a body of evidence that tells me if the company will prosper or not. If I check several research reports on the company and they are as negative as the fundamentals suggest, then I will look elsewhere for a more promising opportunity.

One flaw I have noticed over the years of doing this is that I place too much emphasis on the fundamentals. The numbers are just snapshots in time of how the company did at the end of a quarter or year. A company can win or lose a new contract, sending their business spinning in a new direction. When I have tossed away a company despite a glowing technical picture, I have often regretted it. However, I would rather be safe than sorry. It does not take much to lose money in the markets.

TWO BOOK VALUE TIPS

Some claim that book value has lost its significance since the value of an asset is only worth what someone is willing to pay. Thus, it can be difficult to get an accurate reading of book value. Nevertheless, I still like to see a rising book value over time. That tells me the company is worth more than it used to be.

Any sharp declines in book value may be due to a spin-off, sale of a subsidiary, or stock repurchase. Any sharp increases may be because they bought another firm or merged with one.

Divide price by book value to get price to book value. Numbers below 2.0 are sweet, so that is what I look for.

- Book value should be rising over time.
- Look for price to book value below 2.0, the lower the better.

DO NOT GET SINGED BY BURN RATE

The burn rate is how fast a startup company is spending their cash (negative cash flow). The quicker they spend their cash, the faster they will have to sell more stock or find other ways to fund operations. When they sell more stock, they dilute the value of outstanding shares and the price usually drops.

MannKind (MNKD), for example, closed at 7.15 on August 10, 2010, after steadily trending upward from the low in late May. The next day the company announced that they would sell 36.4 million shares, half to the Mann Group and half to Seaside 88, L.P. The stock closed lower at 6.85, which is no big deal, but the news started a two-week slide. Five days later, the company announced a proposed offering of $100 million senior convertible notes. The stock gapped open 6 percent lower. When the stock bottomed on August 24th, the stock reached a low of 5.50, or 23 percent below the August 10 close.

You can ask shareholder services what the burn rate is and how long it will be before they ask for more money. If you are lucky, they will tell you.

I remember discussing the burn rate for a drug startup with a financial consultant. My crude numbers showed that the company had about a year's worth of cash on hand to fund operations. That meant they would have to issue more stock soon, which implied the stock's price would take a hit. Based on that thumbnail analysis, I decided to wait before buying the stock since I knew that price would be coming down. It took several months, but the announcement came and down went the stock.

- Burn rate applies to startup companies. Determine how fast they are spending cash and how soon they will need to fund operations.

DROP CAPITAL SPENDING!

Capital spending is wonderful since the company is investing in itself. It is spending to build a new plant or buy expensive equipment. However, when capex (capital expenditures) is high, it is not the time to buy. The best time to buy is once the company has finished their pet projects and is about to reap the rewards. Thus, look for a *decrease* in capital spending, preferably for two years in a row.

- Look for a decrease in capital spending. A cut in capex two years in a row is a plus.

CURRENT RATIO 2.0

The current ratio is current assets divided by current liabilities. It signals the ability of a company to fund its short-term obligations. I use a value of 2.0 as a minimum. Below that is a danger signal, but the number will vary from industry to industry.

If you are checking other stocks in the same industry, and all else being equal, go with the stock that has a higher current ratio.

- Current assets ÷ current liabilities must be over 2.0.

PROSPECTING FOR GROWTH USING DIVIDENDS

I like receiving dividends, and I like stocks that pay them. It is like free money, even though there is a cost (price drops an equivalent amount when the company pays a dividend). Stocks that pay dividends tend to outperform those that do not pay dividends.

Also, dividend-paying stocks tend to hold their price better in a declining market. Imagine that a stock pays a 5 percent dividend annually. Now imagine that the stock price drops in half. The dividend is now 10 percent. When investors see such a high dividend rate, and assuming the fundamentals can support the dividend, they buy the stock. That buying will tend to support price more than those stocks not paying a dividend.

- Select stocks paying a dividend.

Usually, the dividend payment will represent a small amount of net income unless it is from a utility. If so, then look at the payout ratio. That is how much the company spends on dividends out of net income.

A utility spending 100 percent (or more) on a dividend has nothing left to spend on itself. They are in danger of cutting the dividend rate unless the high percentage is a momentary blip. A quick check of stocks in the electric utility industry shows that most pay out about 60 to 75 percent of net income. If it gets to 90 percent or higher, then be concerned. Below 60 percent and the utility is being stingy.

- For a utility stock, check the payout ratio to be sure they have enough money left to fund future growth and emergencies.

RISING EARNINGS, NET PROFIT

When I look at Value Line's newsletter, I scan across the earnings-per-share row. I want to see that earnings are climbing consistently, preferably for five years in a row. If a company has a NMF (not meaningful) price-to-earnings ratio, I flip to the next stock. That is especially true when I am searching for stocks to populate a new industry that I want to follow. If a company cannot make money and has not for years, why would I want to own it?

Having said that, if you can find a small-cap stock that has run into trouble, but is digging itself out of the hole, then buy it. In other words, if it lost money last year but appears on its way to turning a profit this year, then that could represent a wonderful opportunity. The stock can soar when that happens.

- Small-cap stocks that transition from losing money to making money tend to outperform.
- Stocks with increasing net profit from one year to the next tend to outperform.

P/E RATIO VERSUS INDUSTRY

Compare the price-to-earnings ratio with other stocks in the same industry. P/Es lower than others can represent value, but you have to figure out why the P/E is low. If they had a lousy quarter, but anticipate that business will turn around in the second half, then they are either dreaming or making a realistic guess. Often it is a bit of both with heavy emphasis on dreaming. Management always puts a positive spin on things, even when their world is ending.

When things go wrong, it has been my experience that the stock almost never views the future the same way as management. That means a hit to the wallet or purse. It takes longer to turn around a business than management expects.

- Select stocks with P/E ratios lower than the industry.
- Listen to what management says about difficult conditions, and be cautious of glowing statements that business will improve soon. Let price be your guide.

LITIGATION: STOP PISSING PEOPLE OFF!

When I read an annual report, I always look for the section on litigation. If people are suing the company too often, then that tells me something is not right. I have discarded stocks because of lawsuits stacking up. Yes, accidents happen and an occasional lawsuit represents the cost of doing business, but when you see suit after suit described, it suggests management is making unwise choices. Look elsewhere for a better-managed company.

- If the company is being sued too frequently, discard the stock.

AVOID TOO MUCH LONG-TERM DEBT

I am a cash person. If I use a credit card, I pay it off completely when the bill comes due. That is also what I like to see in stocks I buy. No debt is best, but as we have learned in this book, companies that go from being debt-free to having manageable long-term debt tend to outperform dramatically. Avoid companies with heavy debt loads.

What does *heavy* mean? If you use Value Line, the capital structure is shown on the middle left of the stock page. There you will see the percentage of capital. For example, Owens & Minor, as of May 2008, showed 25 percent of capital in long-term debt and preferred stock. Flipping through the pages shows the typical value for the industry. Most times, it will be around 33 percent. If it gets to 70 percent or higher then I consider that a risk factor.

Another way to gauge debt is to compute the debt-to-equity ratio. Divide long-term debt into the sum of long-term debt and total shareholders equity. For example, Value Line shows Abbott Labs to have $9,487.8 million in long-term debt and $17,779 million in shareholders equity, giving a ratio of about 35 percent or 9,487.8 ÷ (9,487.8+17,779), which is reasonable.

- No long-term debt is best.
- Companies moving from no debt to some long-term debt tend to outperform.
- Debt to equity should be small, say, below 50 percent.

MARKET CAPITALIZATION: BIG RETURNS BY GOING SMALL

Market capitalization is the current closing price multiplied by the number of shares outstanding. Small-cap stocks have market caps below $1 billion. Large caps are above $5 billion, and mid caps are between those two. Those break points vary from source to source, so when they call a stock a small cap, it could be a mid cap by my definition.

In test after test, small-cap stocks outperform mid- and large-cap stocks. It is fine to have a sprinkling of mid or large caps in your portfolio, but you should concentrate your holdings on small caps.

- Buy small-cap stocks.

RESEARCH SPENDING

I spent most of my professional life in the research and development (R&D) department of major corporations, so I like to see research into new products funded properly. If research funding is increasing from year to year, that tells me the company is serious about its future. The ideas nurtured in the lab turn into products in the market place. That is where sales growth comes from (at least partly. The company can also buy other companies or product lines).

It is okay if a company slips for a year or so and reduces funding. This is necessary in times of economic weakness, and R&D should shoulder its burden just like the rest of the company. Funding might also diminish once a product hits the marketplace. They have to figure out what gizmo to spend on next.

Compare the funding of R&D with other stocks in the same industry. Those with hefty R&D funding may be the powerhouses of tomorrow.

- Is research funding growing from year to year?
- Is R&D funding higher than at other companies?

SALES? THINK MONEY

If sales are exploding, are earnings growing rapidly, too? Many times, a company can grow sales, but cannot translate that into profits. You want to find a company that excels at growing the top and bottom lines (sales and net profit).

I remember reading about Ennis Business Forms and how analysts kept predicting that the stagnant top-line growth (sales) would eventually trickle down to slowing profits, and yet the company continued to find ways to grow earnings faster than sales. They did it for years.

The key was to reduce costs. If overhead is growing faster than sales, then that is a red flag. You can find that in what is called SGA: selling, general, and administrative costs (or just general and administrative) on the income statement. Check the rate of growth of SGA compared to sales.

- Can the company translate sales into profits?
- Is overhead cost rising faster than sales?

PRICE-TO-SALES RATIO: WHAT ABOUT DEBT?

As a benchmark, I like the price-to-sales ratio (PSR), especially if it is below 1.0. A low PSR tells me the stock is cheap relative to sales. However, as Chapter 9 warned, a low PSR is not the only criterion to examine. Do not forget debt. If debt is too high, a low PSR may sucker you into a losing situation.

- Look for a price-to-sales ratio below 1.0.

STOCK PRICE: 5 TO 20

Analysts normally do not consider the stock's price as a fundamental, but I do. I avoid stocks trading below a dollar if I am not familiar with the company. That means if a bear market hammers stocks down by 60 percent, and some slide below a dollar, that is fine. They spent most of their productive life in higher territory. However, if a stock has been trading below a dollar for a year, in a bull market, it is not investment quality. Avoid penny stocks.

Stocks that trade too long below a dollar can be delisted. When they fall below $2, I sell them in the belief that they are on the road to bankruptcy. One investment advisor told me she cannot buy stocks below $2 unless the client requests it. Some mutual funds have a $5 minimum.

On the top end, I do not like to buy stocks that are too expensive, but other traders will disagree (they prefer three-digit prices and high liquidity). When price climbs over 100, or even 70, I shy away from them. My favorite range is between 5 and 20. The chapter on book value said that the best performance came from stocks priced below 16, so my range is in the sweet spot.

- Stocks priced below 16 tend to do well.
- Avoid penny stocks (those below $1) and be cautious of those priced below $5.

VOLUME: THIN ICE AHEAD!

I want to mention volume, too. I read one measure that said if you plan to buy a stock and your share purchase represents more than 1 percent of the average daily volume, then the stock is traded too thinly (or you are a big spender, perhaps both). I like that benchmark.

For example, when the market resumed its upward move after the 2007 to 2009 bear market, I went shopping for stocks. I found Bassett Furniture (BSET) because it had been moving sideways for months. Those types of flat bases are always appealing. Then I noticed the volume: 5,400 shares at $5 a share. Yuck. If I tried to buy several thousand shares, I would move the stock and have problems when I tried to sell it, too.

- Avoid stocks in which your trading volume is more than 1 percent of the average daily volume.

CHAPTER CHECKLIST

Here is a checklist of what I use when tearing apart the annual report to search for buy candidates.

☐ Book value should be rising over time. See the section "Two Book Value Tips."

☐ Look for price-to-book value below 2.0, the lower the better. See the section "Two Book Value Tips."

☐ For startup companies, determine the burn rate to see how soon they will need to fund operations. See the section "Do Not Get Singed by Burn Rate."

☐ Look for a decrease in capital spending. A cut in capital spending two years in a row is a plus. See the section "Drop Capital Spending!"

☐ Current assets/current liabilities must be over 2.0. See the section "Current Ratio 2.0."

☐ Select stocks paying a dividend. See the section "Prospecting for Growth Using Dividends."

☐ For a utility stock, check the payout ratio to be sure they have enough money left to fund future growth. See the section "Prospecting for Growth Using Dividends."

☐ Small-cap stocks that transition from losing money to making money tend to outperform. See the section "Rising Earnings, Net Profit."

☐ Stocks with increasing net profit from one year to the next tend to outperform. See the section "Rising Earnings, Net Profit."

☐ Select stocks with P/E ratios lower than the industry. See the section "P/E Ratio versus Industry."

☐ Listen to what management says about difficult conditions, and be cautious of glowing statements that business will improve soon. Let price be your guide. See the section "P/E Ratio versus Industry."

☐ If the company is being sued too frequently, discard the stock. See the section "Litigation: Stop Pissing People Off!"

☐ No long-term debt is best. See the section "Avoid Too Much Long-Term Debt."

☐ Companies moving from no debt to some long-term debt tend to outperform. See the section "Avoid Too Much Long-Term Debt."

☐ Debt to equity should be small, say, below 50 percent. See the section "Avoid Too Much Long-Term Debt."

☐ Buy small-cap stocks. See the section "Market Capitalization: Big Returns by Going Small."

☐ Is research funding growing from year to year? See the section "Research Spending."

☐ Is R&D funding higher than at other companies? See the section "Research Spending."

☐ Can the company translate sales into profits? See the section "Sales? Think Money."

☐ Are overhead costs rising faster than sales? See the section "Sales? Think Money."

☐ Look for a price to sales ratio below 1.0. See the section "Price to Sales Ratio: What About Debt?"

☐ Stocks priced below 16 tend to do well. See the section "Stock Price: 5 to 20."

☐ Avoid penny stocks (those below $1) and be cautious of those priced below $5. See the section "Stock Price: 5 to 20."

☐ Avoid stocks in which your trading volume is more than 1 percent of the average daily volume. See the section "Volume: Thin Ice Ahead!"

CHAPTER 18

Introduction to Position Trading

A hundred feet below my office as a senior software engineer stood the main branch of the Fort Worth public library. I descended from my office about once a month to visit the library during my lunch hour.

Cosmopolitan was always a hit, because I wanted to understand what the ladies thought we (guys) were thinking, and the quizzes were a lot of fun, too. But *Technical Analysis of Stocks & Commodities* magazine was also a priority even though the pictures were not as sexy. By reading TASC, I began to learn about chart patterns.

In the buy-and-hold years of my flirtation with the markets, I watched stocks I owned double in price and then drop by half—or more. Many times, I was lucky to grab a substantial profit along the way, sometimes by just waiting for another up cycle. *There had to be a better way,* I thought, and there is: position trading. Position trading is what this section is all about. The chart patterns I read about decades ago still play a major part in how I position trade today.

WHAT IS POSITION TRADING?

Position trading means buying a stock and holding it until the trend ends, then selling. Buy and hold means hanging onto a stock for years, but a position trade usually has a hold time measured in weeks and months, not years.

Position trading is more difficult than buy and hold because it is less forgiving. In position trading, you are trading securities, trying to time the market. If you cannot successfully do that, then stick with buy and hold.

- Position traders hold until the primary trend changes direction.

WHO SHOULD POSITION TRADE AND WHY?

Investors who buy and hold gravitate to position trading because of the disgust of watching profits evaporate. For example, Intel began a stair-step move higher in 1995 after moving sideways for almost two years. The split-adjusted price was $4. By the time it peaked in August 2000, the stock had climbed to nearly 76. Then the tech bubble burst, deflating Intel, too. After a decade of trying for a new high, the closest the stock has come is halfway up to its old high.

If you had bought the stock before 2000 and held on, you would have enjoyed the euphoria of holding onto a winner followed by the water-torture agony of seeing profits disappear as air escaped from the stock balloon.

The trend had changed.

Swing and day traders can benefit from position trading as well. If making money is difficult intraday (day trader) or losses outnumber profits from swing trading, then maybe position trading is the style for you. Perhaps you would like a more relaxed trading style, one that makes a lot of money while the market does all the work. Position trading might be the perfect fit.

- Buy-and-hold investors can benefit from position trading by learning to time the market. Swing and day traders can also enjoy a more relaxed style by position trading.

Here is a comparison of position trading to the other styles of trading.

- Done properly, position trading carries less risk of loss than buy and hold. Why? Because timing the exit can minimize losses, meaning drawdowns are shallower. Buy-and-hold investors will ride the roller-coaster, hoping for a recovery and praying they will not have to sell when their stock has lost half its value.
- The risk of a significant one-day loss is reduced because a position trader is out of the market for longer periods than buy and hold. A position trader might be on the sidelines during market crashes like

the 23 percent plunge on October 19, 1987, the 11 percent loss during 9/11, or miss declines suffered by individual stocks after the discovery of accounting irregularities, the failure of human drug trials, or other reasons. Those plunges begin at 15 percent but can exceed 70 percent in *one* day.

For example, I sold Vivus (VVUS) in mid-June 2010 one month before the stock plunged from a close of 12.11 to a low of 4.69 two days later—a drop of 61 percent, when the FDA denied approval of their weight-loss drug.

- If a stock climbs significantly a day after the announcement of earnings (or other good news), a position trader can sell the stock and buy it back later when price returns to earth.

I bought CNO Financial Group (CNO) on August 14, 2009, at 3.33 and sold it on October 15, a day after the stock jumped 29 percent on news that Moody's boosted the outlook for the company to positive and a broker raised its rating to outperform with a $9 target. I sold at 6.35, making 90 percent on the trade. The stock peaked a day later at 7.04, and then dropped to a low of just over $4 in February 2010. Such good news is an event pattern you can trade on, but I will leave a discussion of that for the swing-trading section. See the section in Chapter 21, "CNO Financial Group," for a complete review of the trade.

- Position trading means higher annual commission charges than buy and hold, but lower than swing and day trading.
- Capital gains taxes will likely be higher due to a shorter holding period compared to buy and hold.
- Fewer trades means less paperwork than swing and day trading.
- Position trading is less costly than day trading. You can use free end-of-day data instead of paying extra for real-time quotes and other fees.
- Trading stress is reduced compared to swing and day trading which require more attention than position trading.

Of the list, I consider two most important:

1. I hate seeing a stock I bought drop in value, changing a large profit into a smaller one—or worse—a loss. This happened with Michaels Stores. On 18 occasions while I owned it, the stock dropped at least 15 percent in one day.
2. If a trader is suffering losses in day or swing trading, then the more forgiving style of position trading may lead to profits. Longer hold times can cover a multitude of mistakes. It is like stopping at a red light versus closing your eyes and running it.

WHAT POSITION TRADING WILL NOT DO

Position trading will not work miracles. If you consistently lose money day or swing trading, it is possible that the problem is a reluctance to cut losses short.

Here is an example of the opposite of that. One trader I know keeps his stops placed pennies below the current low such that if the stock burps, he gets stopped out. His losses are so numerous that he cannot begin to dream of making a profit. What is worse, after I pointed out his problem, he acknowledged it, but continued as before. The fear of loss held a grip so tight that his trading capital is on life support.

Here is a short list of what position trading will not do.

- Position trading cannot fix all problems. If you short a stock when you should have gone long, then holding it can be a costly mistake.
- It is likely you will not find a 10-bagger position trading. It often takes several years for a stock to increase in value by a factor of 10, and just 8 percent make the journey in a single year.
- You still have to time the market and doing that is very difficult most of the time. If the market trends, it is easy to make money, but how often does the market trend?
- Buying stocks (long) in a falling (bear) market will hurt your wallet or purse regardless of the trading style adopted.
- Position trading cannot give you the mental discipline to make correct choices.

EXAMPLE POSITION TRADE

If the phrase "time the market" strikes terror in your heart then rest easy. **Figure 18.1** shows that it can be done.

I took interest in Ann Taylor stock during late June 2009. The general market had exited from a horrendous bear market in March and made a strong move higher until May when it started moving horizontally. The S&P 500 index made a head-and-shoulders top from May 7 to July 1, but the drop was minor. In other words, it was what I call a busted head-and-shoulders top. That is when the pattern completes, but price suddenly reverses direction and makes a bold move in the new direction—upward in this case.

Reviewing the fundamentals in late June showed that the stock had almost no debt and that two insiders were buying between 25,000 and 100,000 shares, five times between January and March. The rating agencies

FIGURE 18.1 The sale on this trade is two days before the stock peaked, resulting in a net gain of 78 percent in nine months.

disliked the stock and I did not think it was an exciting value play, either. Same store sales were down 31 percent, which is terrible.

A month later, I made a note to wait for the August earnings announcement before considering the stock again.

Looking at the chart, the stock made a strong advance in line with the market from point A to B and then consolidated while waiting for earnings (circled area).

The valley before A shows the start of a chart pattern called a high-and-tight flag. That is when price moves up by at least 90 percent (look for a double) within two months, which this stock accomplished. After the move up, a flag pattern often appears, which is not really a flag at all because it forms an irregular shape as in this case (the circled area).

The theory behind a high-and-tight flag is that the move up will be replicated when it leaves the flag area. It rarely works that well. This one only climbed 36 percent from the day I bought to the high at E, compared to a 100 percent move from the July low.

The company announced earnings on August 21 and price left the consolidation area, so I bought that day and received a fill at 12.36, which is close to the intraday low of 12.15.

- A buy signaled after price exited a consolidation area setup by a high-and-tight flag chart pattern and news of good earnings.

The stock threw back to the breakout price at C before making another straight-line run higher, peaking at E. Following that, the stock drifted lower to D. As a long-term holding (which was my intent), I did not pay much attention to the stock during the E to D decline. For most of that period, I was making money and since I intended to hold the stock for several years with a target of 29, I did not care about the day-to-day fluctuations.

The higher price climbed, the more nervous I became. Why? Because the general market was sprinting higher, too, and I knew the race to the top would end soon.

A chart pattern called a measured move up (see the section in *Trading Basics*, Chapter 4, "Measured Move Support and Resistance") sees the second leg of a rise equal the duration and price move of the first leg. The first leg is the move from A to E followed by what is called a corrective phase (E to D) and the second leg is from D to F. I show F as the end of the leg because I sold the stock a few days later.

The move from A to E was about 10.5 points. The second leg measured 13 points, so the second leg was longer than the first. In other words, the chart pattern said it was time to take profits unless I wanted to see them evaporate.

I started using conditional orders in late April to protect my profits. Then I noticed that since 2000, the stock peaked in May 60 percent of the time. That obeys the saying, "Sell in May and walk away."

With the market expected to tumble, I decided to take my profits to the bank and sold the stock at the open on May 3 at 22.06. Had I waited another day, I could have captured another $2 when price gapped up on an upgrade by a brokerage firm. I missed selling at the high by a day.

Notice that the upgrade came at a particularly bad time. The stock dropped after that.

This is an example of a position trade. I entered the stock expecting to hold it for years, but events intervened. I bought after the stock had doubled (it is actually much more than that since I bought at 12.36 and the stock bottomed at 2.41 in March), so you can buy high and still make money. I used a high-and-tight flag with a breakout from a congestion area on what I interpreted as good earnings. The stock cooperated by rising. When the general market looked as if it was going to drop, and the stock was already making a strong move down during the week before I sold, I deemed it was time to sell. I made 78 percent on the trade.

- The sale signaled when price fulfilled the measured move-up prediction, seasonal indicators said sell ("sell in May and walk away"), and because of an expected market drop.

CHAPTER CHECKLIST

Position trading is more difficult to do successfully than buy and hold, but it can save you from seeing a large profit turn into a small one by holding too long. Here is a checklist of subjects covered in this chapter.

☐ Position traders hold until the primary trend changes direction. See the section "What Is Position Trading?"

☐ Buy-and-hold investors can benefit from position trading by learning to time the market. Swing and day traders can also enjoy a more relaxed style by position trading. See the section "Who Should Position Trade and Why?"

☐ For a comparison of position trading to other styles, see the section "Who Should Position Trade and Why?"

☐ See the section "What Position Trading Will Not Do" for a list of deficiencies.

☐ A buy is signaled after price exits a consolidation area setup by a high-and-tight flag chart pattern and news of good earnings. See the section "Example Position Trade."

☐ A sale is signaled when price fulfills the measured move-up prediction, seasonal indicators say sell ("Sell in May and walk away"), and there is an expected market drop. See the section "Example Position Trade."

CHAPTER 19

Getting Started in Position Trading

How do you get started position trading? The method shares many of the same entry techniques with buy-and-hold investing. In fact, it is a good idea to reread Chapter 2, "Stock Selection."

Let us begin with this idea from Chapter 2: "Stocks that drop 50 percent or more outperform the following year 68 percent of the time." That is a wonderful tip that puts the odds in your favor. Ann Taylor, from the prior chapter, reached a high in September 2008 of 27.55 (about a year before I bought). The stock bottomed in March 2009 at 2.41 for an astounding skydiver freefall of 91 percent. Of course, the 2007 to 2009 bear market pummeled many stocks, leaving value players salivating at all of the opportunities.

However, you have to be careful. I bought Molecular Insight Pharmaceuticals (MIPI) at 4.81 in July 2009. At the time, they had five drug compounds in various stages of development, with three of them in phase II trials. Reading the information on their website made it sound as if FDA approval would be easy. It never is.

On September 17, I changed my opinion on the stock. Here is what I wrote about the trade in my notebook. "Sell reason: Bottom of symmetrical triangle, and I have changed my mind about this stock. I do not feel it has 'block buster drug' status in any of its compounds and thus is not a good long-term holding. It is not in phase 3 yet, so the risk of failure is too high here."

I sold at 5.20 for a net gain of just 8 percent. A month after I sold, a broker initiated coverage in the stock with a buy recommendation. The next day, the stock peaked at 6.50 before playing dead. In March 2010, the auditor questioned whether the company could survive. In December, they filed for bankruptcy.

The point of this discussion is that if you just buy any stock with a huge drop in price from the prior year, you could see the stock take a beating, carrying your hard-earned money along with it to the morgue.

- Not all value plays represent good value.

CHECK THE NEWS OR LOSE!

Before buying a stock, always check for important news. This is especially true on the day of purchase. You do not want to place a market order to buy the stock the night before the company announces that the president ran off not only with his secretary, but also with millions from the company till.

Patrick O'Hare (May 2004) uses news in a different way to find stocks. He recounts news items on four stocks: Martha Stewart Living Omnimedia (MSO), Toys R Us (TOY), Tyco International (TYC), and Newell Rubbermaid (NWL).

The four stocks were down more than 50 percent from their highs with negative sentiment about each company's future as plentiful as mosquitoes at a baseball game. He says that it was not the news that was as important as how favorably the stocks responded to the bad news.

O'Hare cites Toys R Us as an example. In late 2003, the company released disappointing third-quarter earnings, and prospects for Q4 were dismal, too. As predicted, the January 2004 earnings were lousy, and the company lowered their earnings outlook for the fiscal year. The stock dropped just two cents on the day of the announcement. Clearly, the market had factored in the bad news. Within a month, the stock had climbed 20 percent.

- Look for stocks that respond favorably to bad news, but are also down significantly (50 percent or more) from the yearly high.

I consider how the markets interpret news as key to predicting when the indexes will transition from bull to bear or the reverse. If the markets are bottoming (churning up and down after a decline) and bad news does not push the index lower but good news lifts the index, then that is a good indication the markets are ready to move higher.

Conversely, if the markets make large drops (over 100 points) on bad news and good news does not lift the index like it used to (maybe a gain of 30 points), then the market wants to move lower. Look for that trend to appear when the market is close to making new yearly highs. It signals a time to be cautious, to look for an approaching bear market or a major trend change.

- At market bottoms, if bad news no longer hurts the index like it used to, then that is a buy signal. At market tops, if good news does not lift the index as it did, then the uptrend could reverse.

At the end of each trading day, I go to Yahoo! Finance and scan for news on stocks I own. When I find something of interest, I log the information into my homebrew stock-market program so I can see how the stock behaves around events.

For all securities in my watch list (over 600), I check earnings news, rating changes, and log any that I find. I treat earnings differently than regular news. They appear at the top of my chart as the phrase "Qtr", in red for recent announcements and blue for older ones. All news items have a small red circle just below price, so I can visually identify the timing of those items. A list box on the lower left describes the news items shown in the chart, so if I see something interesting, I can read about it in the box.

All of this helps me to *see* how the stock is behaving and discover the reasons for that behavior. It is a tool I use and perhaps your software has that ability as well. An easy implementation of this is to use Google finance charts. At the time of this writing, you can set up their charts to show events and a list box describes the news item with links to the full articles. I often go there for historical information on stocks.

TREND? WHAT TREND?

Different styles of trading use different timeframes. A day trader relies on intraday charts for analysis and trading. Swing traders find daily charts to be most helpful whereas position traders use the weekly charts. The parallel in nature would be ripples, waves, and tides, respectively. Let us take a closer look.

Ripples

Ripples represent the intraday movement of stock prices as they bob up and down like a twig hit by waves. These fluctuating price movements excite day traders. The taller the waves, the more profitable the opportunity. If they catch the beginning of a swell, they hope to hang on long enough to catch the majority of the wave.

Swing and position traders will wade into the waters intraday to place their trades. Of course, that is truer of swingers than position traders. Why? Because position traders are looking for the homeruns, so saving a few pennies per share is more trouble than the round off error it represents. Swing traders want to make the most of their profits by timing the entry and exit, so trade placement is important to them.

Day traders will monitor prices over several days, perhaps as many as ten days of intraday data, to spot trends and areas of support and resistance. When I day trade, I have the intraday chart as the largest one on the screen, but also have smaller weekly and daily charts displayed. I drill down from the weekly chart to the daily and then to intraday, trying to determine the coming price trend.

If the weekly or daily charts say a storm is brewing, then I will want to know how that will influence the intraday charts. Those storms can be economic reports, earnings announcements, and rating changes by brokerages. How has the stock handled similar storms in the past? I will use the charts to find out.

- Intraday charts are the domain of day traders. They ride the ripples that bob prices up and down each day.

Waves

If day traders ride the ripples, swing traders surf the waves. Waves represent the swings from minor low to minor high and back again. Swing traders are not interested in being rocked by waves while holding on as the tide rises or playing the ripples. Instead, they want to catch each wave and ride it until it ends, and then paddle out for the next one.

Their style of trading uses a range of charts, as do the other styles of trading. Swingers focus on the daily charts, but use intraday data to place their trades and rely on the weekly charts to monitor the primary trend (tide). They know that a rising tide lifts all boats, so they will want to orient their trade swings from minor low to minor high. In a bear market, their focus will reverse, selling when price is high and buying when it drops.

Ignoring the primary trend is a flaw swing traders can avoid by watching the weekly charts. Imagine shorting a stock in a bull market when price is rising! It is much more profitable to go long in a bull market and short in a bear market, and that is why monitoring the tide is so important.

- Swing traders should use daily charts to identify price waves that oscillate higher and lower.

Tides

Beginning position traders sometimes have difficultly determining the primary trend. What does a primary trend mean and what is a bull market anyway?

In our water analogy, the primary trend is the tide. According to Victor Sperandeo (Wiley, 1991), the median duration of a bear market is 1.1 years with 75 percent of them lasting between 0.8 and 2.8 years. That compares to a bull market that lasts a median of 2.3 years, and 67 percent of them last between 1.8 and 4.1 years. My most profitable trades lasted about three years. That fits into the bull market range nicely.

A bull market occurs when price rises from a low by at least 20 percent. A bear market is when price drops by at least 20 percent from a high. Most use a close-to-close measure in the Dow Jones Industrials as the benchmark. Some type of duration should be included with the analysis, though.

For example, the crash of 1987 in which the Dow dropped almost 23 percent on October 19th does not qualify as a bear market because it happened in one day. However, the decline from the peak in August 1987 to the low in October measured 32 percent (high to low). If you were in the market at the time, those three months were like being on a rollercoaster after peaking the first hill. The drop not only took your breath away, but holding on turned your knuckles white.

Many position traders trying to catch the longer trend will do well to use the weekly charts. It is easy to spot the primary trend, and it is easy to ignore the noise created by the ripples and waves.

When I consider selling a position trade, I will flip to the weekly chart to see my price target (which I show as a horizontal line across the chart, at the appropriate price). Maintaining such perspective helps me stay calm and keep the long-term view in mind.

- Position traders focus on the primary trend, the bull and bear market swings shown on the weekly charts.

TRADE WITH THE PRIMARY TREND

When learning to position trade, or adopt any trading style for that matter, you will have more luck if you trade with the primary price trend. Perhaps you have heard the phrases, *go with the flow* and *a rising tide lifts all boats*.

During research and writing of my book *Encyclopedia of Chart Patterns* (John Wiley & Sons, 2005), I discovered that chart patterns with breakouts in line with the bull market outperformed the countertrend ones. That may sound obvious, but proving it helps.

For example, symmetrical triangles are chart patterns that breakout upward 54 percent of the time. That is almost random. Those that breakout upward in a bull market (meaning they are following the primary trend) gained an average of 31 percent before the trend changed. In a bear market, upward breakouts gained just 26 percent (a countertrend move).

Downward breakouts were not as dramatic. Those triangles with downward breakouts in a bull market lost an average of 17 percent (a countertrend move), but those in line with the bear market (meaning a downward breakout) lost 19 percent on average.

- Trade with the primary price trend.

TAKE YOUR PICK: BOTTOM FISHING OR MOMENTUM?

Figure 19.1 shows trading with the trend in visual terms, and I consider it one of the most important figures in the *Evolution of a Trader* series. At point A, price is dropping, but traders think it might be turning, that it has found a bottom. They buy. Do not be one of them. Wait.

If price is trending down and you want to buy, then you know you are on the wrong side of the trend. You are trading against the trend instead of with it. Now look at B. Price is moving up. Yes, it is well past the bottom, but at least you have the primary trend with you, helping push price upward.

My question to you is this: Where would you rather buy, at A or B? Both are at the same price. Point A has price trending down, and B has it moving up. A is bottom fishing, and B is momentum trading. The trend suggests that trade B will outperform trade A.

Trading can be that simple. Switch your bar chart to a line graph and look at your prior trades compared to Figure 19.1. If you find that you are

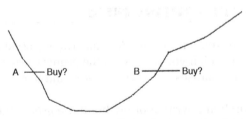

FIGURE 19.1   Points A and B are at the same price. At which point would you rather buy?

buying at A, then you know you are not trading with the trend. You are bottom fishing and drowning in red ink.

- Switch to a line chart and check if you are buying when the primary trend is down (bottom fishing) or if the trend is rising (momentum).

Imagine Figure 19.1 flipped upside down. Where would you rather sell, at A or B? If price is rising at A, then why sell unless you need the money to pay off that loan shark before he breaks your legs?

I read an email from a person faced with such a situation. They asked me to review their trade. My guess is they sold it too soon, that price was still rising, and that other technical factors supported my case. Two weeks later, the stock had continued higher, but he was not in the trade. He sold too soon.

There are times when caution is advised and the smart move is to sell, and there are other times when holding on is the more profitable move. Unfortunately, it is often luck or experience that decides which is correct, and I cannot *give* you either. Care to rent instead?

WHAT IS MARKET INFLUENCE ON STOCKS?

Let us approach trend trading from the market's perspective. How often does the overall market boost an individual stock? I decided to look by comparing the performance of the Dow industrials with the 555 stocks I follow that are not part of the Dow. **Table 19.1** shows what I found.

For the test, I compared the movement in a stock with the movement in the index. For example, if the Dow closed up and so did GumChewers stock, I counted that as a correct up move. If both dropped, then that was also correct for the downward direction. If the Dow closed higher, but the stock dropped, then that was incorrect. I summed the results of correct up totals to the total of both correct and incorrect moves. The table shows the percentages.

TABLE 19.1 Percentage of Time Stocks Close Up or Down versus Major Indexes

Market	Day Up	Day Down	Week Up	Week Down	Month Up	Month Down	Average
Dow Industrials	63%	64%	64%	64%	66%	62%	64%
*S&P 500 Index	64%	65%	65%	65%	66%	63%	65%
*Nasdaq Composite	63%	65%	65%	64%	66%	61%	64%

*Many stocks tested also comprise the indices.

For example, the stocks I tested that did not comprise the Dow Industrials (as of the April 2010 composition) closed higher 63 percent of the
time, following the Dow upward. For the 573 stocks I tested, some of which
may be a member of the S&P 500 or Nasdaq Composite, they followed the
associated index higher or lower between 63 and 65 percent of the time.

For weekly and monthly tests, I used overlapping intervals. In other
words, on day 1, I looked back a week and determined whether the index
closed higher or lower for that week and compared it to each stock using
the same two dates. Then I advanced to the next day, and looked back a
week and did another comparison, and so on until the end of data. I used
this daily overlapping method for both weekly and monthly data.

What the data tell me is that on any given day, stocks follow the averages higher or lower 64 percent of the time (which is the average of all of
the numbers in the table). I am surprised at the weekly and monthly results.
I expected a higher percentage than those shown in the table.

- A stock follows the market higher or lower 64 percent of the time.

WHAT CHART PATTERNS ARE BEST FOR POSITION TRADES?

I like chart patterns because they are the footprints of the smart money. I
want to follow those footprints to navigate through the investing or trading
minefield. However, not all chart patterns are created equal. By that, I mean
some perform better for position trades and some work better for swing
trades. Filling our toolbox with chart patterns that work best for position
trades allows us to match our steps to the smart money's footprints.

To uncover the best chart patterns for position trades, I began with
statistics from my book, *Encyclopedia of Chart Patterns, Second Edition,*
specifically, the average rise or decline and the hold time. Let us discuss
upward breakouts from chart patterns in a bull market first.

I ranked the average rise to the ultimate high (which is the highest high
before price dropped at least 20 percent) and the time it took to get there
(the hold time). Then I summed the ranks and sorted the list. **Table 19.2**
shows a partial inventory of the results with the best performing chart pattern at the top for upward breakouts in a bull market.

I assigned the swing label in the right column to those chart patterns
with hold times less than 62 calendar days (about two months). The position label belongs to those chart patterns with longer hold times. Only
three chart patterns fall into the swing category: high-and-tight flags (first
place for performance), pennants (17th), and regular flags (19th).

TABLE 19.2 The Best Chart Patterns with Upward Breakouts for Swing and Position Trading in Bull Markets

Chart Pattern	Average Rise (%)	Hold Time (Days)	Average Rise Rank	Hold Time Rank	Sum	Swing or Position Trade
Flags, High and Tight	69	39	1	3	4	Swing
Three Rising Valleys	41	125	7	13	20	Position
Scallops, Ascending and Inverted	43	137	5	20	25	Position
Diamond Bottoms	36	119	17	11	28	Position
Islands, Long	31	67	26	4	30	Position
Wedges, Falling	32	116	25	9	34	Position
Triangles, Descending	47	178	2	34	36	Position
Rectangles Bottoms	46	177	3	33	36	Position
Broadening Wedges, Ascending	38	161	11	25	36	Position
Double Bottoms, Adam & Eve	37	160	14	23	37	Position

It is not surprising to see high-and-tight flags in the top position. Since the average hold time is just over a month (39 days), I believe that pattern will work better for swing traders. Three rising valleys as the best position trading tool surprises me. I expected to see one of the three triangles (ascending, descending, or symmetrical) in second place. In fact, scanning down the list shows many surprises, like scallops, diamonds, and long islands. Those chart patterns are not common tools that traders use. Maybe that is why they populate the list; the more obscure the tools the better they tend to work.

Table 19.3 shows the top 10 performing patterns for downward breakouts in a bear market. Why did I choose patterns in a bear market? Because a downward breakout direction matches the direction of the primary trend (which is also downward), and the primary trend is what position traders should focus on. I am *not* recommending that novice position traders short stocks.

Since the hold time is so short, all of the patterns shown in the table would work best as swing trades. The lone position trade is there because I assigned swing or position labels to those below or above the median hold time, respectively, which was 34 days.

Although the two tables give you some idea of the best chart patterns according to the average rise/decline and hold time, labels should not

TABLE 19.3 The Best Chart Patterns with Downward Breakouts for Swing and Position Trading in Bear Markets

Chart Pattern	Average Decline (%)	Hold Time (Days)	Average Decline Rank	Hold Time Rank	Sum	Swing or Position Trade
Broadening Bottoms	−12	24	1	4	5	Swing
Triangles, Symmetrical	−11	30	2	11	13	Swing
Broadening Tops	−10	29	5	10	15	Swing
Double Tops, Adam and Adam	−11	32	2	13	15	Swing
Rounding Tops	−7	25	12	5	17	Swing
Scallops, Inverted and Descending	−7	28	12	8	20	Swing
Scallops, Ascending	−11	35	2	19	21	Position
Scallops, Descending	−7	30	12	11	23	Swing
Pennants	−5	16	23	1	24	Swing
Flags	−5	17	23	2	25	Swing

matter. The statistics do not include busted chart patterns, and that is an area you should focus on. Why? Because busted chart patterns provide exceptional profit opportunity with reduced risk.

BUSTED CHART PATTERNS REVISITED

I mentioned busted chart patterns in *Trading Basics*, Chapter 5, "Busted Patterns for Profit," and also devoted two chapters to them in my book, *Visual Guide to Chart Patterns* (John Wiley & Sons, 2013), so there is little need to repeat the information here. However, a brief review will be helpful to those unfamiliar with busted chart patterns.

Figure 18.1 shows a busted descending triangle in Ann Taylor. Price broke out downward, reversed at D, and then shot out the top of the chart pattern. A strong move up followed, which is typical of busted patterns (but no guarantee, of course).

A busted pattern occurs when price breaks out in one direction and does not move far (less than 10 percent) before reversing direction, breaking out in the opposite direction, and closing beyond the pattern's height (above the top or below the bottom). Most of the time, the new breakout direction provides a strong move. However, symmetrical triangles double bust (the most of any pattern studied). They may breakout upward then downward and then upward again. Although symmetrical triangles are common, it is best to avoid them unless you are an experienced trader.

- Symmetrical triangles tend to double or triple bust.

Figure 19.2 shows another example of a busted descending triangle. Price touches each trend line several times, creating support and resistance zones that contain price—at least for a while. The top trend line slopes downward, giving the chart pattern its name, and the bottom trend line is horizontal.

Descending triangles breakout downward most often, and this is an example. However, after spending a few weeks below the horizontal bottom trend line, price shoots upward, piercing the bottom trendline and soaring out the top. When price closes above the top trendline, it busts the triangle and suggests a strong move ahead. That is what happens, too, with price rising 50 percent from 18.77 (the breakout price) to 28.17 (the April peak) in a near straight-line run higher. Even if you captured only half of that move, it is still a yummy return.

FIGURE 19.2 The descending triangle busts after a downward breakout and sees price move up instead.

A trend line drawn below the valleys on the way up tells when to sell the stock. In late April when price closed below the trend line, that was the sell signal.

- Trade busted chart patterns because they often provide strong moves.

TRADING EXAMPLE: FINDING VALUE IN DISASTER

We have covered much ground, with strings of ideas floating in the wind, so let us tie them together with an actual trading example. **Figure 19.3** shows a chart of Hawaiian Electric (HE) on the daily scale.

The general market had turned down starting in October 2007 when the S&P peaked. Price dropped, changing a bull market into a bear that clawed its way through 2008 and into 2009. The last two weeks of February 2009 were especially brutal. Price made a straight-line run down. On March 6, the decline ended and a bull market began, but no one knew that at the time.

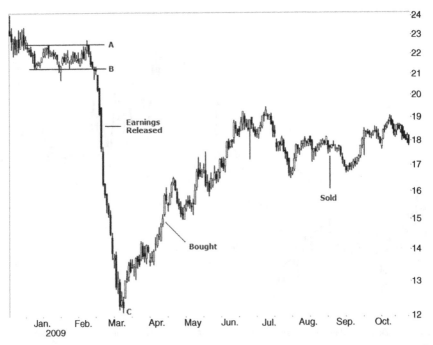

FIGURE 19.3 A swift decline in a bear market suggested a bounce back in a bull market.

The chart shows what happened to the electric utility during those weeks in March. Hawaiian Electric was not alone seeing its stock cut nearly in half in less than a month. Six of nine (67 percent) western U.S. electric utility stocks faced substantial declines during that month.

Seeing the stock become a cliff diver intrigued me. With the stock going splat at 12 and then bouncing, the yield was tasty, but was the dividend safe? I decided to look closer.

The stock moved horizontally between a rectangle bottom chart pattern shown at A and B. It is a bottom chart pattern because price enters the rectangle from the top. If you could go back more in time, you would see that the decline started from a high of almost 30.

My guess was that the stock would return to the AB region and stall there, so 21 to 22 was the target. If the market Gods were kind to me, the rise back to B would mirror the steepness of the February decline, but that is rare. A gentler rise is realistic, and that is what the chart shows after bottoming at C.

Financials

I listened to the quarterly conference call. Questions from the analysts always intrigue me. I remember management discussing that they had factored in a worse-case scenario for their banking subsidiary and made contingency plans based on that.

Let us stop right there. Notice anything unusual? What is an electric utility doing owning a bank? I do not know the answer except to say that it is one strange way to diversify away from the regulated side of the business. My guess at the time was that concerns over the health of the bank subsidiary helped the stock drop 43 percent in about three weeks.

After listening to the quarterly conference call, I delved into the finances. The payout ratio had been in the high 80s for several years, leaving little left to run the business. That is not unusual for utilities, but with worries about the economy taking center stage, I wanted a safe dividend. Three other utilities had cut their dividends, and I did not want this one to be a fourth.

I checked their 10-K for a report on litigation and the company appeared clean. Insurance would help protect the business, and they did not appear to be pissing off people, anyway. That is a good sign.

I was not concerned about earnings and sales growth since this was primarily a stock rebound play with a dividend kicker. However, Value Line reported that for the period ending in May 2008, the stock had it all: rising revenue, declining earnings, and a stagnant dividend. Book value was over $15 a share, according to one source I checked. Cash flow per share had been declining since peaking in 2005—a worrisome trend—but the drop was not severe. My notes say that company pension contributions would hurt results in the next quarter. The rest of the financials were about what you would expect for an electric company with a bank subsidiary.

Insiders seemed to love the stock as it bottomed in March. Five bought between 2,000 and 8,000 shares each, with just one selling 3,000 shares. I like it when insiders share my pain.

The Buy

On February 24 with the stock at 15.50, I decided to buy four times the usual number of shares . . . and then did not. With price dropping in a straight-line run, I held off.

My notes say that price was heading toward a support zone at 15 and another at 13.85, based on the monthly chart going back to 1988. The relative strength index and commodity channel index were both signaling buy. The dividend was 8.2 percent.

I watched as price bottomed and did a V-shaped bounce.

On April 7, I looked at the stock again and decided to buy with much of the preceding discussion concerning financials occurring then. I cut the share size to what it was in the bull market days because I was concerned about the bear market taking price lower. I received a fill at 14.84.

The Sale

The stock climbed almost as I hoped (not quite as vertical as I wanted, but close). In early July, the stock stumbled, but that could have been a delayed reaction to a sell off in the S&P that started in June. The Dow utility index also showed that price dipped in July, but recovered in about a week whereas this stock took twice as long to make the turn.

With the markets moving higher almost daily (except for this stock), I wanted to diversify my holdings away from the slow-growth utility stocks. On August 21, I sold my stock and received a fill at 17.67. With dividends, I made 23 percent.

Since this was a long-term hold, I sold later than I should have, but I did not consider this a position trade at the time. Even so, looking at the chart shows that had I sold up to 1 month earlier, I would not have increased the sale price much. Holding allowed me to collect another dividend payment at 8.4 percent (adjusted for my buy price). I *like* earning that kind of money while I watch my stocks move higher!

Here are the important elements of this trade.

- Sharp downward move: The stock dropped 43 percent in about three weeks, so I anticipated a bounce.

- The general market turned bullish.
- Price already started moving up from the low.
- The dividend appeared safe.
- Financial ratios were acceptable.
- RSI (relative strength index) and CCI (commodity channel index) said buy.
- Overhead resistance was well above the current price.
- Insiders were buying.
- Two above-average dividend payments helped boost the overall return.
- Sold for diversification purposes and because the stock was moving sideways to down.

The next chapter reviews a scoring system so you can get a better feel for how I make position trading work.

CHAPTER CHECKLIST

Based on findings in this chapter, here are some tips to consider when getting started in position trading.

☐ Not all value plays represent good value. See this chapter's introduction.

☐ Look for stocks that respond favorably to bad news, but are also down significantly (50 percent or more) from the yearly high. See the section "Check the News or Lose!"

☐ At market bottoms, if bad news no longer hurts the index like it used to, then that is a buy signal. At market tops, if good news does not lift the index as it did, then the uptrend could reverse. See the section "Check the News or Lose!"

☐ Intraday charts are the domain of day traders. See the section "Ripples."

☐ Swing traders should use daily charts to identify price waves that oscillate higher and lower. See the section "Waves."

☐ Position traders focus on the primary trend, the bull and bear market swings shown on the weekly charts. See the section "Tides."

☐ Trade with the primary price trend. See the section "Trade with the Primary Trend."

☐ Switch to a line chart and check if you are buying when the primary trend is down (bottom fishing) or if the trend is rising (momentum). See the section "Take Your Pick: Bottom Fishing or Momentum?"

☐ A stock follows the market higher or lower 64 percent of the time. See the section "What Is Market Influence on Stocks?"

☐ Table 19.2 shows the best performing chart patterns with upward breakouts in a bull market for swing and position traders. See the section "What Chart Patterns Are Best for Position Trades?"

☐ Table 19.3 shows the best performing chart patterns with downward breakouts in a bear market for swing and position traders. See the section "What Chart Patterns Are Best for Position Trades?"

☐ Symmetrical triangles tend to double or triple bust. See the section "Busted Chart Patterns Revisited."

☐ Trade busted chart patterns because they often provide strong moves. See the section "Busted Chart Patterns Revisited."

CHAPTER 20

Ten Factors Make Chart Patterns Work

Trading comes in two basic styles: discretionary and system. Discretionary trading relies on intuition and experience to determine when to buy and sell. System trading follows a mechanical setup for trading signals. I am a discretionary trader, but sometimes having systems available that point the way are the trader's equivalent of a GPS (global positioning system). In the pages that follow, I describe a scoring system that helps select winning chart patterns, or more importantly, avoid weak ones.

Novice system traders often compile a list of rules that could fill a page. "If the MACD histogram shows bull divergence, and RSI was oversold but has moved above 30 with price above the 200-day SMA, with the ADX showing a strong trend, and it is raining on Monday. . . . "

One novice showed me his list of rules, and it was 21 items long. My guess is he would get one signal every decade, and it would probably fail anyway. Pros know better. They have boiled down their setups into as few rules as possible. Simplest is best.

Try this experiment. Plot all of your indicators on the same chart. If the indicators peak as price peaks and they make valleys as price bottoms, then why not just eliminate them and use price alone? Price tells all. Everything else is just a derivative (distraction?). Are they acting like a busload of kids all yelling to turn right at the next intersection, confirming what the GPS is saying?

- To increase the odds of success, simplify your trading rules.

One novice trader reported that he spent two years testing every indicator he could find only to discover that none tested well enough to use. "I wish I had those two years back," he said. "What a waste of time!"

This chapter tells what I use to position trade chart patterns. I found 10 factors that determine whether a chart pattern will outperform. I wrote about that discovery in my book, *Trading Classic Chart Patterns* (Wiley, 2002), but the following includes updated research that uses samples since the book appeared (in other words, out of sample data). Let us begin by reviewing a popular chart pattern called a double bottom.

WHAT IS A DOUBLE BOTTOM?

A double bottom is just as it sounds—two valleys that bottom near the same price. If price trends downward into the double bottom, then the chart pattern acts as a reversal of the downward trend.

It is rare, but double bottoms sometimes appear in a rising price trend. **Figure 20.1** shows this consolidation double bottom in the inset. Price moves higher into peak A then forms two bottoms near the same price with peak B soaring above the two bottoms. In fact, one of the requirements of a double bottom is that B should be at least 10 percent above the lower of the two bottoms. The upward trend that preceded creation of the double bottom resumes after the pattern ends, and price takes off like a jetliner leaving O'Hare.

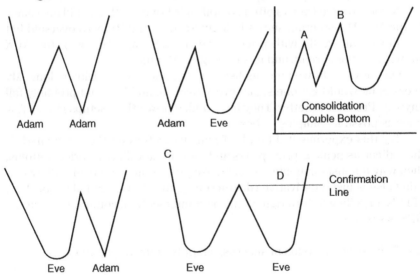

FIGURE 20.1 Shown are four variations of double bottoms.

- A consolidation double bottom acts as a continuation of the upward price trend, not as a reversal. The left side of the double bottom has a peak lower than the peak between the two bottoms (peak A is below B in Figure 20.1).

When technical analysts discuss double bottoms, they are *not* talking about consolidation double bottoms. They are talking about those that act as reversals, specifically, an Eve and Eve double bottom.

Double Bottom Reversals

When price begins its descent from above (point C in Figure 20.1) the double bottom (point D), then the chart pattern acts as a reversal of the price trend. If price closes above the confirmation line, price often (but not always) continues rising.

Double-bottom chart patterns come in four delicious flavors: Adam and Adam, Adam and Eve, Eve and Adam, and Eve and Eve. The Adam and Eve phrases describe the shape of the bottoms with each combination performing differently. I first learned of the Adam and Eve labels from Alan Farley's book (McGraw-Hill, 2001).

Figure 20.1 shows the ideal configurations. Adam bottoms are narrow, often composed of long, one-day, downward price spikes.

Eve bottoms are wider and rounded looking. If they have price spikes, they tend to be shorter and more numerous. If Adam has one long price spike, Eve will have three or four short ones (but allow variations). Eve bottoms tend to get much wider up the price scale compared to Adam, which tends to remain narrow.

Width is a good key for deciding if the bottom shape is Adam or Eve. However, it takes practice to identify correctly the type of double bottom. One tip is to ask if the first bottom looks similar to the second. If so, then you are dealing with either Adam and Adam or Eve and Eve. If the two bottoms look different, then it is either Adam and Eve or Eve and Adam.

Another tip is to look at the price bottoms over the past year or two. Compare the shape of historical bottoms to those of the double bottom. The shape of Adam and Eve bottoms tend to repeat over time (many downward price spikes are Adam bottoms, for example). That may help with identification.

- The type of bottom determines performance.
- Adam bottoms are narrow along their height, pointed looking, often with one long price spike poking downward.
- Eve bottoms look round and wide, with numerous shorter price spikes (or none at all).

- Compare the two bottoms. Do they look alike (Adam and Adam or Eve and Eve) or different (Adam and Eve or Eve and Adam)?
- Compare the double bottoms with other bottoms in the historical price series to help determine the bottom type.

After determining the double-bottom type, wait for price to close above the confirmation price, point D in Figure 20.1. Why is that important? In an updated study I conducted, I discovered that price fails to close above point D 44 percent of the time in a bull market. In other words, price continues to drop, so waiting for confirmation is important.

- Wait for confirmation—price to close above the peak between the two bottoms—before buying.

TEN FACTORS REVEALED

Why spend so many words describing double bottoms? Because I used them as benchmarks to prove that the 10 factors for scoring a chart pattern still work a decade after I discovered the technique. The number of factors varies somewhat from pattern to pattern and it is a bit different from what I proposed in my *Trading Classic Chart Patterns* book.

In the book, I included a bull-trap factor. Bull traps happen when price breaks out upward, climbs less than 10 percent before curling over and dropping below the bottom of the chart pattern. If you could tell when a bull trap was going to occur, you would avoid buying it in the first place. I included it in the book since it seemed like a good idea at the time.

By scoring each factor as plus or minus one (sometimes zero) and adding the scores, I found that chart patterns with scores totaling above zero significantly outperformed those with totals below zero.

Unfortunately, a chart pattern with a high score does not mean it will outperform. It means it has the characteristics common to the best performing chart patterns, but that is no guarantee of success. Besides, you can botch a winning trade, turning a potential 10-bagger into a loss. I use the information to avoid buying a chart pattern that has a low probability of success.

The following 10 factors are used for any chart pattern *with an upward breakout*. For downward breakouts or pattern-specific factors, then consult my *Trading Classic Chart Patterns* book.

Trend Start

Figure 20.2 shows an example of an Adam and Adam double bottom. You may quibble about the Adam designation on the second bottom, that it should be Eve. Contrast the second Adam bottom with E. E is a rounded turn that better represents what an Eve turn should look like. In fact, if you used an erasure on the left Adam spike (remove the price bar), what remained would be a nice Eve turn, too.

Both Adam valleys plunge downward from horizontal price movement, like table legs setting the foundation for a strong advance. Both valleys bottom near the same price (the two prices do not have to match, but they should be close).

Where does the price trend leading to the start of the chart pattern actually begin? The answer is to find where price rises or falls more than 20 percent. The 20 percent benchmark is what separates a bull market from a bear market, so I just applied that measure to the trend start. In this example, the trend start is at A because price drops at least 20 percent before that peak.

I found that patterns with short-term trends leading to the start of chart patterns tend to outperform. Short-term means less than three months. In this example, the trend starts more than three months before the first bottom, so the trend is not short-term. Score +1 for short-term trends, otherwise score 0. For CALM (the stock in Figure 20.2), the running total is 0.

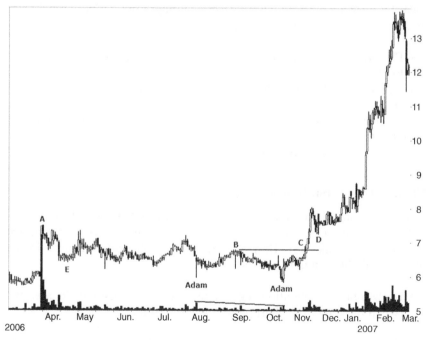

FIGURE 20.2 An Adam & Adam chart pattern sees price rise 220 percent after the breakout. Note the linear scale.

- The trend start is either the highest high *before* which price drops at least 20 percent or the lowest low *before* which price rises at least 20 percent.

Flat Base

I discussed a flat base in *Trading Basics*, Chapter 5, "Flat Base Entry Pattern." Here is a review. The ideal flat-base pattern has a flat top and a flat bottom with narrow up and down price fluctuations that can last for months. That flat movement is called a flat base, a springboard from which large price moves can occur.

To locate a flat base, look for horizontal price movement of several weeks to several months (the longer, the better) duration. I like to see three or four months' worth of horizontal price movement with peaks and valleys staying between two parallel lines.

Figure 20.2 shows a flat-base pattern starting after A. A double bottom, like the one shown, often pokes below the bottom of a flat base. What is important, is that price moves horizontally for months leading to the start of a chart pattern. It acts as a springboard to a future advance.

When searching for flat bases, switch to the linear price scale. The logarithmic scale tends to make mountains ranges out of flat bases. Figure 20.2 uses the linear scale.

- Flat bases appear as horizontal price movements, often several months long.
- Use the linear price scale when hunting for flat bases.

If your chart pattern has a flat base, score +1; otherwise subtract 1 from the total.

For CALM, the running total is +1.

Horizontal Consolidation Regions

Horizontal consolidation regions, or HCRs as I call them, are like flat bases only they appear *between the trend start and the top of the chart pattern* (for upward breakouts). They are regions of overhead resistance in the predicted flight path of the stock.

- Horizontal consolidation regions are overhead resistance located between the top of the chart pattern and the trend start.

The HCR has to loom like an impenetrable cloud floating above future price movement, hence the emphasis on location.

When I search for a HCR, I am looking for at least three peaks or three valleys that share the same price and are close together. It is rare that I find one. In 1,289 double bottoms, I found 420 HCRs, or 32 percent of the total.

If price trends upward leading to the start of a chart pattern with an upward breakout, then you are in luck. There is no HCR in the way of future price movement, by definition.

Score –1 if a HCR floats above the predicted price path, otherwise score +1. For CALM, the stock does not have a HCR in the way (+1), so the running total increases to +2.

- On the way to the ultimate high, price either never rises to a horizontal consolidation region (which happens 9 percent of the time) or stops within 5 percent of it 50 percent of the time.

Position in Yearly Range

Where in the yearly price range does the breakout from the chart pattern reside? Use the price range: split it into thirds of the 12 months before the start of the chart pattern. The breakout is often where price pierces a chart pattern trend-line boundary or closes above the top of a chart pattern.

For double bottoms, we use the highest high in the chart pattern (point B) as the breakout price. Figure 20.2 shows the breakout in the middle of the yearly price range.

Score your chart pattern +1 if the breakout price is within a third of the yearly low, –1 if it is in the middle, and 0 if it is within a third of the yearly high. For CALM, the running total is +1.

- Chart patterns within a third of the yearly low tend to outperform.

Height

The height of a chart pattern is perhaps the strongest indication that the chart pattern will do well after the breakout. Tall patterns beat the pants off short ones (not always, mind you).

Compute the height of the chart pattern from the highest high price to the lowest low and divide by the breakout price. Compare the result to 15.36 percent, which is the median height of all 1,289 double bottoms in the study. Tall chart patterns have percentages higher than 15.36.

The double bottom shown in Figure 20.2 is short (–1) for a running total of 0. Tall patterns score +1.

- Tall chart patterns perform better than short ones.

Volume Trend

I do not particularly like using volume as an indicator. In fact, I do not show it on the charts I view on a daily basis. However, testing reveals that it is useful. The *linear regression* volume trend often slopes downward throughout many chart patterns. In fact, volume can drop to a very low level a day before the actual breakout.

What is linear regression? It is a 10-gallon phrase for mathematically fitting a line between points such that the distance from the line to all of the points is at a minimum. The slope of that line shows the trend. Often you can guess the slope of the linear regression line just by looking at the volume chart.

For example, Figure 20.2 shows volume trending downward (see diagonal line), but I used linear regression to prove it. If linear regression on volume from the start of the chart pattern to the end (bottom to bottom) shows it trending lower, then score it +1, otherwise score it –1. Running total for CALM is +1.

- Volume often trends downward throughout the chart pattern and can be very low the day before a breakout.

Breakout Day Volume

Volume on the day price breaks free of the chart pattern is the next factor that helps determine how well a chart pattern performs.

When I wrote *Trading Classic Chart Patterns*, I manually compared the breakout day's volume with the prior three months, splitting the breakout day's volume into one of five categories. That is too subjective.

In this study, I find the average volume over three months. If breakout day volume is ≥25 percent above the average, then rate it high. If it is 25 percent below average, then classify that as low volume. Between those two, breakout day volume is just average.

Score +1 for high volume, and –1 for everything else. It is difficult to see volume on the chart, but it is above the three-month average. For CALM, the running total is +2.

If I want to buy on the breakout day (or have a buy stop already in place), I just assume that breakout-day volume will be average.

- High breakout-day volume is like a rocket engine propelling the stock higher.

Throwbacks

Throwbacks are annoying diseases that strike chart patterns about half the time. Price breaks out upward from a chart pattern and then reverses after an average of six days and after rising 8 percent. Then it takes another four days for the stock to return to the breakout price. After that, anything goes, but 65 percent of the time, price resumes its upward run.

If a throwback occurs, it kills upward momentum, resulting in performance that is worse than from chart patterns not showing a throwback (I proved this). Score –1 if a throwback occurs within a month and +1 if it does not.

If you do not want to wait to see if one will occur, then look for nearby overhead resistance. Price can usually push through resistance that is within 5 percent of the breakout price, but will return if resistance is just beyond that (like the 8 percent figure I mentioned).

Most of the time I just assume that a throwback will occur.

For the stock shown in Figure 20.2, point D is the throwback attempt, but price did not return to the breakout price, so no throwback actually occurred. This scores +1, for a running total that now stands at +3.

- Throwbacks hurt performance by killing upward momentum.

Breakout-Day Gaps

Breakout-day gaps occur when traders pile into a stock before the opening bell and the buying pressure forces price to open above the prior high. If price can remain above the prior high throughout the day, it leaves a price gap on the chart. No breakout-day gap appears at C (the day price closed above the peak between the two bottoms) in Figure 20.2.

When a gap occurs, it often means a better performing stock, so score it +1 if a gap occurs on the breakout day and –1 if it does not. For CALM, the running total is +2.

If the breakout has not occurred yet, I just assume that a breakout day gap will not occur.

- Breakout-day gaps mean traders are excited about the stock, helping to push price higher.

Market Cap

The final factor in determining which chart patterns will tend to outperform is market capitalization. Market cap is the number of shares outstanding multiplied by the current price. I consider small-cap stocks as having market caps below $1 billion, large caps are over $5 billion, and mid caps are everything between those two values.

If you were not asleep when I discussed fundamentals, you know that small caps tend to outperform. Score large caps as –1 and everything else as +1. CALM is a small-cap stock so the final total is +3.

- Small caps perform best; large caps perform worst.

On average, scores above 0 outperform those below 0, so a +3 score suggests that the stock will do well. In fact, it does. The ultimate high, which is the highest high before a 20 percent change in trend, does not appear on the chart. The stock reached 21.70 in July, for a gain of 220 percent above B.

I chose this stock because of the large advance, positive score, and to show what a flat base looks like. Just because a stock shows a positive score is no guarantee that price will climb above the median rise. On average, however, the scoring system adds value to stocks selected for chart patterns.

I will discuss performance in a moment and then give additional case studies of how the system works.

SCORING SYSTEM CHECKLIST

Table 20.1 shows the generic system for scoring chart patterns. Although it is based on double bottoms, each factor is common to all chart patterns, so the technique should work for other types of chart patterns, too.

SCORING PERFORMANCE

How well does the scoring system do? **Table 20.2** shows the results.

I used 566 stocks and found 1,289 double bottoms. Those I split into bull and bear markets, and the various combinations of Adam and Eve. The bear markets were from March 24, 2000, to October 10, 2002, and October 12, 2007, to March 6, 2009, as shown by the S&P 500 index. The bull market is outside of those two ranges. In this study, I used out-of-sample double bottoms from August 14, 2001, (catching the tail end of the bear market) to August 20, 2010.

I scored the double-bottom chart patterns using the same method I did when preparing my *Trading Classic Chart Patterns* book, with the exception of bull traps and the treatment of breakout-day volume, as I mentioned earlier. The scoring system is slightly different in the book for some of the double bottoms than presented in the "Ten Factors Revealed" section earlier. For example, I used a market trend in the book, but found that it does not add value in out-of-sample tests, so I removed it from the generic model (the last line in Table 20.2).

TABLE 20.1 A Scoring System Checklist

Factor	Score
Trend start: Price trends less than three months leading to the start of a chart pattern.	+1 otherwise 0.
Flat base: A flat base appears near the start of a chart pattern.	+1 otherwise −1.
Horizontal consolidation region: A HCR does *not* appear in the way of price movement (meaning it is located between the trend start and the top of the chart pattern). A HCR that spans the trend start is valid.	+1 otherwise −1.
Position in yearly range: The breakout price is within a third of the yearly low.	+1 otherwise −1 for the middle third and 0 for the highest third.
Height: Patterns taller than 15.36% (height divided by breakout price).	+1 otherwise −1.
Volume trend: Volume trends lower from start to end of the chart pattern. Use linear regression if not sure.	+1 otherwise −1.
Breakout day volume: A high volume (at least 25% higher than the 3-month average) breakout occurs.	+1 otherwise −1.
Throwbacks: Price does *not* throwback to (or come that close to) the breakout price within a month.	+1 otherwise −1.
Breakout day gaps: A price gap (regardless of size, providing you can see it on a price chart) appears on the breakout day.	+1 otherwise −1.
Market cap: The stock has a market cap below $5 billion (it is not a large-cap stock).	+1 otherwise −1.

TABLE 20.2 Scoring System Results for Double Bottoms

Bottom Type	Bull Market Scores > 0	Bull Market Scores < 0	Bear Market Scores > 0	Bear Market Scores < 0	1991 – 2001 Scores > 0	1991 – 2001 Scores < 0
Adam and Adam	70%	39%	28%	17%	45%	18%
Adam and Eve	45%	33%	21%	18%	44%	19%
Eve and Adam	57%	44%	31%	27%	45%	24%
Eve and Eve	49%	40%	26%	19%	47%	25%
Generic	53%	38%	28%	16%	None	None

As Table 20.2 shows, Adam & Adam double bottoms with scores above 0 in a bull market had gains that averaged 70 percent. Those with scores below 0 gained an average of 39 percent. Those numbers compare to the 1991 to 2001 bull/bear combination market of 45 percent and 18 percent, respectively. Since the book lumped both bull and bear markets together, the two periods are not directly comparable, but they do show how performance has changed over time.

Do not expect your double bottom to gain 70 percent in a bull market. That is for hundreds of perfect trades, buying in at the breakout price and cashing out at the highest high just before price tumbles at least 20 percent. No one can duplicate such results repeatedly. You could do better, or worse.

The last row in the table (Generic) uses the Ten Factors to score double-bottom chart patterns (regardless of their Adam and Eve designations). In a bull market, double bottoms with scores above 0 gained 53 percent compared to 38 percent for those with scores below 0. In a bear market (upward breakouts), the gains are closer, 28 to 16 percent. The book did not have a generic scoring system so there are no comparable numbers to discuss.

- In each bottom type shown in Table 20.2, chart patterns with scores above 0 outperform those with scores below 0.

When I score a chart pattern and it is below 0 that means there is an increased risk of a failed trade or one that could underperform the median. I may take the trade, but it causes me to recheck my work. If the score is 0 or above, then I feel more confident that the trade will do well.

HIGHER SCORES WORK BEST

The higher the score, the better the chart pattern tends to perform. To determine this, I used the high and low range of scores (from –8 to +10) and logged the average rise for each score in bull and bear markets, using the generic scoring system (the Ten Factors, discussed above). **Table 20.3** shows the results.

For example, double bottoms with –5 scores in a bull market showed gains averaging 21 percent (using 27 samples, which is few). Those with +5 scores gained 62 percent (also 27 samples). Graphing the results for all of the individual scores shows two up-sloping lines, one for bull markets and one for bear markets. The lines are jagged because the sample counts can be small, but the upward trend is clear in both cases.

TABLE 20.3 Higher Positive Scores Mean Better Performance.

Score	Bull	Samples	Bear	Samples
−8	23%	2		0
−7	50%	8	20%	4
−6	75%	6		0
−5	21%	27	26%	8
−4	41%	33	12%	8
−3	36%	73	16%	28
−2	50%	93	15%	20
−1	47%	101	20%	30
0	48%	117	21%	30
1	34%	94	24%	35
2	56%	102	23%	43
3	54%	45	24%	14
4	54%	68	24%	29
5	62%	27	81%	1
6	98%	25	50%	7
7	46%	3	40%	2
8	52%	4	76%	1
9	375%	1		0
10	285%	1		0

While it is possible that an individual chart pattern with a high score will underperform, and one with a very low score will outperform, the table shows that chart patterns with higher scores tend to do better, on average.

- The higher the total score the better performance tends to be.

CASE STUDY: STILLWATER MINING

Figure 20.3 shows the first case study using Stillwater Mining as the guinea pig. The general market finished a bear market in late 2002 and tested the low in March 2003, right when the double bottom shown at AB appeared.

This double bottom is a good example of a Big-*W* chart pattern. The *W* begins at E, bottoms at A and B, and then recovers more slowly back up to the price level of E and beyond.

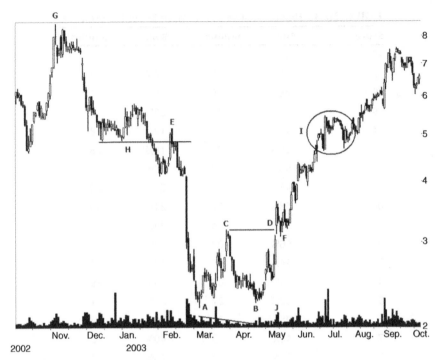

FIGURE 20.3 A big-*W* chart pattern with a good score suggests a strong move, carried higher by a rising general market.

Seeing the twin bottoms at AB form, a good target would be a rise to E. So, even without a scoring system, this was a compelling position or swing trade.

Briefly, let's use the generic scoring system to rate this chart pattern. Refer to Table 20.1 for the scoring guidelines.

The trend starts at G because *before* that peak, price drops at least 20 percent. The time between G and A is more than three months, so that scores 0.

Does a flat base precede this stock? No. Score –1 for a total of –1.

A horizontal consolidation region appears at H. H is between G and C, the trend start and the top of the chart pattern. When price rises, I would expect the stock to stall or reverse at H, the flat-bottomed congestion region. As the chart shows, the stock got hung up at I (circled), right at the price level of the HCR. Score a HCR as –1 for a total of –2.

As you might guess, the breakout (D) is within a third of the yearly low. Score that +1 for a total of –1.

The height of the chart pattern measures from C, 3.18 to the lowest bottom, A, 2.20, for a height to breakout of (3.18 – 2.20) ÷ 3.18, or 31 percent. The pattern is tall for a +1 score. Total: 0.

Volume trends downward for a +1 score. Total: +1.

Breakout-day volume (J) is also high for a +1 score. Total: +2.

The stock has a throwback at F. That scores –1 for a +1 total.

The stock also gaps higher on the breakout day, but it may be hard to see on the chart (it is a small gap). That scores +1 for a total of +2.

The stock is a small cap for a +1 score. Final score: +3.

The stock peaked in April 2004 (the ultimate high) at 18.18 for a gain of 472 percent above C.

Yes, that is a big gain, but remember that the general market had just left a bear market, tested the low, and was on the way to a recovery when this chart pattern broke out upward. The chart pattern benefited from a rising tide (trade with the trend), but it also outperformed many other stocks. The scoring system correctly identified this stock as a winner.

CASE STUDY: LSB INDUSTRIES

This case study looks at LSB Industries, but in a bear market. The S&P 500 index peaked in October 2007, so the index had been sliding downward for about six months before the double bottom in LSB appeared. In fact, as the stock bottomed, the index was completing an upward retrace of the downward trend. In other words, after mid-May, the index resumed its long downtrend even as the stock climbed.

Figure 20.4 shows the chart and it looks similar to the last figure. It is another double bottom, but also a Big-*W* pattern with a tall left side and a weaker right one. This Big *W*, however, did not make it back up to the start of the W, at E (price rose only to K).

Let us score this pattern beginning with the trend start. I show that at point G, which is less than three months from the start of the chart pattern (A), for a +1 score.

Does a flat base precede the double bottom? No. Score –1 for a total of 0.

Is there a horizontal consolidation region in the way of price? Yes, at H, but it does not qualify because it occurs *before* the trend start. The HCR must appear after G and before A (in time), and between G and C (in price). H does not qualify, for a +1 score or a total of +1.

Where is the breakout in the yearly price range? It is near the yearly low for a +1 score. Total: +2.

The chart pattern is tall (barely) for a +1 score. Total: +3.

Volume trends downward (J) for a +1 score. Total: +4.

Breakout day volume is just average for a –1 score. Total: +3.

Price attempts a throwback at F, but it never quite reaches the horizontal breakout line at D for a +1 score. Total: +4.

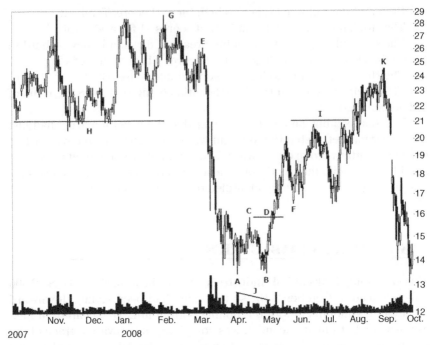

FIGURE 20.4   A double bottom during a bear market still powers the stock to a good gain, just as the scoring system predicted.

The stock does not gap higher on the breakout day for a –1 score. Total: +3. Finally, the stock is a small cap for a +1 score. Final total: +4.

The stock climbed to K, the ultimate high, before the general market or industry conditions sucked the stock lower. Nevertheless, the stock gained 55 percent in a bear market. That kills the bear market stocks that scored less than 0 and climbed only 16 percent (from Table 20.2). The scoring system said the stock would do well and it did, even in a bear market.

CASE STUDY: LUMBER LIQUIDATORS

The last case study completes our tour of the decade. **Figure 20.5** shows the setup. The general market was in the midst of a major bull run after recovering from the 2007 to 2009 bear market. The run up from the 2009 lows was a near straight-line run (with one pause in June 2009). The market peaked in January 2010, retraced until the start of February, and then shot off again. In other words, the drop from K to F in the figure was a counter market move.

Let us score this double bottom to see what the system says about trading it. I kept the letters the same as on the two previous charts, by the way. Notice that this is also a Big *W* except that the right side failed to rise far enough to reach E, the top of the *W*.

The trend starts at G for a short-term trend. Score: +1.

There is no flat base. Score: –1. Total: 0.

There is no horizontal consolidation region in the way of price climbing. That is good news. Score: +1. Total: +1.

The breakout price (C) is within a third of the yearly high. Score: 0. Total: +1.

The double bottom is short. Score: –1. Total: 0.

Volume trends upward (J). Score: –1. Total: –1.

Breakout day (D) volume is low. Score: –1. Total: –2.

Price breaks out at D and throws back to F. Score: –1. Total: –3.

There is no breakout day gap. Score: –1. Total: –4.

The stock is a small cap. Score: +1. Final total: –3.

The stock climbed to the ultimate high at K before closing below the bottom of the chart pattern. The rise from D to K measured just 5 percent, in line with the scoring system suggesting that this pattern would underperform.

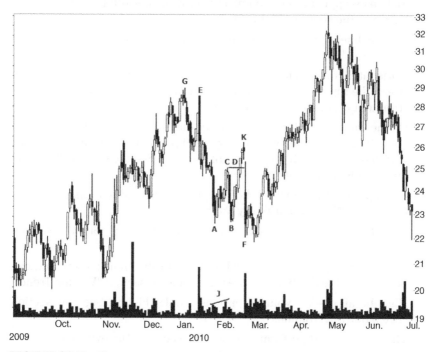

FIGURE 20.5 The scoring system predicted this stock would not do well, and it lived up to expectations.

CHAPTER CHECKLIST

Not all of your chart pattern trades using the scoring system will work as well as the case studies. However, if you add this system to your technical toolbox, you will find that it helps predict when a stock will outperform (compared to the median performance) and when it will not.

Here is a checklist of the things we learned in this chapter.

☐ To increase the odds of success, simplify your trading rules. See this chapter's introduction.

☐ A consolidation double bottom acts as a continuation of the upward price trend, not as a reversal. See the section "What Is a Double Bottom?"

☐ Wait for confirmation—price to close above the peak between the two bottoms—before buying. See the section "Double Bottom Reversals."

☐ The trend start is either the highest high *before* which price drops at least 20 percent or the lowest low *before* which price rises at least 20 percent. See the section "Trend Start."

☐ Flat bases appear as horizontal price movements, often several months long. See the section "Flat Base."

☐ Use the linear price scale when hunting for flat bases. See the section "Flat Base."

☐ Horizontal consolidation regions are overhead resistance located between the top of the chart pattern and the trend start. See the section "Horizontal Consolidation Regions."

☐ On the way to the ultimate high, price either never rises to a horizontal consolidation region (which happens 9 percent of the time) or stops within 5 percent of it 50 percent of the time. See the section "Horizontal Consolidation Regions."

☐ Chart patterns within a third of the yearly low tend to outperform. See the section "Position in Yearly Range."

☐ Tall chart patterns perform better than short ones. See the section "Height."

☐ Volume often trends downward throughout the chart pattern and can be very low the day before a breakout. See the section "Volume Trend."

☐ High breakout-day volume propels stocks higher. See the section "Breakout-Day Volume."

☐ Throwbacks hurt performance. See the section "Throwbacks."

☐ Breakout-day gaps mean traders are excited about the stock, helping to push price higher. See the section "Breakout Day Gaps."

☐ Small caps perform best; large caps perform worst. See the section "Market Cap."

☐ For a scoring system checklist, see Table 20.1.

☐ Table 20.2 shows the statistical results of the scoring system for chart patterns.

☐ Chart patterns with scores above 0 outperform those with scores below 0. See Table 20.2.

☐ The higher the total score the better performance tends to be. See Table 20.3.

CHAPTER 21

Three Winning Trades and a Funeral

M y ideal discretionary position trade begins with some type of bottom reversal, like a double bottom or head-and-shoulders bottom. Price launches into the sky like a rocket. It climbs and climbs until it cannot climb any higher. Then another reversal pattern forms in the shape of a double top or head-and-shoulders top, signaling an end to the up move.

Is discretionary position trading like that? No.

An actual position trade begins when the seas are calm and you are searching and waiting for the perfect entry, when all of the signals align and say buy. After buying, things grow tense, especially at the start. Colors that were vivid, even crisp just yesterday feel muted today, like storm clouds hiding the sun. The worrying begins.

"Will the stock continue moving higher? Will I miss the exit signal?" are questions asked, hoping to find the right answers at the right time.

Months later, after worry about the liftoff subsides, something in your mind wakes up and a voice speaks to you. "It's time to sell," it says. If you are smart, you will listen to that voice because it is the voice of experience. It is right more often than not. So you sell, and the cycle begins again.

I can teach you when to buy because the entry signals are easy, but a millisecond after you put your money down things get hairy. After 30 years in the markets, I still have not figured out which trades will work and which ones will not.

This chapter dissects three winning trades to learn the lessons they have to offer, but first I discuss my inner voice. The next chapter focuses on losing trades.

THE INTEL FIASCO

Speaking of the inner voice, I am reminded of a day trade I made in Intel on January 16, 2008. After the close on the 15th, the company announced earnings that were worse than expected, so I decided to short 2,000 shares when the market opened the next day.

Before going to bed, I placed the trade with my broker, but then could not sleep. Something was bothering me. I tossed and turned, but was it a chew toy my dog left buried under the covers that was keeping me awake?

No. The voice inside my head was telling me something. I got up and cut the position size to 1,000 shares because I did not have much luck trading large positions in recent days.

The next morning, I searched for news that would uncover a flaw in my analysis. Everything seemed fine. I expected the stock would gap lower and close down even more.

When the market opened, the stock tanked as I expected, but instead of continuing down, it barely budged during the first minute. That was when I planned to exit—in the first minute. Analysis showed that holding longer meant a higher risk of the stock bouncing.

Nothing happened. Sometimes the drop takes two to four minutes before it occurs, so I decided to hold on.

In seconds, price shot from 20.05 to 20.18. The sudden move and extent surprised me. As quick as I could, I closed out the short for a small loss. Then I did something stupid.

I bought the stock (long).

I received a fill at 20.37, just 2 cents below the day's high. Uh-oh.

The down move I originally predicted finally came. It was not a skydiver plunge, but more like water traveling down rapids. Price broke though 20 then pulled back to 19.98 where I sold, before heading south to a low of 19.70. Eventually the stock recovered to close down 12 percent from the prior day.

I lost $550 on the two trades in 30 minutes. If I continued to lose that kind of money every 30 minutes for a trading year, I would be down $929,500. In other words, we are talking real money despite the modest loss.

The good news about this trade was the second exit. I sold the stock on the pullback, near my $20 mental stop price. I was also right on the direction—down—but the upward bounce surprised me.

Fortunately, I listened to the voice that told me to cut the position size in half, to 1,000 shares. How do I teach that? How do I give you the voice of experience?

- Discretionary trading means developing an inner voice and obeying it.
- It also helps if you are lucky.

HUDSON HIGHLAND HICCUP

Figure 21.1 shows a trade I made in Hudson Highland Group (HHGP) on the daily chart. I begin most trades by seeing a stock make a move that interests me. In this case, it was a head-and-shoulders bottom chart pattern. LS marks the left shoulder and RS marks the right one. Between the two shoulders is the head that drops below the other two. The two shoulders bottom near the same price and are near the same distance from the head. The head low is not too far from the two shoulder lows. In other words, the chart pattern looks like an upside down human torso, not a mutant.

The traditional buy signal occurs when price closes above the neckline. The neckline is a line connecting the two armpits (see Figure 21.1). When the neckline slopes upward, I use a close above the right armpit high as the buy signal because price might not hit a steep up-sloping neckline. This neckline slopes downward. I show the traditional buy signal near point B on the chart.

Notes to the trade says the score was –1 (see Chapter 20, "Ten Factors Make Chart Patterns Work"), suggesting mild underperformance with a target of 9.11 based on the median rise of 29 percent for all head-and-shoulder bottoms.

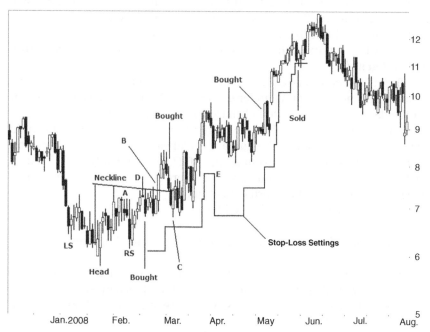

FIGURE 21.1 Trades in Hudson Highland Group begin with a head-and-shoulders bottom and end when price hits a stop-loss order.

Overhead resistance began at 8 (you can see part of it on the far left of the chart, in December 2007) with more at 12 to 13, so those would be areas of concern where price might reverse.

The company announced earnings about a week earlier, meaning earnings would not be an issue for another three months (I do not buy within three weeks before an earnings announcement—too risky).

Flipping to the weekly scale, I checked other stocks in the same industry and found that eight were hitting bottom and had begun to turn up (good) with four still continuing lower. Nearly all of them were in stage 4 declines (not good). If that does not ring a bell then reread the section, "The Weinstein Setup," in Chapter 16.

On the monthly scale, several stocks were resting on long-term trendlines (support). All of this suggested that the market had bottomed, but I was not taking any chances. I cut my position size to ¼ of normal.

I made note of a "solid block of congestion," which sounds like some type of nasal condition, but it refers to the horizontal price movement at point A. I felt that the area marked by a flat top at 7.25 would support price, but it extended down to 6.50. As the chart shows, this region did support price since it dropped only as low as C.

The general market was weak, having started a bear market on October 11, 2007, but no one would know about that until the S&P 500 index had dropped 20 percent, which it did in July 2008, well after I sold the stock. I felt the stock would throw back to the breakout price, helped by the outgoing tide of a falling market. The throwback occurred and ended at C.

To find the entry price, I computed the 38 percent retrace of the move from the low at the right shoulder to the high at D and placed a limit order for the day to buy at 7.06. On February 15, I bought the stock.

If you look at a chart showing more of the price action (not shown in Figure 21.1), it shows that I bought a reversal pattern just as the stock bottomed after trending down from a high of 22.55 in mid July 2007. Finding such a bargain is like shopping at a sale where the merchandise is marked down 69 percent. In other words, great timing.

Here is a recap of what I looked for.

- A head-and-shoulders reversal marked the change from trending down to up.
- A score of –1 suggested caution, but a rise to 9.11 if the stock performed as well as the median head-and-shoulders pattern.
- Overhead resistance began at 8, with more at 12 to 13—both potential reversal targets.
- Earnings were announced a week before the trade, so earnings were not a concern.

- 8 of 12 stocks in the industry were turning higher.
- Position size cut to ¼ normal due to a weak general market.
- The day before buying (point D), price climbed above a support area (A).
- A 38 percent Fibonacci retrace of the move up from the right shoulder to D set a buy price of 7.06.

Buy More

The chart shows where I bought the stock in mid-February (the day after D, not the later buy points), before the traditional neckline pierce because I felt comfortable with the technical indications discussed above.

I placed an initial stop at 6.05, shown by the jagged line that looks like a staircase pulled from the set of a horror movie.

On February 27, I made note that insiders were buying the stock: ". . . a ton of it in the last month," I wrote. A day later, I raised the stop to 6.60 as price climbed away from the congestion area.

The next day, I doubled my position when price approached the congestion area to the right of D. I felt the area would support price, so the risk of failure was small.

The stock moved sideways before heading up again. I raised the stop twice in quick succession.

On April 1, I did something unusual. I placed a limit order to buy the stock at 8.40 and *lowered* the stop. I show that on the chart at E. In my trading notebook, I noted, "I feel the stop is too close, and I want this trade to be a long-term holding. The new stop is below a support line at 6.80." That support line matches the low at C, but extending back to the day I bought.

A week later, I made a mistake. I day traded the entry to another ¼ position, but forgot that I had an outstanding limit order to buy the stock, which also triggered. The two buys nearly doubled my position, which started at ¼ of normal, but was now fully funded.

I felt that the stock would complete its rounding turn and push higher. The rounding turn is a reference to a bowl-shaped move that began off the left of the chart in November 2007. It is irregular in shape, but price tends to pause at or near the bowl lip, which is between 9 and 10 on the chart.

I raised the stop again on April 19 when price seemed to be moving out of the congestion area.

Ten days later, I placed a buy stop for another ¼ position that hit on May 1. I raised the stop to just below the round number 8. That purchase marked the end of the buying spree.

As price climbed, I raised the stop as the jagged line shows. Sometimes I used a volatility stop to determine the price; at other times, I tucked it below a minor low.

Notice the vertical distance between the stop and the day's low price. In April, the stop was far away, but as price climbed, I narrowed the distance. On May 21, with the stock near 12, I narrowed the distance even more to limit the giveback. Why? Because price dropped 5 percent in one day, in concert with a large drop in the general market. That swift move down made me nervous so I tightened the stop, expecting it to hit, but hoping it would not.

The stock sold a day later.

I made between 15 and 55 percent on the various trades, with an overall gain that averaged 33 percent in two months. I sold about two weeks before the stock peaked. Ten months later, with the bear market in full swing, the stock was trading below $1.

- A stop-loss order closed out the trade automatically.

CNO FINANCIAL GROUP

The next trade (**Figure 21.2**, daily scale) is simpler than the last one and it makes more money. The trade begins by noticing a symmetrical triangle

FIGURE 21.2 A retrace of the move from D to A signaled a buy with an exit after the stock gapped up.

forming on July 17 (point E), about a week before the breakout. What action did I take? I logged the chart pattern into my computer and moved on to the next chart!

At point D, the company made a Form 8-K disclosure announcing the preliminary financial results for the quarter ended June 30. The stock gapped higher on the news, quickly rising to A, a climb of 111 percent. Such a quick rise (a double in less than two months) qualifies it as a high-and-tight flag, but I missed that chart pattern and probably would not have cared anyway. High-and-tight flags can mean another rise averaging 27 percent, but have a high failure rate (14 percent breakout downward and 19 percent fail to rise at least 5 percent after the breakout, for a combined failure rate of 33 percent).

When the company released final financial results after the close on August 4, point A, traders had already factored in the news and the stock eased lower, forming a pennant or the flag portion of the high-and-tight flag (the flag portion often takes any shape it darn well pleases).

I became interested in the stock when it retraced 38 percent of the move from D to A. I show the retrace options (38 percent, 50 percent, and 62 percent) as three horizontal lines on Figure 21.2. Price has a tendency to reverse at those three locations, or so traders believe. Those types of beliefs can become self-fulfilling prophecies if enough trade it.

Since the company just released earnings, I did not have to worry about that for another three months.

Overhead resistance shown on the long-term chart was at 10, 17, and 20. Near-term resistance was at 4, 5, and 8, set up by recent peaks.

A volatility stop calculation suggested placement at 2.57, or 23 percent below the close on August 13. A volatility stop warns that placing a stop closer risks being stopped out on normal price movement. The large potential drop (23 percent) to the stop told me that the risk of a large loss loomed if I wanted to trade this stock. I would not use a stop because doing so on such a highly volatile stock increased the risk of being stopped out prematurely.

Scoring the chart pattern (the symmetrical triangle) using the generic system showed the pattern had a +6 score with a 2.44 target based on a median rise for symmetrical triangles of 28 percent. With the stock sitting at 3.33, the scoring system had already fulfilled its promise for the triangle.

I bought the stock at 3.33 on August 14, just 4 cents below the high for the day.

The stock plunged the next day to the low at C, a stomach-churning drop of 16 percent below my buy price. Having a sensibly placed stop (like 8 percent) would have cashed me out of the trade before it had a chance to work.

The stock began to recover immediately, but I did not give it much attention. I was hoping it would climb to 20, but would settle for 8, and that meant more than a double from my purchase price. That could take a year or more (but in one week I made 111 percent in the same stock back in early May, so you never know).

- Buy when the stock retraces 38 percent of the prior up move.

That's a Wrap

On October 14, point F in the figure, Moody's changed the outlook for the company from negative to positive and a broker upgraded the stock while raising its target price from 4 to 9.

When someone hands me 29 percent more money, I grab the wad and run to the bank. On the technical side, the stock made an event pattern that I call an inverted dead-cat bounce. In that event pattern, the stock typically gaps up and then eases lower.

That is what I expected to happen despite the broker calling for a rise to 9. I also found a potential double top (points F and G) or 2B pattern. Victor Sperandeo (Wiley, 1991) coined the 2B Rule. The 2B name comes from an exception to step two of his three steps for detecting a change in the price trend (for more information, refer to *Trading Basics*, Chapter 5, "Timing the Exit: The 2B Rule" and (this book) Chapter 16, "1-2-3 Trend Change for Up/Down Trends").

The 2B rule describes how price may climb a bit higher or fall just short of a prior high, but when it stalls, it suggests a short-term reversal. The stock may or may not drop far, but it does indicate weakness, and it is a good opportunity to take profits.

The final sell kicker came from the company. They started making noises about issuing more shares. When a company issues shares, the stock takes a hit since it dilutes the value of existing shares. I did not want any part of that.

I sold the stock the next day at the market open and received a fill at 6.35, making 90 percent in two months. I missed selling at the yearly high by one day. On February 5, 2010, the stock bottomed at 4.18, 35 percent below the buy price and well below the $9 broker target.

- Sell when the stock jumps 29 percent, placing it at the price level of a prior high, and the company suggests they would issue new shares.

COMPLETE PRODUCTION SERVICES

Chart pattern recognition is an art, despite automated tools for finding them. **Figure 21.3** (daily scale) is an example. Points A and B show two peaks near the same price level with a drop to C between them. Point C is 28 percent below the higher of the two peaks (B), which places it outside the typical range of 10 to 20 percent needed to qualify as a double-top chart pattern. It means the decline is a significant one, but at these low prices, any drop can become a huge percentage move.

At D, the twin-peak pattern becomes a true double top when price closes below the confirmation line. The confirmation line extends from the lowest valley between the two peaks. Price must close below this price level to become a valid double top, which it does.

What happens next? After a skydiver plunge of 36 percent from B to D, the body hits the earth and bounces. Perhaps some traders expected a bounce, given the strength of the decline, but for those shorting the stock at D, expecting a further drop, they were surprised to see the stock recover. It eased higher over the coming weeks to close above the top of the chart pattern at E.

That is when I got interested.

I show a horizontal line from A to E along price tops, and if you draw another one from C to D, it would outline a chart pattern called a broadening formation, right-angled, and descending. A partial decline at G suggests an immediate upward breakout when it touches the top trend line, which is

FIGURE 21.3 The stock busts a double top, signaling a purchase.

what happened. Point F is a throwback to the breakout price. Throwbacks happen 52 percent in these types of broadening formations.

Points A, B, and E are three tops in a row. Is this a triple top? No. Why? Because price never confirms the chart pattern by closing below the lowest valley between the three tops.

The double top did confirm, so it is a valid chart pattern and so is the broadening formation. Instead of those two patterns, I interpreted the price movement as a busted double top. That means price did not drop very far after confirmation before reversing course and closing above the top of the chart pattern. When a busted pattern occurs, it often—but not always— means a powerful move.

Fundamental analysis said the stock was a middling value play. The important ratios were all over the place like balls after the opening shot on a billiards table. Insiders were buying the stock for a year, but only one was snatching lots of it.

I bought the stock three days after the pattern busted, receiving a fill at $9 even. Notice that I was not buying the stock when it was cheap. The stock bottomed at J (far left), which is also at the bottom of the bear market. I did not buy then because there was no reason to (no chart patterns formed except a V-shaped turn, which is difficult to trade and easily recognized only in hindsight).

The drop from H to I measured 31 percent, and yet I held onto the stock. My target was 21 to 25, and that meant it was a long-term holding. With buy-and-hold positions, I rarely use a stop unless I am nervous about the market changing from bull to bear.

- Entry on busted-double-top chart pattern.
- Insiders are buying, none selling.

The Exit

Figure 21.4 (daily scale) shows how the trade progressed. Notice the potential double top at D and E with the valley between them bottoming at F. It is not a double top since price at G fails to close below the low at F and closes above the top of the chart pattern, near H. As the chart shows, the stock makes a toboggan-style run downhill.

When price bottomed at I, I wrote in my notebook, "I think this will find support at an up-sloping trend line (not shown) connecting the 8/5/2009 low. The company sees some firming in demand, but says it will remain weak. This has already dropped 30 percent, and I missed it [selling sooner]. Sigh. I can see this dropping back to 9, giving back all of my gains and returning to the November 2009 launch price. Even so, it will find support and, in the coming year, I think this will recover. Also, I expect this to form

FIGURE 21.4 After a good earnings surprise, it was time to sell the stock.

a right shoulder mirroring the October 2009 peak. That would see a recovery to about 12.50."

In other words, I was concerned with the volatility shown by the stock, by the large swings, and that it could move lower.

A month later, I placed a stop at 10.78, which is a nickel below the low at I. The horizontal stop line I show on the chart and the length of it shows how long I left it active. I reminded myself that this was a long-term holding and using a stop may limit losses, but it also takes you out of potential winners.

Things changed in early July when I found that the five indices I follow began trading below the 12-month simple moving average. On July 6, I placed a stop at 13.33, below the minor low at J.

It is difficult to see on the chart, but I raised the stop a day later then lowered it to below the symmetrical triangle trend line to "give this one room to play," as I wrote in my notebook, and then trailed it higher after the close each day, placing it a few pennies below the day's low.

The stock closed above the top of the triangle signaling an upward breakout, so I canceled the stop on July 13th to let price run.

Then the company announced earnings that were better than expected. At the open the next day, the stock gapped higher (point A) and continued to move up until peaking at C. A day later, the stock opened high, but closed almost a dollar lower. Time to sell. This is another example of taking profit after an inverted dead-cat bounce. In my notebook, I wrote, "The stock gapped up and now it is going to retrace its gains. I am taking the money and running. I can buy back in when it hits 16 if I want."

I received a fill at 18.98 for a gain of 110 percent in slightly less than a year.

- Sold after surprisingly good earnings formed an inverted dead-cat bounce.

Review the two figures. The drop from H to I in both figures measured over 30 percent each. The potholes on the road to doubling my money were filled with luck, helped by a rising market, and surprisingly good earnings. The stock slid back to 16, just as I predicted.

I include this trade not as a template for how to position trade, but as a lesson that sometimes you can do very well just by having good luck. I doubled my money despite seeing drawdowns of over 30 percent—twice—during the trade. A year later, the stock hit a high of 42.62. If you think a hemorrhoid is a pain in the butt, think about missing that kind of a run.

CHAPTER CHECKLIST

Here are some of the lessons and trading signals discussed in this chapter.

- ☐ Discretionary trading means developing an inner voice and obeying it. See the section "The Intel Fiasco."
- ☐ A head-and-shoulders bottom marked the entry into the Hudson Highland trade with a stop loss closing it out. See the section "Hudson Highland Hiccup."
- ☐ A buy in CNO Financial began when price retraced 38 percent of the prior up move, and ended with an inverted dead-cat bounce chart pattern. See the section "CNO Financial Group."
- ☐ A trade in Complete Production Services began with a busted double top and insider buying, and ended with another inverted dead-cat bounce. See the section "Complete Production Services."

CHAPTER 22

What Not to Do: Three Botched Trades

I have read often enough that you can learn more from your failures than your successes. Thanks for that tip, but I would rather learn from my successes because it is more profitable! I make mistakes in either type of trade, so there are plenty of opportunities to learn.

If you read the last chapter, it may seem that making money position trading is easy. You just buy any chart pattern and hold the stock until it is time to sell. The next three trades show how dangerous that assumption can be. One trade highlights selling too late, one sells too soon, and the last one really screws up. Yes, I try to cover all of the territory.

MEDIVATION: SELLING TOO LATE

If you own stocks long enough, you may get hammered by the dead-cat bounce (DCB). I will discuss the event pattern in the section on swing trading (Swing and Day Trading, Chapter 5, "Event Pattern Setups"), but a position in Medivation (MDVN), shown in **Figure 22.1** (daily scale), is an example. I exited 12 trades in my career because of DCBs and rode the rollercoaster waves of many more.

DCBs are not a fun chart pattern because each entails a loss of between 15 and 70 percent in one session, and that is just the start. Once the bounce ends, the decline begins. If earnings are involved, one DCB sometimes follows another in three months.

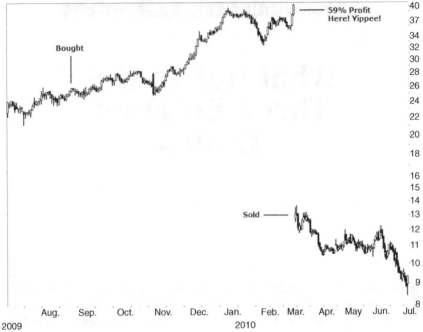

FIGURE 22.1 Failure of a drug in clinical trials amputates 67 percent of the stock's price in one session.

The Medivation trade was a risky biotech play, so I knew the dangers involved before I took a position. By buying the stock, I was betting that the company would get approval of their Dimebon drug by the FDA in 2011. Here are some background milestones related to buying the stock, according to the company's website.

- April 2008: Alzheimer's patients showed improved thinking and memory over a one-year period after taking Dimebon. The results of the first phase 3 trial in 183 patients were successful.
- June 2008: Begins second phase 3 trial of Dimebon with 525 patients.
- July 2008: Announces positive results from phase 2 Dimebon study for Huntington's disease.
- September 2008: Company announces it is partnering with Pfizer to co-develop Dimebon for Alzheimer's and Huntington's disease.
- April 2009: Begins 12-month phase 3 trial of Dimebon with Donepezil for Alzheimer's disease.
- July 2009: Begins phase 3 trial of Dimebon for Huntington's disease.

Based on the events shown and other research, it seemed that the company had a winning Alzheimer's drug. It passed one phase 3 trial and was promising enough that Pfizer decided to add the drug to its payroll.

My notebook has the following entry. "7/11/09. This stock seems priced for perfection. Has $200M in the bank (cash, most recent quarter) with quarterly revenues of $28.92M, current ratio of 2.595, $11K debt, cash/share of $6.66. Revenue may be due to Pfizer deal, because prior years had no revenues. Last year cost $62m, so they have more than three years of cash on hand at current spending."

The cash on hand is most important for startups. How long can a company continue if it is burning cash? That is called the burn rate, and it is worth finding out. If the company blows through cash like my neighbor spends on water drowning his lawn each summer, then they will need additional financing. That means selling stock (often private placements), and a hit to the stock's price.

I bought a small position in the stock on August 21, 2009, and received a fill at 25.54 as Figure 22.1 shows. In my notes for the purchase, I wrote, "Buy reason: Long-term play on drug prospects. Must hold until approval in 2011. Short term, breakout of congestion area in August 2009. Has Dimebon in phase 3 trial in patients with mild to moderate Alzheimer's disease and is in phase 3 clinical trials in patients with Huntington's disease (as of July 2009). This is an orphan drug trial for Huntington's that will last six months. The Alzheimer's study is to last 1 year."

The stock continued moving higher except for October when the general market stumbled. After that, though, it resumed plodding upward like ants rebuilding a mound after a rainstorm.

On the stock chart that I look at each day, I placed a note that said, "Sees FDA approval in 2011." I forgot that the company had to finish the drug trials first before filing with the FDA. That meant another hurdle for the company to jump over. However, with positive results logged so far, both the Street and I thought the company had a winning drug. On March 2, 2010, (the day before the big plunge), my profit was almost 60 percent.

- Biotech plays are bets that the stock's price will rise by a multiple or suffer a massive drop. Invest only a small portion of your portfolio or skip them altogether.

Emergency Room

The next day the company announced that Dimebon had failed the second set of phase 3 trials. The stock gaped open lower a heart-stopping 68 percent! Three-hundred Joules. Clear!

After using the paddles to restart my heart, I pulled the plug on the corpse the same day and sold the thing, receiving a fill of 13.33. Instead of a 60 percent winner, I lost 48 percent. Fortunately, I held a small position, so even though the percentage loss was huge, it represented a minor dollar hit.

The rose-tinted glasses worn by the person who bought my stock hid the blood smeared all over the patient. The stock continued declining until reaching a low of 8.43, an additional drop of 37 percent.

- If a stock makes a massive drop (a so-called dead-cat bounce), sell as quickly as you can.

COLDWATER CREEK: SELLING TOO SOON

Figure 22.2 shows a trade in Coldwater Creek (CWTR) on the daily scale. Here is what I wrote in my notebook about the stock on 4/17/2009. "Small cap growth, rated hold by S&P, high risk. $276M market cap, beta 2.5. Insiders like the stock. Four bought since December with three of them buying in March from 11K to 100K shares. Ford says sell. Has not made money since January 2008 when book value stood at 3.38. Return on equity is negative. Ratios are at bottom of scale except for price to earnings, which is not meaningful. Not a compelling value play, but I do like the insider buying. This is showing an ugly double bottom with a potential to move higher."

If you pick any stock chart and look at every major turn from down to up, most will show higher lows and higher highs. The name for that turning pattern is an ugly double bottom if price separates the two bottoms by at least 5 percent.

I do not show the left bottom in Figure 22.2, but it happens in November 2008 at 91 cents. The second bottom is at B, 1.42. A close above the peak between those two bottoms confirms the ugly double bottom as a valid chart pattern.

About a week after completing analysis of the stock, price broke out of a small, flat-topped, congestion region (circled). I bought the next day and received a fill of 3.14. The buy point appears on the chart.

On 4/30, I doubled my position (combined it was still ¼ of normal since it was not clear the bear market had ended, which it did in March 2009) because the stock had broken through overhead resistance from December to February (shown by the horizontal line).

Here is a short review of the buy reasons.

- Ugly double bottom on entry with breakout from a small congestion area.

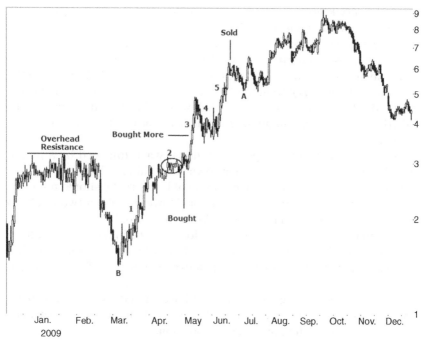

FIGURE 22.2 Exiting the trade too soon leaves profit behind.

- The general market completed the bear market and turned bullish.
- Fundamentals were weak.
- Insiders were buying.

Psst. Time to Exit

I rode the stock higher, but in June price neared overhead resistance set up by prior peaks starting in February 2008 and valleys from June to August 2008. Both centered near $6.

Here is what I wrote for the exit. "6/11/09. I am placing a day order, stop order at 5.73, two cents below the prior candle's low, because this is in stage 5 (Elliott wave), and I expect an ABC correction. Overhead resistance is coming. If the strong uptrend continues, then I will trail the stop upward, otherwise, it will take me out for a nice gain.

"This was stopped out at 5.76. Oops. I expected this to continue rising in a strong up trend, but it reversed. I guess that is what the stop was there for. If this continues down, it will be a brilliant move, but my guess is it was a mistake. Plus, I gave up some profit by not selling closer to the high. I feel as if selling was a mistake."

Since every Elliott wave can have an extension, I am not a lover of Elliott wave. It is too subjective. Nevertheless, I show what I thought were the five waves on the chart. Advancing waves 1, 3, and 5 pushed the stock upward whereas countertrend waves 2 and 4 pulled it lower.

The idea behind wave counting is that five waves push the stock in the direction of the primary trend and three waves form a correction against that trend. The five-wave push can be downward followed by an upward correction, so keep that in mind. You will see that combination often in a bear market.

The ABC correction I expected (a down wave followed by a partial upward retrace followed by another down wave) did not happen.

Price peaked at 6.27 the day before I sold, so I really should not complain about missing the top. The stock eased lower for about two weeks to bottom at 5.11, a drop of 11 percent below where I sold.

My notebook entry speaks of indecision, that the inner voice may have whispered, "sell," but changed its mind just after I sold. I hate it when that happens! As the chart shows, the stock moved sideways before peaking at 9.20.

If I had perfect timing, I could almost have tripled my money. Instead, I made 83 percent on the first trade and 61 percent on the second. That is a good return for a botched trade. I sold too soon.

- A tight stop forced an exit too soon.

HOVNANIAN: SELLING AT THE BOTTOM

This trade is representative of many that I have made, and if you have traded often enough, you will run across these types of trades, too. If you are into a losing trade and it is well past the proper sell point, you will suspect that:

1. If you do not sell, the stock will continue down.
2. If you do sell, you will be selling within a week or two of the bottom.

In other words, regardless of what you do, you are screwed. Even if you sell sooner, the 1–2 combination will apply, so you might as well sell sooner and save more money. Let me give you an example of what I mean using Hovnanian (HOV), shown on the daily scale in **Figure 22.3**.

The bear market officially ended in March 2009, but I did not know it at the time. However, the housing stocks seemed to be perking up. I wrote in my notebook: "4/25/09. Debt is high, at 88 percent of market cap. S&P

FIGURE 22.3   Bad timing marked this trade.

says hold but high risk. Insiders are buying. Ford says sell. Price to book is pegged high at 5.74. Price-to-sales ratio is 0.05, almost at lowest. Price/value is mid range exactly. Other financial ratios are not meaningful. New homes sales seem to have bottomed, according to one Associated Press report on 4/24. S&P debt rating agency calls this stock a high risk, 'acknowledging the potential for additional defaults in the near term' among homebuilders."

Looking at support and resistance, I determined a near-term upside target of 6, with a buy-and-hold target of 25. Overhead resistance appeared at about 4.50. I base those targets on prior minor highs, lows, or horizontal consolidation regions. On the weekly scale, I saw additional resistance at 13 and then 33.

Quarterly earnings were set for June 10, about six weeks away, too distant to be of concern.

Using the Stan Weinstein method of determining a buy, price entered stage 2 (see the section in Chapter 16, "The Weinstein Setup" for details). Stage 2 is the time to be in the stock. It means price has climbed above the 30-week simple moving average on high volume and the sky is the limit.

Here is a note of caution. I checked three indicators: RSI, CCI, and BBs. The relative strength index (RSI) was overbought on 4/27, the commodity channel index (CCI) said buy three days ago, and the stock was poking out the top of the Bollinger bands (BBs). I wrote in my trading notebook, "These suggest a drop in price."

Since the price trend could have been a bull market rally in a bear market, and coupled with my amazing ability to lose money on nearly every housing stock I have ever bought, I cut my position size even more, to 1/8 of normal.

I bought on April 28, receiving a fill at 2.74, and placed a stop at 1.39. A volatility stop was at 1.68 or 37.6 percent below the prior close, which suggests a highly volatile stock. With a buy price of 2.74 and a stop about half that, it is almost like having no stop at all. Why did I bother?

Notes from the purchase are: "Buy reason: Breakout from a congestion zone, rounding turn. On the intraday chart, this has formed a rising wedge in the last few minutes, suggesting a drop in price, but only to 2.63 from 2.69. I am just going to buy at the open and pray. With 25 percent of float short, as of March, this could be a nice short squeeze play, if it has not already happened. But this is high risk. They could have a liquidity crisis and with earnings coming out from other homebuilders next month (first week in May), this may get whacked then."

I show the rounded turn at A, although it is not exactly smooth. The congestion area I spoke of is a loose one circled at B.

- The stock was above the 30-week moving average on high volume.
- Breakout from a congestion area after a rounding turn suggested higher prices ahead.
- RSI and Bollinger bands warned of an overbought state. CCI said go for it, dude!
- Earnings season would begin in a month and if the reports were weak, the stock would likely drop.

Checkout Time

The stock did not cooperate since it dropped for three days after I bought before launching to a new high. Looking at the price action throughout May and into June shows that the stock went sideways to down slightly. That is fine. That happens when a stock gathers strength to make another run at the summit. If you look at a chart of the S&P during 2009, you will see that the general market moved sideways to down during the same period (and into July). I was not concerned.

Things started to take a turn for the worst when the company announced earnings on June 2. Yes, the stock made a nice move up that day (point E on the chart), breaking out upward from a symmetrical triangle, but then dove back under cover.

Two days later, a brokerage house increased earnings estimates, but warned that a higher stock price would depend on the overall housing market. The stock seemed to ignore the good news. Two trading days later, another broker downgraded the stock. Price opened lower and did not recover that day.

On the downgrade day, price busted the triangle (an upward breakout followed by a downward one) and that often means a strong move ahead . . . except for symmetrical triangles. Those have a nasty habit of double busting. That means price will breakout upward then downward, only to resume moving upward as the final direction.

As the chart shows, this stock did not double bust. It just kept tumbling.

Which broker do you believe, the one that raised estimates or the other that cut its rating on the stock? Price shows how traders answered that question by heading lower during the move from E to C.

I became concerned when price closed below the support area shown at C. Those tails (lower shadows on the candles) bottoming near the same price looked like someone's comb. I reasoned that since the stock had pierced that support area, it could tumble back to the launch price, A (often price stops short of dropping that far such that you see a higher bottom). When a cheap stock has the potential to sell below $1, I get nervous. I think bankruptcy.

Having said that, many quality stocks were selling at unbelievably cheap prices after the 2007 to 2009 bear market ended.

Instead of waiting for the stock to hit my 50 percent stop-loss order, I sold it on July 8, receiving a fill of 2.03 for a loss of 27 percent in about 2.5 months.

As bad as the exit was, it would have looked brilliant had the stock continued lower to, say, 81 cents, but that is not what happened.

At D, I show a sliver of support that actually extends backward in time to December 2008. It is a horizontal consolidation region, where price bottoms near the same level, and it is also positioned in the 1.50 to 1.60 range. Of course, with the stock at $2, waiting to see if it bounces at 1.50 meant another 25 percent loss, something I was unwilling to risk.

As the chart shows, the stock surprised me and two days after I sold, the blasted thing took off in a straight-line run to the stars, leaving me back on the ground watching it soar with a 27 percent hole in my wallet.

- Do not trade an industry (like housing) if you have had difficulty making money trading it before.
- Sometimes a broker gets it right.

CHAPTER CHECKLIST

Here are some lessons I learned from these trades.

- ☐ Invest only a small portion of your portfolio in high-risk, high-reward trades. See the section "Medivation: Selling Too Late."
- ☐ If a stock makes a massive drop (a so-called dead-cat bounce), sell as quickly as you can. See the section "Medivation: Selling Too Late."
- ☐ Insider buying and an ugly double bottom lead to purchasing Coldwater Creek, but a tight stop forced an exit too soon. See the section "Coldwater Creek: Selling Too Soon."
- ☐ Hovnanian looked like a buy since the stock was trading above the 30-week simple moving average on high volume after breaking out of a congestion area. Two indicators warned of trouble ahead. See the section "Hovnanian: Selling at the Bottom."
- ☐ Do not trade an industry (like housing) if you have had difficulty making money trading it before. See the section "Hovnanian: Selling at the Bottom."

CHAPTER 23

What We Learned

This book focused on buy and hold (value investing) and position trading. Those two styles are complementary since knowing when to exit a long-term holding is often the key to making and keeping money when investing in the stock market.

This chapter lists all of the discoveries I shared with you in these pages, sorted by chapter.

CHAPTER 2: STOCK SELECTION

☐ See this chapter's introduction for criteria I use to select stocks.

☐ Stocks that double substantially outperform the following year 53 percent of the time. See the section "What Comes After Large Price Moves?"

☐ Stocks that drop 50 percent or more outperform the following year 68 percent of the time. See the section "What Comes After Large Price Moves?"

☐ Stocks that drop most in a bear market bounce higher one year after the bear market ends. Stocks that drop least perform worse. See Table 2.1

☐ Pick stocks of companies that you know and like. See the section "Stock Selection the Easy Way."

☐ Check for poor earnings or earnings warnings in other stocks in the same industry. See the section "Two Tips for Stock Selection."

☐ Check for rating upgrades or downgrades of other stocks in the industry. See the section "Two Tips for Stock Selection."

☐ Select quality stocks beaten down in price but with solid prospects. See the section "Buy Fallen Angels."

☐ Spin-offs can represent a good opportunity to buy an established company with management motivated to succeed. See the section "Buy Fallen Angels."

☐ The chart pattern found most often before a merger announcement is a double bottom. See Table 2.2.

☐ Stocks trend higher 63 percent of the time before a merger or buyout announcement. See the section "Overpaying?"

☐ Look for many different insiders buying a ton of stock when price is low, with few selling, but selling small amounts is fine. Does the buying appear regularly, as if on a schedule? If so, that is not as good as insiders buying value at a low price. See the section "What Are Insiders Doing?"

CHAPTER 3: BOOK VALUE

☐ Book value is net worth minus preferred stock divided by common shares outstanding. See the section "Book Value Defined."

☐ Book value can be unreliable when the value of intangible assets is inflated. See the section "Value Assets Properly."

☐ Book value is not the same as market value. See the section "Investing Using Book Value."

☐ Book value is important if the company goes out of business, merges with another, or is bought for its hidden assets. See the section "When Is Book Value Important?"

☐ A company selling above book value has limited upside potential if everything goes right, but a huge downside if things go wrong. A company selling below book value has big potential when things turn around. See the section "The Value of Hidden Assets."

☐ See the section "Limits of Book Value" for a list of problems associated with relying on book value.

☐ Share buybacks can change book value. See the section "Buybacks Lower Book Value."

☐ Greater returns were achieved by companies with low book value. See Historical Research.

☐ Low price to book value won 73 percent of contests when held for three years and won all contests when held for five years. See the section "Historical Research."

☐ Stocks with low price to book value outperform in good and bad times. See the section "Historical Research."

☐ Using a low price to book value approach does not lead to greater downside risk. See the section "Historical Research."

☐ Find stocks selling below the 2.11 median price to book value. See Table 3.1.

☐ Small-cap stocks with low price to book values outperform, so consider buying stocks priced below $1 billion in market capitalization. See Table 3.2.

☐ Select stocks priced below about $16 for the best results. See Table 3.3.

☐ Stocks with a falling price to book value and a rising return on shareholders equity (ROE) result in the best performance the following year. Avoid stocks in which price to book value and ROE are both falling. See Table 3.4.

☐ Stocks with price to book values below 1.0 tend to do well. See Table 3.5.

☐ Table 3.6 lists combinations of fundamentals to limit the number of stocks qualifying and to boost performance.

☐ Annually buying the Dow's ten lowest price-to-book-value stocks remains a winning strategy. See the section "Trading Strategy: Beating the Dow."

☐ To beat the performance of the Dow industrials, buy eight Dow stocks with the lowest price to book value each year. See the section "The Eight-Stock Setup."

☐ Hold your low price-to-book-value stock for one to three years. See Table 3.8.

CHAPTER 4: CAPITAL SPENDING

☐ Capital spending is the amount of money a company spends annually to buy property, divided by the number of shares outstanding. See this chapter's introduction.

☐ When companies cut capital spending, their stocks tend to outperform the next year, but the improvement only applies to half of the stocks. See Table 4.1.

- ☐ Companies with capital spending decreases for two consecutive years have the best year-ahead stock performance. This method works 58 percent of the time. See Table 4.2.
- ☐ As capital spending increases, stock performance suffers. If capital spending decreases, stock performance rises. See Table 4.3.
- ☐ Invest in small-cap stocks because they show the best performance over time, especially if they cut their capital spending. See Table 4.4.

CHAPTER 5: CASH FLOW

- ☐ Free cash flow is operating cash flow minus capital expenditures. See this chapter's introduction.
- ☐ Historical research confirms that stocks with low price to cash flow outperform and are no more risky. See the section "Historical Research Review."
- ☐ Read the section "Cooking the Books" to understand how companies can manipulate financial results.
- ☐ Look for decreasing price to cash flow. See Table 5.1.
- ☐ Companies with price to cash flow per share below the median 9.17 tend to have their stocks substantially outperform up to five years later. See Table 5.2.
- ☐ The performance of small-cap stocks beat the performance of mid- and large-cap stocks. See Table 5.3.
- ☐ Price-to-cash-flow ratios below their respective median show stocks with better performance up to five years later 73 percent of the time (11 out of 15 contests). See Table 5.3.
- ☐ The best price-to-cash-flow ratio is between 1 and 2, but few companies qualify. Generally, the higher the ratio, the worse the stock's performance a year later. See Table 5.4.

CHAPTER 6: DIVIDENDS

- ☐ Dividends are a portion of the company's net earnings returned to shareholders. They can come in a variety of forms. See this chapter's introduction.
- ☐ Stocks with high yield and low payout ratios do well. See the section "Historical Research Review."

□ Dividend yield alone is not sufficient to select a stock. See the section "Historical Research Review."

□ Stocks with a high yield tend to outperform. See Table 6.1.

□ The best performance comes from stocks with a high yield and low payout ratio. See Table 6.2.

□ Owning dividend-paying stocks is better than owning stocks not paying a dividend. See Table 6.3

□ Stocks that cut their dividend rates outperform a year later, but samples are few. See Table 6.4.

□ In the year when a company cuts its dividend, expect price to drop substantially. See Table 6.4.

□ Buy stocks after they cut their dividend and price bottoms. See the section "When Disaster Strikes."

□ Stocks that pay a dividend outperform for up to five years, with small caps doing best. See Table 6.5.

CHAPTER 7: LONG-TERM DEBT

□ Long-term debt is borrowed money not due within 12 months. See this chapter's introduction.

□ Companies with no long-term debt outperform for three years. See Table 7.1.

□ Companies decreasing long-term debt levels outperformed over time. Those eliminating long-term debt also did well. See Table 7.2.

□ Companies moving from being debt-free to taking on long-term debt outperform dramatically the first year but suffer in later years. See Table 7.2.

□ Small caps do best with decreasing long-term debt loads and outperform mid- and large-cap stocks. See Table 7.3.

□ Small-cap stocks with debt outperform over time. See Table 7.4

CHAPTER 8: PRICE-TO-EARNINGS RATIO

□ The price-to-earnings ratio is the current stock's price divided by a year's worth of earnings. See this chapter's introduction.

□ For the best performance, select stocks with a P/E ratio below the median 17.1. See Table 8.1.

☐ Pick stocks with a decreasing P/E from one year to the next. See Table 8.2.

☐ Stocks from companies with a falling price and rising earnings (year to year) have the best year-ahead performance. See Table 8.3.

☐ Small caps with below median 16.0 P/E ratios outperform mid- and large-cap stocks for up to five years. See Table 8.4.

☐ If a stock's P/E ratio is above the average highs of the last three years, then consider selling. See the section "High P/E: Time to Sell?"

☐ A stock with a historically high P/E that drops to unusually low levels could represent value. See the section "Three P/E Tips."

☐ Avoid buying stocks with historically low P/Es. See the section "See Three P/E Tips."

☐ Avoid cyclical companies sliding downhill (falling P/Es). Pick them on the rebound (rising P/Es). See the section "Three P/E Tips."

CHAPTER 9: PRICE-TO-SALES RATIO

☐ The price-to-sales ratio compares the stock's current price per share by its annual sales per share. See this chapter's introduction.

☐ The market capitalization of the stock divided by its annual revenue describes how much value the market places on each sales dollar. See this chapter's introduction.

☐ Avoid companies with a low price-to-sales ratio and awful fundamentals, like too much debt. See this chapter's introduction.

☐ The average price-to-sales ratio varies by industry. See this chapter's introduction.

☐ Companies with price to sales below 1.0 tend to have stocks outperform for at least five years. See Table 9.1.

☐ Companies with a falling price-to-sales ratio from one year to the next have stocks that outperform over time. See Table 9.2.

☐ Small-cap stocks beat the other market caps and those with PSRs below 0.76 do even better. See Table 9.3.

☐ Select stocks with annual sales higher than their market capitalization. See the section "Market Cap versus Sales."

☐ Since the price-to-sales ratio can vary by industry, check the PSR in other industry-related companies to see if your stock is expensive or not. See Table 9.4.

CHAPTER 10: RETURN ON SHAREHOLDERS EQUITY

☐ Return on equity is annual net profit divided by shareholders' equity. See this chapter's introduction.

☐ Stocks with ROE below the median 13.4 percent outperform. See Table 10.1.

☐ Stocks with high ROE (over 26.8 percent) underperform those with ROE below 6.7 percent. See Table 10.1 discussion.

☐ Whether ROE increases or decreases in one year makes little difference in a stock's long-term performance. See Table 10.2.

☐ Sorted by return on equity, small caps outperform mid- and large-cap stocks. See Table 10.3.

CHAPTER 11: SHARES OUTSTANDING

☐ Shares outstanding are shares issued by a company, sold to the public, and still publicly available (not repurchased). See this chapter's introduction.

☐ The larger the share buyback, the better the performance. See Table 11.1.

☐ A Dutch auction tender offer is an auction in which the offering price is raised within a range until a fixed number of shares is acquired. See the section "Event Pattern: Dutch Auction Tender Offers."

☐ See the section "Should You Sell?" for a list of findings associated with Dutch auctions.

☐ In a Dutch auction tender offer, tendering shares at a price midway in the offering price range will succeed 75 percent of the time, on average. See Table 11.2.

☐ When a company sells more shares in a common stock offering, price gaps lower, often making a U- or J-shaped move. See the section "Event Pattern: Common Stock Offerings."

☐ See the section "Event Pattern: Common Stock Offerings" for a list of findings that may help you understand the behavior of common stock offerings.

☐ Small-cap stocks tend to outperform and do especially well if the number of shares outstanding decreases. See Table 11.3.

CHAPTER 12: FUNDAMENTAL ANALYSIS SUMMARY

☐ See the chapter for a list of fundamentals sorted by how well stocks did over one, three, and five years.

CHAPTER 13: HOW TO DOUBLE YOUR MONEY

☐ Of those stocks that doubled in five years, 63 percent took less than three years. See Table 13.1.

☐ Most doubles (63 percent) begin with a price between $5 and $20. See Table 13.2.

☐ Small-cap stocks, those worth less than $1 billion, double most often. See Table 13.3.

☐ Stocks that doubled started with low price to book values (half the time below 1.5). See Table 13.4.

☐ Capital spending decreased from the prior year in stocks that doubled. See Table 13.5.

☐ Stocks that double have low price-to-cash-flow values (63 percent below 8). See Table 13.6.

☐ To double your money, avoid stocks paying dividends. See the section "Dividends."

☐ Long-term debt is not a factor for stocks that double. See Table 13.7.

☐ Check other stocks in the same industry to see what level of long-term debt they carry and compare it to the stock you want to buy. See the section "Long-Term Debt."

☐ The most popular P/E ratio for stocks that double is between 10 and 15 with 20 coming in second. See Table 13.8.

☐ Stocks that double tend to have a lower P/E ratio in year 0 than do those failing to double. See Table 13.8.

☐ Stocks that double have low price-to-sales ratios, most below 0.75. See Table 13.9.

☐ Return on equity often ranges between 6 and 14 percent in stocks that double. The return on equity is lower than for stocks that fail to double. See Table 13.10.

☐ Shares outstanding is not a significant contributor to a stock doubling in price. See Table 13.11.

☐ Stocks that double show strong first-year performance. See Table 13.12.

☐ Stocks that double in price have a lower than normal chance of seeing price drop in half until year 4. See Table 13.12.

☐ Using the nine selection criteria boosts the chance of finding stocks that double from 26 to 67 percent. See the section "Testing the Setup."

CHAPTER 14: 10-BAGGERS

☐ Fully 41 percent of 10-baggers take five years to complete the move. See Table 14.1.

☐ Most (55 percent) 10-baggers begin their move at prices below $5. See Table 14.2.

☐ Most (59 percent) 10-baggers double in price during year 0 with a median rise of 116 percent. See Table 14.3.

☐ Year 1 is when price often moves up the most. See Table 14.4.

☐ Small caps represent 77 percent of 10-baggers. See the section "10-Bagger by Market Cap."

☐ The year before a 10-bagger starts shows that half the samples have a price to book value below 1.5. See Table 14.5.

☐ 10-baggers show decreasing capital spending in year 0 from the prior year 59 percent of the time. See Table 14.6.

☐ Many 10-baggers (40 percent) had price to cash flow below 1.0. See Table 14.7.

☐ 10-baggers do not pay dividends at birth; only 13 percent did. See the section "Dividends."

☐ Most 10-baggers (72 percent) hold long-term debt. See Table 14.8.

☐ Most 10-baggers (64 percent) lose money in the year before they achieve 10-bagger status. See Table 14.9.

☐ As profits increase, the P/E ratio for 10-baggers drops leading to year 0. See Table 14.10.

☐ In the year preceding a 10-bagger, sales are considerably weaker than non-10-baggers. However, 10-baggers see a dramatic improvement in sales during year 0 but remain about half the rate of non-10-baggers. See Table 14.11.

☐ In the year before year 0, over half (56 percent) of 10-baggers had price-to-sales ratios of 1.0 or lower. See Table 14.12.

☐ High return on equity is not a good measure for selecting 10-baggers since 51 percent of them had ROE below 8 percent. See Table 14.13.

☐ Most of the time (84 percent), 10-baggers had more shares outstanding at the end of year 0 than the prior year compared to 68 percent for non-10-baggers. See Table 14.14.

☐ Of the 60 industries included in the study, the semiconductor industry and homebuilders had the most 10-baggers from 1992 to 2007. See Table 14.15.

☐ Most 10-baggers begin their move up just after a bear market ends. See Table 14.16.

☐ 10-baggers are not immune to price drops. See Table 14.17.

☐ See the section "Backward Testing" for ideas on parameter selection choices.

CHAPTER 15: TRADING 10-BAGGERS

☐ Many 10-baggers (46 percent) start from a flat base. See the section "10-Baggers Start from a Flat Base."

☐ Switch to the linear scale and look for a flat base pattern. See the section "10-Baggers Start from a Flat Base."

☐ Buy when price closes above the top of the flat base. See the section "10-Baggers Start from a Flat Base."

☐ Most 10-baggers begin life with a V-shaped start. See the section "Some 10-Baggers Prefer a V-Shaped Start."

☐ Look for a confirmed ugly double bottom to signal a trend change. See the section "Moving Up: A Higher Valley Turn."

☐ Use the weekly measured move-up chart pattern to predict the ending price and time. See the section "Weekly Measured Move Up."

☐ The most frequent retrace in a weekly measured move up is between 25 and 45 percent with a 35 percent median. See Table 15.1.

☐ Weekly measured moves appear most often between price doubling and tripling, but the frequency distribution is quite wide. See Table 15.2.

☐ Where the measured move appears on the time scale spreads almost evenly between 0 and 80 percent from start to end of the 10-bagger. See Table 15.3.

☐ The first leg of a weekly measured move up is shorter than the second 79 percent of the time. See the section "MMU Measure Rule."

☐ The measure rule on the calendar scale for weekly measured moves works only 48 percent of the time. See the section "MMU Measure Rule."

☐ The hump-shaped 10-bagger is a twin-peak pattern with the second peak taller than the first. See the section "Two Hump Shape."

☐ Humped 10-baggers are rare, occurring 16 percent of the time, and lasting an average of 3.3 years. See the section "Two Hump Shape.

☐ Trend lines can be invaluable when trading humped 10-baggers. See the section "Trading Humps."

☐ The line-shaped 10-bagger has an average duration of 2.3 years, occurs 42 percent of the time, and has the fewest appearances of measured moves (0.9) of the four shapes. See the section "Line Shape."

☐ The rounded turn 10-bagger is just as it sounds, a long slow turn. It only happens 19 percent of the time and takes an average of 3.5 years to reach 10-bagger status. See the section "Rounded Turn Shape."

☐ The stair-step 10-bagger happens 23 percent of the time, but takes an average of 3.5 years to complete. See the section "Stair-Step Shape."

☐ Use prior price action that forms shapes to help determine what the 10-bagger's end will look like. See the section "10-Bagger Death."

☐ 10-baggers have two shapes at the end, a rounded turn or an inverted V. See the section "10-Bagger Death."

☐ In the year after a 10-bagger ends, the average decline is 66 percent. See the section "The Numbers" and Table 15.4.

☐ A head-and-shoulders top ends a 10-bagger 16 percent of the time. See the section "Head-and-Shoulders Top."

☐ Double tops form at the end of 10-baggers 22 percent of the time. See the section "Double Top and the 2B Rule."

☐ Rarely (9 percent of the time) will a triple top end a 10-bagger. See the section "Triple Top."

☐ Inverted V shapes end 10-baggers most often: 29 percent of the time. See "Inverted V."

☐ Look for similar shaped peaks to help predict the ending shape of a 10-bagger. See the section "Rounded Turn."

☐ Ugly double tops end 10-baggers just 6 percent of the time. See the section "Ugly Double Top."

CHAPTER 16: SELLING BUY AND HOLD

☐ Buying a stock in stage 1 and selling in stage 2 often results in profitable trades. See Table 16.1.

☐ Technicals are more timely than fundamentals. Evaluate the risk of both and trade accordingly. See the section "Example: Savient Pharmaceuticals."

☐ Use the 1-2-3 trend change method to determine a change in trend. See the section "1-2-3 Testing."

☐ The cloudbank pattern is an easy way to determine when to sell. See the section "The Cloudbank Pattern."

☐ A double bottom happens 17 percent of the time after a cloudbank. See the section "The Shape of Bottoms."

☐ An ugly double bottom occurs after a cloudbank 12 percent of the time. See the section "The Shape of Bottoms."

☐ The v-shaped turn occurs most often—63 percent of the time—after a cloudbank. See the section "The Shape of Bottoms."

☐ The horizontal bottom is the rarest of the four types of turns. It happens 8 percent of the time after a cloudbank. See the section "The Shape of Bottoms."

☐ A cloudbank can represent a short-term bonanza, too. See the section "Investing in Cloudbanks."

☐ 82 percent of stocks with cloudbanks returned to the cloud within 1.5 years. See Table 16.2.

☐ It takes longer for price to return to the cloudbank after a large decline than a short one. See Table 16.2.

☐ Over half the stocks with cloudbanks (58 percent) dropped less than 15 percent below the buy price, but 18 percent plunged more than 35 percent. See Table 16.3.

☐ Sell a cloudbank stock when it returns to the bottom of the cloud. See the section "Selling Cloudbanks."

☐ Place a trailing stop below the 30-week moving average. See the section "Using Trailing Stops to Sell."

☐ If price rises in a straight-line run, use a volatility stop. See the section "Using Trailing Stops to Sell."

☐ When price breaks out to a new high, find the most recent minor low. Raise the stop to below the 30-week moving average at the time of the minor low. See the section "Using Trailing Stops to Sell."

☐ If you think you are going to be stopped out, then just sell the stock. See the section "Using Trailing Stops to Sell."

☐ Trend lines can signal a sale earlier than other methods. See the section "Timely Trend-Line Exits."

☐ A 12-month simple moving average of closing prices on the S&P 500 index can help determine when you should be in or out of the market. See the section "Can Moving Averages Help?"

☐ When using a monthly moving average, plot prices using a line chart, not a bar chart. See the section "Can Moving Averages Help?"

☐ If insiders buy the stock, it could represent value, but they can sell for any number of reasons. See the section "Follow Insider Transactions."

☐ If market cap exceeds annual sales, then consider selling. See the section "Selling: Two Ratio Tips."

☐ If the P/E ratio is higher than the three-year maximum, consider selling. See the section "Selling: Two Ratio Tips."

☐ If a blue chip drops 10 percent from a high, consider selling it. See the section "Selling Down from a High."

☐ The most common retrace is between 5 and 7 percent. Over half of the samples retraced between 4 and 8 percent. See the section "Selling Results."

CHAPTER 17: FUNDAMENTALS, WHAT I USE

☐ Book value should be rising over time. See the section "Two Book Value Tips."

☐ Look for price to book value below 2.0, the lower the better. See the section "Two Book Value Tips."

☐ For startup companies, determine the burn rate to see how soon they will need to fund operations. See the section "Do Not Get Singed by Burn Rate."

☐ Look for a decrease in capital spending. A cut in capital spending two years in a row is a plus. See the section "Drop Capital Spending!"

☐ Current assets/current liabilities must be over 2.0. See the section "Current Ratio 2.0."

☐ Select stocks paying a dividend. See the section "Prospecting for Growth Using Dividends."

☐ For a utility stock, check the payout ratio to be sure they have enough money left to fund future growth. See the section "Prospecting for Growth Using Dividends."

☐ Small-cap stocks that transition from losing money to making money tend to outperform. See the section "Rising Earnings, Net Profit."

☐ Stocks with increasing net profit from one year to the next tend to outperform. See the section "Rising Earnings, Net Profit."

☐ Select stocks with P/E ratios lower than the industry. See the section "P/E Ratio versus Industry."

☐ Listen to what management says about difficult conditions, and be cautious of glowing statements that business will improve soon. Let price be your guide. See the section "P/E Ratio versus Industry."

☐ If the company is being sued too frequently, discard the stock. See the section "Litigation: Stop Pissing People Off!"

☐ No long-term debt is best. See the section "Avoid Too Much Long-Term Debt."

☐ Companies moving from no debt to some long-term debt tend to outperform. See the section "Avoid Too Much Long-Term Debt."

☐ Debt to equity should be small, say, below 50 percent. See the section "Avoid Too Much Long Term Debt."

☐ Buy small-cap stocks. See the section "Market Capitalization: Big Returns by Going Small."

☐ Is research funding growing from year to year? See the section "Research Spending."

☐ Is R&D funding higher than at other companies? See the section "Research Spending."

☐ Can the company translate sales into profits? See the section "Sales? Think Money."

☐ Are overhead costs rising faster than sales? See the section "Sales? Think Money."

☐ Look for a price-to-sales ratio below 1.0. See the section "Price-to-Sales Ratio: What About Debt?"

☐ Stocks priced below 16 tend to do well. See the section "Stock Price: 5 to 20."

☐ Avoid penny stocks (those below $1) and be cautious of those priced below $5. See the section "Stock Price: 5 to 20."

☐ Avoid stocks in which your trading volume is more than 1 percent of the average daily volume. See the section "Volume: Thin Ice Ahead!"

CHAPTER 18: INTRODUCTION TO POSITION TRADING

☐ Position traders hold until the primary trend changes direction. See the section "What Is Position Trading?"

☐ Buy-and-hold investors can benefit from position trading by learning to time the market. Swing and day traders can also enjoy a more relaxed style by position trading. See the section "Who Should Position Trade and Why?"

☐ For a comparison of position trading to the other styles, see the section "Who Should Position Trade and Why?"

☐ See the section "What Position Trading Will Not Do" for a list of deficiencies.

☐ A buy signaled after price exited a consolidation area setup by a high and tight flag chart pattern and news of good earnings. See the section "Example Position Trade."

☐ A sale is signaled when price fulfills the measured move-up prediction, seasonal indicators say sell ("Sell in May and walk away"), and there is an expected market drop. See the section "Example Position Trade."

CHAPTER 19: GETTING STARTED IN POSITION TRADING

☐ Not all value plays represent good value. See this chapter's introduction.

☐ Look for stocks that respond favorably to bad news, but are also down significantly (50 percent or more) from the yearly high. See the section "Check the News or Lose!"

☐ At market bottoms, if bad news no longer hurts the index like it used to, then that is a buy signal. At market tops, if good news does not lift the index as it did, then the uptrend could reverse. See the section "Check the News or Lose!"

☐ Intraday charts are the domain of daytraders. See the section "Ripples."

☐ Swing traders should use daily charts to identify price waves that oscillate higher and lower. See the section "Waves."

☐ Position traders focus on the primary trend, the bull and bear market swings shown on the weekly charts. See the section "Tides."

☐ Trade with the primary price trend. See the section "Trade with the Primary Trend."

☐ Switch to a line chart and check if you are buying when the primary trend is down (bottom fishing) or if the trend is rising (momentum). See the section "Take Your Pick: Bottom Fishing or Momentum?"

☐ A stock follows the market higher or lower 64 percent of the time. See the section "What Is Market Influence on Stocks?"

☐ Table 19.2 shows the best performing chart patterns with upward breakouts in a bull market for swing and position traders. See the section "What Chart Patterns Are Best for Position Trades?"

☐ Table 19.3 shows the best performing chart patterns with downward breakouts in a bear market for swing and position traders. See the section "What Chart Patterns Are Best for Position Trades?"

☐ Symmetrical triangles tend to double or triple bust. See the section "Busted Chart Patterns Revisited."

☐ Trade busted chart patterns because they often provide strong moves. See the section "Busted Chart Patterns Revisited."

CHAPTER 20: TEN FACTORS MAKE CHART PATTERNS WORK

☐ To increase the odds of success, simplify your trading rules. See this chapter's introduction.

☐ A consolidation double bottom acts as a continuation of the upward price trend, not as a reversal. See the section "What Is a Double Bottom?"

☐ Wait for confirmation—price to close above the peak between the two bottoms—before buying. See the section "Double Bottom Reversals."

☐ The trend start is either the highest high *before* which price drops at least 20 percent or the lowest low *before* which price rises at least 20 percent. See the section "Trend Start."

☐ Flat bases appear as horizontal price movements, often several months long. See the section "Flat Base."

☐ Use the linear price scale when hunting for flat bases. See the section "Flat Base."

☐ Horizontal consolidation regions are overhead resistance located between the top of the chart pattern and the trend start. See the section "Horizontal Consolidation Regions."

☐ On the way to the ultimate high, price either never rises to a horizontal consolidation region (which happens 9 percent of the time) or stops within 5 percent of it 50 percent of the time. See the section "Horizontal Consolidation Regions."

☐ Chart patterns within a third of the yearly low tend to outperform. See the section "Position in Yearly Range."

☐ Tall chart patterns perform better than short ones. See the section "Height."

☐ Volume often trends downward throughout the chart pattern and can be very low the day before a breakout. See the section "Volume Trend."

☐ High breakout-day volume propels stocks higher. See the section "Breakout-Day Volume."

☐ Throwbacks hurt performance. See the section "Throwbacks."

☐ Breakout-day gaps mean traders are excited about the stock, helping to push price higher. See the section "Breakout-Day Gaps."

☐ Small caps perform best; large caps perform worst. See the section "Market Cap."

☐ For a scoring system checklist, see Table 20.1.

☐ Table 20.2 shows the statistical results of the scoring system for chart patterns.

☐ Chart patterns with scores above 0 outperform those with scores below 0. See Table 20.2.

☐ The higher the total score the better performance tends to be. See Table 20.3.

CHAPTER 21: THREE WINNING TRADES AND A FUNERAL

☐ Discretionary trading means developing an inner voice and obeying it. See the section "The Intel Fiasco."

☐ A head-and-shoulders bottom marked the entry into the Hudson Highland trade with a stop loss closing it out. See the section "Hudson Highland Hiccup."

☐ A buy in CNO Financial began when price retraced 38 percent of the prior up move, and ended with an inverted dead-cat bounce chart pattern. See the section "CNO Financial Group."

☐ A trade in Complete Production Services began with a busted double top and insider buying, and ended with another inverted dead-cat bounce. See the section "Complete Production Services."

CHAPTER 22: WHAT NOT TO DO: THREE BOTCHED TRADES

☐ Invest only a small portion of your portfolio in high-risk, high-reward trades. See the section "Medivation: Selling Too Late."

☐ If a stock makes a massive drop (a so-called dead-cat bounce), sell as quickly as you can. See the section "Medivation: Selling Too Late."

☐ Insider buying and an ugly double bottom led to purchasing Coldwater Creek, but a tight stop forced an exit too soon. See the section "Coldwater Creek: Selling Too Soon."

☐ Hovnanian looked like a buy since the stock was trading above the 30-week simple moving average on high volume after breaking out of a congestion area. Two indicators warned of trouble ahead. See the section "Hovnanian: Selling at the Bottom."

☐ Do not trade an industry (like housing) if you have had difficulty making money trading it before. See the section "Hovnanian: Selling at the Bottom."

Visual Appendix of Chart Patterns

Broadening Bottoms

Broadening Formations, Right-Angled and Ascending

Broadening Formations, Right-Angled and Descending

Broadening Tops

Broadening Wedges, Ascending

Broadening Wedges, Descending

Bump-and-Run Reversal Bottoms

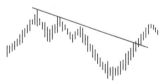

Bump-and-Run Reversal Tops

283

Cup with Handle

Cup with Handle, Inverted

Dead-Cat Bounce

Dead-Cat Bounce, Inverted

Diamond Bottoms

Diamond Tops

Double Bottoms, Adam & Adam

Double Bottoms, Adam & Eve

Double Bottoms, Eve & Adam

Double Bottoms, Eve & Eve

Double Tops, Adam & Adam

Double Tops, Adam & Eve

Double Tops, Eve & Adam

Double Tops, Eve & Eve

Flags

Flags, High and Tight

Gaps

Head-and-Shoulders Bottoms

Head-and-Shoulders Bottoms, Complex

Head-and-Shoulders Tops

Head-and-Shoulders Tops, Complex

Horn Bottoms

Horn Tops

Island Reversals, Bottoms

Island Reversals, Tops

Islands, Long

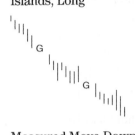

Measured Move Down

Measured Move Up

Pennants

Pipe Bottoms

Pipe Tops

Rectangle Bottoms

Rectangle Tops

Rounding Bottoms

Rounding Tops

Scallops, Ascending

Scallops, Ascending and Inverted

Scallops, Descending

Scallops, Descending and Inverted

Three Falling Peaks

Three Rising Valleys

Triangles, Ascending

Triangles, Descending

Triangles, Symmetrical

Triple Bottoms

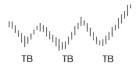

Triple Tops

Wedges, Falling

Wedges, Rising

Bibliography

Active Trader Staff. "Intraday Swing Extremes." *Active Trader* 12, no. 5 (May 2011).

Bandy, Howard. "Scaling Out as an Exit Technique." *Active Trader* 10, no. 9 (September 2009).

Bandy, Howard. "Scaling In as an Entry Technique." *Active Trader* 10, no. 10 (October 2009).

Bulkowski, Thomas. "A Trend Channel Trade." *Technical Analysis of Stocks & Commodities* 14, no. 4 (April 1996).

Bulkowski, Thomas. *Encyclopedia of Candlestick Charts.* Hoboken, NJ: John Wiley & Sons, 2008.

Bulkowski, Thomas. *Encyclopedia of Chart Patterns*, 2nd ed. Hoboken, NJ: John Wiley & Sons, 2005.

Bulkowski, Thomas. *Getting Started in Chart Patterns.* Hoboken, NJ: John Wiley & Sons, 2006.

Bulkowski, Thomas. *Trading Classic Chart Patterns.* Hoboken, NJ: John Wiley & Sons, 2002.

Bulkowski, Thomas. *Visual Guide to Chart Patterns.* Hoboken, NJ: John Wiley & Sons, 2013.

De Bondt, Werner F. M., and Richard H. Thaler. "Further Evidence on Investor Overreaction and Stock Market Seasonality." *Journal of Finance 42*, no. 3 (July 1987).

Desai, H., and P. Jain. "Long-Run Common Stock Returns Following Stock Splits and Reverse Splits." *Journal of Business* (1997).

Fama, Eugene F., and Kenneth R. French. "The Cross-Section of Expected Stock Returns." *Journal of Finance* 47, no. 2 (June 1992).

Fama, Eugene F., Lawrence Fisher, Michael C. Jensen, and Richard Roll. "The Adjustment of Stock Prices to New Information." *International Economic Review* 10 (February 1969).

Farley, Alan S. *The Master Swing Trader.* New York: McGraw-Hill, 2001.

Fischer, Robert, and Jens Fischer. *Candlesticks, Fibonacci, and Chart Pattern Trading Tools.* Hoboken, NJ: John Wiley & Sons, 2003.

Fosback, Norman G. *Stock Market Logic: A Sophisticated Approach to Profits on Wall Street.* Fort Lauderdale, FL: The Institute for Econometric Research, 1976.

Frost, A. J., and Robert R. Prechter. Jr. *Elliott Wave Principle: Key to Market Behavior*. Chichester, England: John Wiley & Sons, 1999.

Garcia de Andoain, Carlos and Frank W. Bacon. "The Impact of Stock Split Announcements on Stock Price: A Test of Market Efficiency." *Proceedings of ASBBS* 16, no. 1 (2009).

Glass, Gary S. "Extensive Insider Accumulation as an Indicator of Near Term Stock Price Performance." PhD diss., Ohio State University, 1966.

Grinblatt, Mark S., Ronald W. Masulis, and Sheridan Titman. "The Valuation Effects of Stock Splits and Stock Dividends." *Journal of Financial Economics* (1984).

Guppy, Daryl. "Matching Money Management with Trade Risk." *Technical Analysis of Stocks & Commodities* 16, no. 5 (May 1998).

Guppy, Daryl. "Exploiting Positions with Money Management." *Technical Analysis of Stocks & Commodities* 17, no. 9 (September 1999).

Hall, Alvin D. *Getting Started in Stocks*, 3rd ed. New York: John Wiley & Sons, 1997.

How to Invest in Common Stocks. The Complete Guide to Using The Value Line Investment Survey. New York: Value Line Publishing, Inc., 2007.

Ikenberry, David, G. Rankine, and E. K. Stice. "What Do Stock Splits Really Signal?" *Journal of Financial and Qualitative Analysis* (1996).

Investopedia.com. "Keep Your Eyes on the ROE." www.investopedia.com/articles /fundamental/03/100103.asp.

Jaenisch, Ron. "The Andrews Line." *Technical Analysis of Stocks & Commodities* 14, no. 10 (October 1996).

Kaplan, Peter. "Finding the Value in Losses." *Stocks, Futures and Options*, September 2006.

Kaufman, Perry J. *A Short Course in Technical Trading*. Hoboken, NJ: John Wiley & Sons, 2003.

Knapp, Volker. "Top Stop Exit." *Active Trader* 9, no. 9 (September 2008).

Knapp, Volker. "Insider Buying." *Active Trader* 9, no. 10 (October 2008).

Knapp, Volker. "Insider Selling." *Active Trader* 9, no. 11 (November 2008).

Lakonishok, Josef, Andrei Shleifer, and Robert W. Vishny. "Contrarian Investment, Extrapolation, and Risk." *Journal of Finance* 49, no. 5 (December 1994).

Landry, Dave. "Trading Trend Transitions." *Active Trader* 11, no. 12 (December 2010).

Lynch, Peter, and John Rothchild. *One Up on Wall Street: How to Use What You Already Know to Make Money in the Market*. New York: Penguin Books, 1990.

Mamis, Justin, and Robert Mamis. *When to Sell: Inside Strategies for Stock-Market Profits*. New York: Cornerstone Library, 1977.

Martell, Terrence F., and Gwendolyn P. Webb. "The Performance of Stocks that Are Reverse Split." New York: Baruch College/The City University of New York, 2005.

McClure, Ben. "Keep Your Eyes on the ROE." www.Investopedia.com/articles /fundamental/03/100103.asp.

Nicholson, S. Francis. "Price-Earnings Ratios." *Financial Analysts Journal 16*, no. 4 (July–August 1960).

Nilsson, Peter. "Money Management Matrix." *Technical Analysis of Stocks & Commodities* 24, no. 13 (December 2006).

O'Hare, Patrick. "Looking for Bottoms in Individual Stocks." *Stocks, Futures & Options* 3, no. 5 (May 2004).

O'Higgins, Michael, and John Downes. *Beating the Dow*. New York: HarperCollins, 1992.

O'Shaughnessy, James. *What Works on Wall Street*. New York: McGraw-Hill, 1997.

Patel, Pankaj N., Souheang Yao, and Heath Barefoot. "High Yield, Low Payout." *Credit Suisse*, August 2006.

Pugliese, Fausto, "Daytrading Rule 1: No Overnights." *Technical Analysis of Stocks & Commodities* 30, no. 7 (June 2012).

Rogoff, Donald T. "The Forecasting Properties of Insider Transactions." PhD diss., Michigan State University, 1964.

Sperandeo, Victor, with Sullivan Brown. *Trader Vic—Methods of a Wall Street Master*. New York: John Wiley & Sons, 1991, 1993.

Stowell, Joseph. "Teacher, Trader Still Teaching: Joseph Stowell." *Technical Analysis of Stocks & Commodities* 13, no. 7 (July 1995).

Subach, Daniel. "Stock Analysis and Investing for the Small Investor." *Technical Analysis of Stocks & Commodities* 24, no. 13 (December 2006).

Tweedy, Browne Company LLC. "What Has Worked in Investing: Studies of Investment Approaches and Characteristics Associated with Exceptional Returns." Revised 2009.

Vakkur, Mark. "The Basics of Managing Money." *Technical Analysis of Stocks & Commodities* 15, no. 9 (September 1997).

Vakkur, Mark. "New Tricks with the Dogs of the Dow." *Technical Analysis of Stocks & Commodities* 15, no. 12 (December 1997).

Vince, Ralph. *The Handbook of Portfolio Mathematics: Formulas for Optimal Allocation & Leverage*. Hoboken, NJ: John Wiley & Sons, 2007.

Weinstein, Sam. *Stan Weinstein's Secrets for Profiting in Bull and Bear Markets*. New York: McGraw-Hill, 1988.

Wisdom, Gabriel. *Wisdom on Value Investing*. Hoboken, NJ: John Wiley & Sons, 2009.

OTHER SITES OF INTEREST

www.Activetradermag.com—website for *Active Trader* magazine.

www.ThePatternSite.com—Mr. Bulkowski's website.

www.traders.com—website for *Technical Analysis of Stocks & Commodities* magazine.

www.Yahoo.finance.com—a general finance website.

About the Author

Thomas Bulkowski is a successful investor with more than 30 years of experience trading stocks. He is also the author of the John Wiley & Sons titles:

- *Visual Guide to Chart Patterns*
- *Getting Started in Chart Patterns*
- *Trading Classic Chart Patterns*
- *Encyclopedia of Candlestick Charts*
- *Encyclopedia of Chart Patterns, Second Edition*
- *Evolution of a Trader: Trading Basics*
- *Evolution of a Trader: Swing and Day Trading.*

Bulkowski is a frequent contributor to *Active Trader* and *Technical Analysis of Stocks & Commodities* magazines. Before earning enough from his investments to *retire* from his day job at age 36, Bulkowski was a hardware design engineer at Raytheon and a senior software engineer for Tandy Corporation.

His website and blog are at www.thepatternsite.com, where you can read over 500 articles and the latest research on chart patterns, candlesticks, event patterns, and other investment topics, for free, without registering.

Index

Printed and bound by CPI Group (UK) Ltd, Croydon, CR0 4YY

16/04/2025

14658449-0003